PENGUIN BOOKS

FAITH AND CREDIT
THE WORLD BANK'S SECULAR EMPIRE

Susan George was born in the United States and educated at Smith College. After moving to France, she received her *Licence* in philosophy at the Sorbonne and a doctorate from the École des Hautes Études en Sciences Sociales. She is an Associate Director of the Transnational Institute in Amsterdam with which she has been associated since it was founded in 1973. *Faith and Credit* is her eighth book; other titles published by Penguin are *How the Other Half Dies* (1976), *A Fate Worse than Debt* (1987), and *Ill Fares the Land* (1990). *The Debt Boomerang* (1992) was published by Pluto Press in its Transnational Institute series. Her work centres on major development issues and North–South power relations and has been translated into a dozen languages. She works with a number of non-governmental organizations and serves on the boards of Greenpeace International and Greenpeace France.

Fabrizio Sabelli was born in Rome and educated at the Jesuit College of Massimo and the University of Rome, where he took a degree in law. He later studied anthropology in Geneva and Neuchâtel before doing his field work in northern Ghana. He then settled in Switzerland, taking his doctorate at the University of Neuchâtel. He is now a Professor of the Institute of Development Studies of the University of Geneva and at the University of Neuchâtel. Alone or with colleagues, he has written several books, most recently *La Mythologie Programmée* and a book on methodology – *Recherche Anthropologique et Développement*. The links between development and religion have been a constant theme in his work.

Susan George and Fabrizio Sabelli

FAITH AND CREDIT

THE WORLD BANK'S SECULAR EMPIRE

PENGUIN BOOKS

PENGUIN BOOKS

Published by the Penguin Group
Penguin Books Ltd, 27 Wrights Lane, London W8 5TZ, England
Penguin Books USA Inc., 375 Hudson Street, New York, New York 10014, USA
Penguin Books Australia Ltd, Ringwood, Victoria, Australia
Penguin Books Canada Ltd, 10 Alcorn Avenue, Toronto, Ontario, Canada M4V 3B2
Penguin Books (NZ) Ltd, 182–190 Wairau Road, Auckland 10, New Zealand

Penguin Books Ltd, Registered Offices: Harmondsworth, Middlesex, England

Published in Penguin Books 1994
1 3 5 7 9 10 8 6 4 2

Filmset by Datix International Limited, Bungay, Suffolk
Printed in England by Clays Ltd, St Ives plc
Set in 10/12 pt Monophoto Photina

Table of Contents

Introduction and Basics

The World Bank is a unique invention of the second half of the twentieth century. Nineteen ninety-four marks its fiftieth birthday, if one counts, like the Chinese, from conception rather than birth. The Bank is respected and admired by some; feared and reviled by others; but to most people it is simply unknown, scarcely a household name; even though it has influenced, directly and indirectly, more lives in those countries euphemistically called less developed than any other institution since the Second World War.

The Bank's charter affirms that it is a purely economic institution but the billions* of dollars it lends are only part of the story; it has come to wield immense political power as well. As a supranational agency in an increasingly globalized world, from Africa to the new republics of the former Soviet Union, the Bank now has more to say about state policy than many states.

We will argue that this institution is filling a gap left by the near-total absence of coherent North-South strategy formulated by anybody else. By accident or design, attribution or default, the policy the Bank chooses to apply in its borrowing countries becomes *de facto* the dominant one. The end of the Cold War has given rise to a mixture of indifference and confusion on the part of the rich, industrialized nations towards the South and towards much of the East as well.

Before, no place on earth was unimportant; the poorest, most obscure country could be the scene of superpower rivalry. In the 1990s, the US acts *vis-à-vis* the South only when it must (and even then often regrets it); or concentrates on trade-related objectives like the North American Free Trade Agreement (NAFTA) and the

---

* A billion is one thousand million; a trillion is one thousand billion.

General Agreement on Tariffs and Trade (GATT). Europe has been incapable of adopting a common view on North–South questions as on a host of others. In the twenty-first century, the rich countries – the Organization for Economic Cooperation and Development (OECD) members, led by the G-7 – will represent at best one-sixth of humanity yet they have no overall vision of a desirable relationship with the other five-sixths.

The Bank, on the other hand, at the topmost levels, knows what it wants and has the means to translate its views into *realpolitik*. Some observers of the Bank claim that it has lost its way, that it 'urgently needs a more focused mission and a smaller number of operational priorities'.[1] This is true enough if one assumes that the Bank is an economic institution only, with no political functions. If, however, one sees the Bank as an extremely powerful player with considerable freedom of movement on a largely empty political terrain, its wide-ranging mission and numerous priorities make much more sense.

The Bank was conceived for the noblest of reasons; its founders firmly believed it would contribute to human betterment in the postwar world. And indeed, the Bank soon became the largest supplier of infrastructure, providing the underpinnings for industry in the so-called developing countries. Its critics charge, however, that many of its projects also left a wide swathe of physical and social destruction in their wake. Bank projects have been known to dislocate entire communities, displace thousands of people, destroy forests, turn grasslands to desert or concentrate land and wealth in the hands of a few rich farmers or entrepreneurs – all in the name of development. Since the 1980s, its 'programme' loans designed to encourage widespread policy changes (better known as structural adjustment) have forcibly reoriented entire economies.

Over its half-century of existence, the Bank has had much to say about itself and its works, producing archives so voluminous they can no longer all be housed in Washington: 65,000 cubic metres are kept in cheaper storage space in Pennsylvania. The Bank is highly self-conscious, constantly reflecting on its own theory, practice and stature.

Outsiders, too, have concerned themselves with the institution and its role in development. Their output is necessarily more modest, but the Bank's activities have gone neither unnoticed nor unreported. Critical literature began to form a trickle towards the end of the 1960s; it swelled to an uninterrupted flow of fault-finding publications in the late 1980s and early 1990s as environmental and non-governmental development organizations brought relentless pressure to bear upon the Bank, particularly because of its structural adjustment policies and its environmentally destructive megaprojects. This river of literature emanating from insiders and outsiders, 'pros' and 'antis', is likely to flood as the half-centennial proceeds (the Bank's fiftieth 'birthday' lasts in fact from 1994 until sometime in 1997).

This book does not seek to be another bulletin on the Bank's failed projects, although of necessity it will allude to some of them; nor is it intended to disparage the institution. Whatever market remains for this literature will doubtless be satisfied by others, although most of academia is reconciled to a Bank which provides fat consultants' fees to so many of its members. In the social science community today, the sport of Bank-bashing is mostly considered *passé* and vulgar, the academic equivalent of mud-wrestling.

We hope, instead, to explain not only the interests the Bank serves but also its internal culture and its broader significance. An out-of-fashion philosopher who influenced us both, once wrote that 'philosophers have interpreted the world in one way or another; the point, however, is to change it'. We now believe that one can also try to change it, at least if one is a scholar and writer, by interpreting it as accurately and as systematically as possible. There is no need to 'bash' an institution whose own documents and practice do the job so thoroughly in the scholar's stead.

Still, why choose the Bank as an object for interpretation? Because, like the proverbial mountain, it is very much there; it is an institution that has successfully reproduced itself and prospered since the Second World War, constantly increasing its physical size, extending its economic grasp and augmenting its political power. Mere scale of resources cannot explain this performance. Crucially, the Bank has managed to make its own view of the world appear the norm. We think its real success has been not so much economic – however great the economic power it wields – as cultural, ideological and, in a not entirely metaphorical sense, religious.

An eminent, world-class institution must learn to command at least the respect, if not the love and loyalty, of political, financial and intellectual élites. We duly admire the Bank's capacity to impose its view of reality (especially since this view is so often later proven wrong) as the one all reasonable men and women ought normally to share. The Bank's hegemony in defining development and correct policy, its legitimacy in interpreting the world for others and the deference it commands are signs of its achievement.

It has usually managed as well to make those holding contrary opinions (a.k.a. the bashers) look like spoilsports or ill-informed outsiders – sometimes by seeking to refute their arguments, more often simply by ignoring them and refusing to take them seriously. Institutionally speaking, these attainments are not just a managerial *tour de force* but are in a sense axiomatic: if the Bank weren't hegemonic, intellectually dominant, respected, it would not still be around. Our apparently simple question is, then, why is it there?

Thus we come neither to bury the Bank nor to praise it – the first course would be pretentious and the second superfluous. More engaging for us, more interesting, we hope, for the reader and more ethically valuable in the long run for everyone is, instead, *an attempt to understand how and what the Bank itself thinks; how and why it can impose its truth and its doctrine on others.* In other words, we are interested in conveying the Bank's values, its culture, its belief system and its reigning myths as well as its actions.*

An establishment employing several thousand people and dispensing billions – in 1993 the World Bank's lending commitments exceeded two and a half million dollars an hour – could not function without a deep and shared conviction that it has not just reasons but Reason on its side. This would be true even if its purpose were merely to lend money, full stop. But the World Bank is at once a bank with a small b, specializing in commercial loans to sovereign governments, and a development institution whose

---

* The term 'myth' is not derogatory and in particular does not imply something fictitious or 'not true'. In its anthropological usage, myth is closer to 'narrative' and provides the symbolic foundations of society. In *La Mythologie Programmée* (Presses Universitaires de France, 1992), Marie-Dominique Perrot, Gilbert Rist and Fabrizio Sabelli examined the meaning of myth in modern society and showed the importance of religion in powerful modern institutions.

philosophy, choices and actions now affect huge numbers of people. It is the only bank that claims not merely an economic function but a humanitarian purpose as well.

Such an institution must, collectively, believe in its mission and maintain the faith inside and out that, although it makes massive profits (in recent years well over a billion dollars annually), it acts in the name of values higher and nobler than those of a mere profit-making enterprise. Even if the philosophy of such an institution has never been stated systematically or set forth in a single text, it is still there to be unearthed and made manifest.

Some critics have approached the Bank as a kind of quintessential Evil Empire, imposing its projects in the teeth of public opinion, the local inhabitants' wishes and, sometimes, the Bank's own experts' advice. At one time or another, all these things have occurred. But if one tries, rather, to understand *why* it should upon occasion behave in such a way, one is struck by an inescapable though perhaps irreverent analogy: *this supranational, non-democratic institution functions very much like the Church, in fact the medieval Church. It has a doctrine, a rigidly structured hierarchy preaching and imposing this doctrine and a quasi-religious mode of self-justification.*

Or, to borrow from a wholly different tradition, the Bank is reminiscent of a centralized political party characterized by opacity, authoritarianism and successive party lines. Could the World Bank be the Last of the Leninists? Perhaps so: we tend, however, to favour the religious analogy.

Although such comparisons may offend believers and non-believers alike, a Church or a monolithic political party is an entity which may well resort to public relations; but which at bottom brooks no opposition or contradiction and which claims a monopoly on Truth. To be sole guardian of the Truth imposes a sacred duty in whose name inquisitions, purges, large-scale loss of livelihood or the forced displacement of hundreds of thousands from their homes can all be legitimized and justified in the name of a greater good which shall come to pass at some future time.

Some friends and colleagues have asked why we should look so far afield for a rationale of the Bank's activities. It's quite enough, they tell us (each according to his or her preferred explanation), to be at the heart of a vast and lucrative procurement network; to be the primary international institution reinforcing United States (or G-7) control over the rest of the planet, or simply to embody in a particularly successful way the desire of all such institutions to perpetuate their own existence. They all have a point and we do not deny the power of these motivations or explanations. Still, we do not believe that the Bank's implicit philosophy and its overt behaviour can be reduced to any of these ingredients, nor that our own approach is far-fetched.

There are no societies without religion, even, or especially, those which believe themselves to be entirely secular. In our century, in our society, the concept of development has acquired religious and doctrinal status. The Bank is commonly accepted as the Vatican, the Mecca or the Kremlin of this twentieth-century religion. A doctrine need not be true to move mountains or to provoke manifold material and human disasters. Religious doctrines (in which we would include secular ones like Leninism) have, through the ages, done and continue to do precisely that, whereas, logically speaking, not all of them can be true insofar as they all define Truth as singular and uniquely their own.

Religion cannot, by definition, be validated or invalidated, declared true or false – only believed or rejected. Facts are irrelevant to belief: they belong to another sphere of reality. True believers, the genuinely pure of heart, exist in every faith, but the majority generally just goes along lukewarmly out of cultural habit or material advantage. When, however, the faith achieves political hegemony as well, like the medieval Church (or the Bolsheviks, or the Ayatollahs), it is in a position to make people offers they can't refuse, or to make their lives extremely uncomfortable if they do.

The religion of development cannot be validated or invalidated either. It doesn't matter whether it works or not, nor how many ordinary people's lives are damaged or destroyed, nor how much nature may be abused because of it. Development theory and practice cannot be validated because they are not scientific. They have not established reliable and recognized criteria for determining whether development has in fact occurred, except for internal economic indicators like the rate of return of an individual project or the growth of Gross National Product – themselves artificial constructions and articles of faith. This being so, there is no established way to identify, correct or avoid error either. When Susan George wrote the Afterword to *A Fate Worse than Debt*, she put it this way:

> Scientists are trained to avoid error by testing their hypotheses systematically. Normally, development theorists and practitioners should also be trained to test their hypotheses by observing *what they do to people,* since human welfare is presumably the goal of development. 'People' here does not mean well-off, well-fed elites but poor and hungry majorities whose fundamental needs are presently not being met. If decades of application of the reigning development paradigm have failed to alleviate their suffering and oppression or, worse still, have intensified them ... the paradigm ought to be ripe for revolution.[2]

She then asked, naïvely, 'In short, how many people have to die before the ruling paradigm is beaten back and we are rid of it once and for all?' thereby largely missing the point. The point is that priesthoods are not elected and they need not answer to the faithful; they are specially invested with the truth and with sacramental functions from which, by definition, the common herd is excluded. The faith they serve is itself a greater good in whose name present suffering is mysteriously transformed into future salvation. Or to borrow an old favourite from secular religion, eggs must and will be broken. One's children, or theirs, or theirs, will eventually sit down to enjoy the omelette.

This, for us, is the final and most compelling reason not to concentrate on pointing out yet again how multifarious are the World Bank's ill-conceived projects, how unresponsive its leaders, how impervious to criticism its doctrine. Such things may be entirely or partially true, but are at bottom expressions of a world-view. It is the foundations of that world-view we shall try to dig for.

The Bank resembles the Church and this will be a guiding analogy in these pages. Both believe themselves invested with a mission, both (the Church historically, the Bank at present) have set themselves against the state. Both celebrate the poor rhetorically while refraining from actually improving their capacity to change their earthly lot.

The Church, more than the Bank, is like God himself 'a mighty fortress, a bulwark never failing' in the words of the splendid hymn. The Bank has lost many of its fortress aspects – particularly compared to the International Monetary Fund (IMF) – and is more open to exchanges with outsiders. The overall vision that guides its practice cannot, however, seem to transcend the narrowest of economic orthodoxies serving a smaller and smaller fraction of transnational élite interests worldwide. The Bank's declared new, or at least renewed, 'poverty focus' shows that it is groping for a mission but in practice it has no grand design beyond the casting of all economies in the neo-classical mould and the refashioning of all men and women as *Homo economicus*.

When we started on this task, we expected to be dealing with a monolithic institution, 'sure of itself and dominating' ('sûr de lui-même et dominateur' as General de Gaulle once said in an unfortunate and much-decried remark about the Jewish people). What we found was, instead, an institution which began marked for a great destiny but is now tragically behind the times; one which craves 'intellectual leadership' but cannot necessarily recognize it even in-house; which seems condemned to reproducing a worn-out, bankrupt development paradigm, and thus to do much harm, occasionally responding to criticism but unable to pre-empt it through genuine change.

Different forces inside and outside the Bank are pulling it in different directions but, on the whole, prolonging its own economic and political power seems to have become an end in itself. The Bank may talk about the poor but its policies have so far ensured their continued exclusion.

We fear that in years to come this situation will worsen. The number of practical links between North and South could become drastically reduced; with relationships between the rich and poor worlds increasingly experienced as clashes between the Empire and the Barbarians (see Chapter VII). As more and more avenues of communication, aid and cooperation are blocked, superseded or destroyed – to us this seems almost inevitable – the Bank will surely be called upon to palliate or repair this state of affairs. It is not now in a position to do so.

If the Bank does not soon emerge of its own accord from dinosaur-hood into mammaldom, if it does not undertake an intellectual, cultural and strategic revolution, nothing anyone outside does or says can prevent its irrelevance and eventual collapse. The obstacles to change are political and ideological as well as institutional. If the Bank intends to make good on its solemn declaration that 'sustainable poverty reduction is the overarching objective ... and the benchmark by which our performance as a development institution will be measured',* it will have to abandon its obsession with the market. Not even an institution as powerful as the Bank can reconcile logical opposites and mutually exclusive objectives.

The market and development, as practised to date, have incorporated a certain segment of developing country societies into the global economy – ten to forty per cent depending on the country. But the market has no plans for those who are not useful either for consumption or for production. The market works for those whose signals it can hear, but the voices of the poor are literally inaudible. So long as the Bank's decisions are based on what the market says, it will be condemned to impotence with regard to the poor. Only a different politics can change their lot and promote 'sustainable poverty reduction'. It is pointless to ask the market to accomplish what it was never cut out to do.

Now for some less speculative, more practical remarks and a brief guide to the chapters that follow. After some basic introductory information ('Basics') we open with the Bretton Woods Conference that gave birth to the Bank in 1944; then skip ahead to the long presidency of Robert McNamara (1968–81), which deeply marked the Bank's thought and action (Chapters i and ii).

The doctrine and the limitations of structural adjustment are the subjects of Chapter iii, while in Chapter iv we show how, despite the Bank's claims to near-infallibility, it has consistently miscalled major economic trends with dire consequences for its borrowers. The most nearly perfect embodiment of the Bank's neo-liberal canon is perhaps its former chief economist, Larry Summers, whom we call the 'Fundamentalist Freedom Fighter', the subject of Chapter v. In Chapter vi we turn to the Bank's internal culture and the traumatic 1987 Reorganization which set the Bank's end-of-the-century agenda.

* See Chapter ii note 2.

Part of this agenda is also shaped by a recent preoccupation with governance, which may also provide a rejuvenated mission for the Bank (Chapter VII). Chapter VIII deals with the challenge environmentalists pose to the Bank's Standard Operating Procedures and its economic orthodoxy, while Chapter IX takes up the Bank's claims to intellectual leadership and its self-defeating, negative attitude towards unconventional or dissenting ideas. In Chapter X we try to determine who really runs the Bank and, in Chapter XI, what others think of it and why it should be so preoccupied with its external image. The final pages justify and strengthen our central analogy of the Bank as a hierarchical, policy-making Church.

At irregular intervals throughout the book are scattered a few shorter texts in the form of stories we call 'Interludes' (in Middle English a 'light dramatic item between acts of a morality play'). The reader must judge if these are recreational or the most serious parts of the book. Anyone put off by these stylistically distinct pauses should just skip them and stick with our own, more – dare we say – orthodox approach, going from one chapter to the next.

BASICS

No prior knowledge of the World Bank, of economics or of the general area of development is necessary to read and, we hope, to enjoy this book. Here is all the background information needed to plunge ahead.

WHEN, HOW MUCH AND TO WHOM

The *International Bank for Reconstruction and Development* (*IBRD*), along with the *International Monetary Fund* (*IMF*), was born at an international conference held in Bretton Woods, New Hampshire in 1944. The Bank and the Fund are thus sometimes called the Bretton Woods Institutions (BWI). The Bank was set up in 1945–6 and made its first loan in 1947. At first, the Bank made loans to European nations for postwar reconstruction, but soon (1948) began lending to southern hemisphere countries as well, for development.

From its inception through fiscal year 1993, the IBRD had loaned or committed $235 billion in more than 3,500 loans. Its all-time largest borrowers are, in descending order: Mexico (which displaced traditional front-runner India in 1993), India, Brazil, Indonesia, Turkey, China, the Philippines, Argentina, Korea, Colombia, Morocco and Nigeria.

IBRD loans are individually negotiated but typically include a five-year grace period (no repayments required); then borrowing governments have fifteen to twenty years to pay back at market interest rates. In 1993, this rate averaged about 7.5 per cent. The Bank never reschedules (stretches out) or cancels a loan. Because it has enormous influence over other public and private sources of capital, its clients put the Bank at the top of their lists of creditors to be repaid.

The *International Development Association (IDA)* was established in 1960 to make 'soft' loans to the world's poorest countries unable to afford IBRD terms. Since then it has lent on its own a total of nearly $78 billion (this is additional to the above-mentioned $235 billion of IBRD loans). More than forty countries, including India and China, are currently eligible for IDA assistance. The IDA formally calls its loans credits to distinguish them from the IBRD's loans; they are virtually interest free ($\frac{3}{4}$ per cent), require no repayments for ten years, then allow forty years to repay. The terms are indeed soft but the loan principal must be repaid – these credits are not gifts. A significant proportion of the present debt burden of the poorest countries consists of money owed to the IDA.

The IDA's funds are 'replenished' from time to time by donor countries as a part of their Overseas Development Aid. The tenth Replenishment took place in 1993. Many countries receive both Bank loans and IDA credits – for example, India, by far the Bank's largest overall customer. By 1993, India had borrowed nearly $28 billion from the Bank and a further $20 billion from the IDA. India, China, Bangladesh and Pakistan together have taken nearly half of all IDA credits. Other countries that have received over a billion dollars from the IDA since it opened its doors in 1960 are, in descending order, Tanzania, Ghana, Kenya, Sri Lanka, Uganda, Ethiopia, Sudan, Egypt, Nepal, Malawi, Zaïre, Madagascar, Yemen, Senegal and Zambia.

Together, the IBRD and IDA make up the World Bank; when we use that term, or simply 'the Bank', we mean the IBRD plus the IDA.

In addition to the IBRD and IDA, there are two other members of the World Bank Group which we do not deal with in this book:

The *International Finance Corporation (IFC)* was established in 1956 as an affiliate of the Bank, although it remains legally and financially separate. The IFC makes loans exclusively for private enterprise in Bank borrowing countries and may for that purpose bring together local and foreign, public and private capital, as well as its own. In addition to providing credit to local companies, IFC has helped many transnational corporations to establish themselves in developing countries.

The *Multilateral Investment Guarantee Agency (MIGA)* is the latest addition to the World Bank Group. Founded in 1988, its purpose is also to encourage direct foreign investment in developing countries. To that end, MIGA provides insurance guaranteeing investments against non-commercial risks and gives policy advice to developing country governments concerning foreign investment.

WITH WHOM

Since their respective birthdates, the IBRD and IDA together have loaned a total of $312 billion of their own funds, but this figure seriously understates their real financial influence. The Bank's involvement in a project routinely generates substantial co-financing. For example, in 1992, the IBRD committed $15 billion. Half its projects attracted other lenders who committed a further $13 billion. A World Bank seal of approval is also seen as an indispensable guarantee before foreign private investors will become involved in a country or private banks will provide them with capital.

WHAT FOR

The categories of projects financed by the Bank have changed little over the years although the emphasis placed on each one may have shifted. Energy and transport used to head the list; now agriculture/forestry/rural development receives more loans than either. For the entire period of the Bank's existence, the order is agriculture 19 per cent, energy 18 per cent, transport 14 per cent. Smaller proportions of total Bank lending have been devoted to education, urban development, development finance institutions, population/health/nutrition, water/sewerage, industry, public sector management, telecommunications, technical assistance. In 1993, the two categories of education and population/health/nutrition received proportionally higher amounts than their historical shares.

We will often use the terms 'structural adjustment' or 'sectoral adjustment' lending. These loans comprise what the Bank also calls its 'non-project' or 'policy-based' lending. Structural adjustment loans – SALs – and sectoral adjustment loans – SECALs – are paid out faster than project loans (they are 'quick-disbursing' in the Bank's jargon) and are meant to help debt-stricken countries reorganize their entire economies or large sectors of them.

Launched by the Bank in 1979, SALs and SECALs act as catalysts and facilitate liberalization of a country's rules and regulations in the desired direction. When the government initiates the policy changes – which may be exceedingly broad and detailed – specified by the Bank, the Bank in turn provides a multimillion-dollar loan intended to help ease the pain of restructuring. SALs and SECALs thus underpin the Bank's 'policy dialogue' with governments and assumed considerable importance during the 1980s: they amount to about fifteen per cent of the Bank's all time lending and about a third of IBRD loans (less for the IDA), for a grand total of about twenty per cent from the mid-1980s through 1993.

HOW: MONEY, VOTES AND PROCUREMENT

All the components of the World Bank Group are owned by member countries – 176 for the IBRD; 152 for the IDA at the end of fiscal 1993. When a country joins the Bank (it must first become a member of the International Monetary Fund to qualify), it pledges a capital subscription but pays in only a small percentage of this pledge. The rest of the money is 'on call' and serves as an iron-clad guarantee should a borrower ever default on a loan, which very few have done so far. The capital subscription assigned is proportional to a country's wealth, based on its IMF quota.

In practice, Bank members are divided into two categories – those who take out loans and those who don't. Inside the Bank, the rich countries are referred to as Part I countries; the borrowers are Part II countries.

Most of the Bank's loanable funds do not come from capital subscriptions at all. It raises billions by selling its own bonds on world financial markets; then charges its borrowers a marginally higher interest rate than it must pay its own bondholders. Because the Bank's bonds are ultimately guaranteed by the world's governments, they are considered remarkably sound investments and are given the top AAA grade by securities rating houses like Moody's or Standard & Poor's. Many institutional investors (like pension schemes) buy them, as do individuals.

Financially speaking, the Bank is very conservatively managed. It never lends out more than it actually possesses in capital: This is called the 'gearing ratio' of loans to capital; in the Bank's case thus 1:1. A conservatively managed commercial bank would routinely have a gearing ratio of 10:1 or 15:1. The Bank consistently makes a handsome profit and, as of 1993, had accumulated 'retained earnings', in effect a surplus, of over $14 billion. The Bank is a bank, and a rock-solid one at that.

Capital subscriptions also determine the country's voting strength in the Bank: for example as of 1993 (in the IBRD), the United States controls 17.2 per cent of the voting stock; Japan 6.6 per cent; Germany, France and the United Kingdom about 5 per cent.

In contrast, forty-five African countries together control only 4 per cent of the total.

The Bank is a big spender as well as a big lender. It tenders contracts on which potential suppliers from any part of the world may bid. Since it opened for business, the Bank (the IBRD and IDA) has spent over $212 billion for procurement of materials, machinery, consultants, et cetera, sometimes inside, but mostly outside, the borrowing country. Historically, the foreign/local contractors split has been about 60/40 but this percentage is gradually being improved in favour of local suppliers who obtained 45 per cent of total contracts in fiscal 1993.

Not surprisingly, the United States has received more procurement contracts than any other country, followed by Japan, Germany, the United Kingdom, France, Italy, Switzerland and Canada. Other countries which have obtained total IBRD contracts worth more than a billion dollars are Austria, Belgium, Brazil, China, Korea, the Netherlands, Spain and Sweden.

WHERE

The Bank's headquarters are in Washington, DC; its official address is 1818 H Street but it has offices at twenty-one different addresses, including the entire city block bounded by G, H, 18th and 19th Streets. It also maintains offices in New York, Paris, Geneva, London and Tokyo; plus 'regional missions' in East and West Africa and Thailand and fifty-two 'country missions', run by Resident Representatives, in borrowing countries.

WHO

As of 1993, about 7,000 people were on its staff. The Bank also employs a great many consultants, again mostly supplied by the rich, donor countries. In 1993, it hired 672 consultants: American (16 per cent), French (13.7 per cent), British (13.5 per cent), Canadian (8.3 per cent), German (7.3 per cent), Japanese (4.2 per cent). In 1993, no developing country supplied more than a fraction of one per cent of these consultants, except for India (1.3 per cent – seven or eight people).

The President of the Bank is by tradition an American. A Resident Representative is never a national of the country where s/he serves. The staff consists of dozens of nationalities, but Americans are still the biggest contingent, with the British second. Oddly, the Philippines seems to rank third (Filipinos occupy mostly secretarial or clerical positions).

The Bank's administrative budget for fiscal 1994 is nearly $1.4 billion, eleven per cent more than in 1993. About two-thirds of the budget is devoted to staff costs, broadly defined. Salary increases between 1993 and 1994 averaged six per cent, twice the rate of inflation.

WHY

That is a question we hope this book may help to answer. Meanwhile, it is important to understand why the Bank's loans in several different categories give it a synergistic power quite disproportionate to its actual size. With four types of loans and the capacity to co-ordinate them strategically, the World Bank controls many aspects of investment, institutional development and public policy (or the lack of same) in nearly 150 nations.*

1) *Project Lending*

2) *Sector Lending*

3) *Institutional Lending*

4) *Structural Adjustment Lending*

5) *Integration Policy*

---

* We are grateful to David Batker for his research assistance in compiling the following typology of the Bank's lending, with examples for each type.

1) Project Lending

This is the classic Bank loan: coal plants, oil development, fisheries, forestry, and agriculture projects, dams, roads, education, population, water/sanitation and health projects, et cetera.

EXAMPLES: $1.2 billion in present and expected future loans for the National Thermal Power Corporation of India (which will require $8 billion in total financing) to finance some fourteen coal and gas thermal power plants (see Chapter VIII); a loan to revamp Russia's fishing fleet, the second largest in the world; $500 million for the Russian oil sector, facilitating transnational corporation (TNC) penetration of Russian oil development; and so on.

2) Sector Lending

These loans govern an entire sector of a country's economy (energy, agriculture, industry). A single loan carries conditions determining the policies and national priorities for the sector.

EXAMPLE: Mexico has received both energy and agriculture sector loans. The energy sector loan set the priorities for $7 billion worth of Mexico's own energy investments, promoted privatization and supplied the legal framework for future penetration by foreign corporations. The agriculture sector loan has helped to further convert Mexican farming from small-scale production for domestic consumption to large-scale export-oriented production. These loans have facilitated the Mexican shift to free trade. For dozens of other countries the process has been similar.

3) Institutional Lending

The World Bank lends in order to reorganize government institutions, orienting their policies towards free trade and open access for TNCs. Privatized utilities but also regulatory bodies in many countries are products of World Bank lending.

EXAMPLES: The National Thermal Power Corporation of India

was formed with a World Bank loan (1975); EGAT, the energy authority in Thailand, and the Brazilian energy ministry were similarly instituted. In 1993, the World Bank made a loan to create a Department of Energy in the Philippines and to revamp the National Power Corporation of the Philippines, structured according to the Bank's usual guidelines. The 'institutional loan' also serves to bring about basic alterations in governing structures without the need for approval by parliaments.

4)   *Structural Adjustment Lending*

Structural adjustment loans were nominally intended to relieve the debt crisis, convert domestic economic resources to production for export and promote the penetration of TNCs into previously restricted economies. Most Southern countries have now undergone structural adjustment – often called austerity programmes by local people – under World Bank and International Monetary Fund auspices. In the 1990s, these programmes were extended to the former Soviet Union, the former socialist countries of Eastern Europe and to India as well. Structural adjustment lending is characterized by:

– privatization of government corporations and severe 'downsizing' of public employment and government bureaucracy, exacerbating unemployment and tending to affect public service ministries most (health, education, transport, housing, environment, et cetera) through drastic budget reductions;

– promotion of exports of raw materials and of export industries to earn foreign exchange; import liberalization and elimination of trade barriers or quotas;

– elimination or sharp reduction in subsidies for agriculture, food staples, health care, education, and other areas (generally excluding the military, however);

– restrictive monetary policies and high interest rates to curb inflation;

– a reduction in real wages (especially for lower wage earners), which is called 'demand management', also intended to control inflation.

Structural adjustment loans invariably encourage the free-market, competitive, individualistic ethos broadly known as Thatcherism in the UK or Reaganomics in the US.

5) Integration Policy

These four types of lending are coordinated in practice, particularly since the Bank reorganized in 1987, to provide a much stronger 'country focus'. The Bank's goal is now to make sure that *all* its loans to a given country contribute to the achievement of adjustment policy objectives there.

EXAMPLE: Project lending (for coal, geothermal, and transmission projects) was withheld from the Philippines in April and May 1993 until the government increased electricity rates to the level required by the World Bank under the restructuring of the energy sector. At the same time Philippines Department of Energy has been set up under Bank auspices. Funds from other donors are made subject to Bank approval: on this account, the Asian Development Bank also refused to approve a coal thermal power plant loan until the Philippine government agreed to a rate increase.

In practice, Western transnational corporations are usually first in line for procurement contracts. In many previously isolated countries, from Bhutan to Rumania, World Bank projects provided the first contracts for TNCs to enter these countries.

Some critics of the Bank have expressed outrage at its close connections with business in general and modern transnational corporations in particular, either through procurement arrangements or by facilitating their operations in this country or that. Such criticism is misplaced: this is part of what the Bank is supposed to do. Article 1 of its charter specifies five purposes, two of which concern the Bank's relationship with private capital. It is expected to 'promote private foreign investment' and 'conduct its operations with due regard to the effect of international investment on business conditions in the territories of members'.

The Bank has certainly fulfilled this part of its mandate. Its founders, however, saw such measures as means rather than ends: the ultimate purpose of the Bank's activities was described as 'the development of the productive resources of members, thereby assisting in raising productivity, the standard of living and conditions of labour'. In this regard, the Bank's record leaves much to be desired.

Chapter I

In the Beginning

Great institutions, like great families or nations, have great ancestors. Humanity looks to its founding fathers and mothers for
guidance, inspiration and strength. Some celebrate warriors,
others law-givers, still others prophets, but no society on earth can
do without ancestors. The word comes from the Latin *antecessor*, one
who comes before, but in a real sense they are also intercessors –
between us and the divine or between us and the values we
cherish, even if we do not always honour them. Ancestors are not
just examples to be followed but the bearers of vital messages for
the present.[1]

The World Bank, like its sister the International Monetary Fund,
has two recognized ancestors, a lesser and a greater. The lesser is
the American, remembered now mostly by specialists. His name
was Harry Dexter White and he later became a victim of Senator
Joseph McCarthy's vicious anti-communist witch-hunts. The greater
is the Englishman, known at least by name even to those who have
never read a line of his work: John Maynard Keynes.

The Bank and the Fund were the crowning achievements of
Keynes's remarkably productive life. But even he, with all his
prestige, could not shape the Bretton Woods twins precisely in his
own image. This chapter tells how they came to be born, the hopes
they incarnated and why they were intended to change the world.

Besides the sprawling Mount Washington Hotel, there isn't much
in Bretton Woods, New Hampshire and there was literally nothing
there but the hotel in July 1944 when 800 people – four-fifths of
them support staff – arrived for the United Nations Monetary and
Financial Conference, known ever since as the Bretton Woods
Conference.[2]

The choice of venue could have been calculated to keep everyone out of mischief, as they would be required to attend meetings around the clock. The scenery of the White Mountain National Forest, whose nearly one million acres entirely surround the hotel complex, is superb and there were free Coca-Cola dispensers on the verandas; but otherwise, Temptation cannot have loomed large in Bretton Woods.

Twenty-seven of the forty-four country delegations came from countries we still euphemistically refer to as 'developing' and which, fifty years later, appear on the World Bank's rosters as such. Three – the Soviet Union, Poland and Czechoslovakia – were soon to disappear behind the Iron Curtain. Only twelve came from the group of rich countries that now belong to the OECD.* And, it could be argued, only two of those – the United States and Great Britain – really counted. It was none the less a remarkable feat to bring together so many diplomats and statesmen while war was still raging in both Europe and Asia.

They came at the invitation of the President of the United States, Franklin D. Roosevelt. Their task was to provide for postwar financial stability and, above all, to ensure unfettered international commerce. Again and again, the *Proceedings* of Bretton Woods stress the ruling obsession of these leaders of a war-torn world: never to revert to the 'competitive currency depreciations, imposition of exchange restrictions, import quotas and other devices which had all but stifled trade' and plunged the planet headlong into its most devastating conflict ever.

The Americans had been planning for this moment almost from the time the war began. In the 1930s, they had themselves suffered from trade blocs – above all the sterling area which their British

---

* The complete list of 'governments and authorities' – this latter term coined to accommodate the Free French and exclude the Vichy government – participating in the conference is: Australia, Belgium, Bolivia, Brazil, Canada, Chile, China, Colombia, Costa Rica, Cuba, Czechoslovakia, Dominican Republic, Ecuador, Egypt, El Salvador, Ethiopia, French Committee of National Liberation, Greece, Guatemala, Haiti, Honduras, Iceland, India, Iran, Iraq, Liberia, Luxembourg, Mexico, the Netherlands, New Zealand, Nicaragua, Norway, Panama, Paraguay, Peru, Philippine Commonwealth, Poland, Union of South Africa, Union of Soviet Socialist Republics, United Kingdom, United States of America, Uruguay, Venezuela and Yugoslavia.

cousins had used to maintain control of the world's most lucrative markets as well as of raw materials. The United States now intended to obtain unimpeded access to both.

Even before the Americans entered the Second World War, Roosevelt had already made his conditions clear to Churchill when the two leaders met on shipboard off Newfoundland in August 1941. The President told the Prime Minister that after the war free trade would be needed to guarantee the peace – there should no longer be any special trade agreements, especially not those of the British empire with its colonies. Churchill replied hotly that the trade agreements lay at the heart of an empire which Britain had no intention of dismantling. Roosevelt countered that peace would require equality among peoples which would in turn imply free trade between them: Britain's trade agreements were the reason its colonies were so 'backward', according to the President.

Britain was in the midst of Hitler's *blitzkrieg* and Churchill was beaten. He said to Roosevelt, 'Mr President, I think you want to abolish the British empire . . . everything you have said confirms it. But in spite of that, we know you are our only hope. You know that we know it. You know that we know that without America, the British empire cannot hold out'. Next day, they announced the Atlantic Charter, whose fourth point specified that after the war, 'all countries large or small, victorious or defeated [should] have access on an equal footing to the markets and the raw materials of the world necessary for their economic prosperity'.[3]

Assistant Secretary (soon to become Secretary) of State Dean Acheson put the matter even more bluntly three years later. When the hostilities ceased, the booming US war economy would necessarily shut down. What was to be done with all that excess manufacturing capacity? Said Acheson:

> No group which has studied this problem . . . has ever believed that our domestic markets could absorb our entire production under our present system . . . we need those markets [abroad] for the output of the United States . . . we cannot have full employment and prosperity in the United States without the foreign markets.[4]

And again in 1944 another influential US State Department spokesman weighed in with:

Our metals are running out and so may our oil eventually ... other
essentials must come from abroad and in fifty years, like the British,
we shall have to export to pay for the things we need for life.[5]

From the US point of view, then, the postwar world had to have
three major characteristics. First, the Americans wanted free trade
with no discrimination against US goods – easy enough to obtain,
since the US was virtually the only country left with a surfeit of
goods for sale. Next, they wanted a favourable climate for American
investment in foreign economies – again, non-negotiable, since the
US was also the only major country left with substantial disposable
savings. Finally, they wanted unimpeded access to raw materials.
The Bretton Woods Institutions were intended to provide for all
three.

After Roosevelt made his unrefusable offer to Churchill, the US
leadership began seriously to prepare for the postwar world. Only a
week after the Japanese bombing of Pearl Harbor in December
1941 brought the Americans into the war, Roosevelt's trusted
Treasury Secretary, Henry Morgenthau, set his assistant, Harry
Dexter White, the task of planning postwar international financial
policies. On the British side, John Maynard (by then Lord) Keynes
had taken on an identical assignment. White kept the three objectives of free trade, private investment and raw material access at
the top of his agenda; Keynes worked especially on what he called
at the time the International Clearing Union.

The US and the UK were allies; their rivalry for markets and
influence none the less remained keen. By 1944 Britain was ex-
hausted and the US finally had the chance to realize Morgenthau's
prime objective, which was, as he later wrote to President Truman,
'to move the financial center of the world from London and Wall
Street to the United States Treasury'.

Keynes, meanwhile, was informing the House of Lords that *his*
plan would be the 'indispensable means' to maintain the 'long
tradition by which most empire countries, and many other countries, too, have centred their financial systems in London'.[6] Both
Keynes and Morgenthau were counting on the Bretton Woods
Conference to put their political and financial objectives in place.

Whatever the competition between them, the two powers agreed on the basics. Through the darkest years of the war, White and Keynes laboured separately to provide a postwar system able, in White's words,

> to prevent the disruption of foreign exchanges and the collapse of the monetary and credit systems; to assure the restoration of foreign trade; and to supply the huge volume of capital that will be needed virtually throughout the world for reconstruction, for relief and for economic recovery.[7]

White was convinced that if these three goals were not achieved,

> [we will] drift from the peace table into a period of chaotic competition, monetary disorder, depressions, political disruption and finally into new wars within as well as among nations.[8]

Bretton Woods was thus expected to produce nothing less than a detailed blueprint for a global peace-keeping machine which had to succeed if future disasters were to be averted. From August 1942 onwards, the two countries worked together on postwar financial planning.

Still, obstacles remained and some were internal to the United States. The name Keynes was associated in the Republican Party psyche with 'that man' – the hated Roosevelt – and American bankers were less than keen on the idea of Keynesian postwar financial institutions. Nor did they welcome Morgenthau's proposed shift of financial gravity from Wall Street to Washington. The bankers insisted – and Treasury eventually gave in – that 'the greatest possible freedom be given to our businessmen engaged in international trade'. American labour unions and the smaller banks were, on the other hand, enthusiastically in favour of institutions promising to safeguard free trade, from which they believed they had everything to gain.

The outcome of Bretton Woods was, perhaps, a foregone conclusion: everyone understood that what the Americans wanted, the Americans would get. Even so, other countries besides Britain had, since mid-1943, helped this dossier to take shape in a series of formal and informal international meetings. Three months before the Bretton Woods Conference convened, a top team of financial technicians had already produced the 'Joint Statement of Experts on the International Monetary Fund' – a detailed document published simultaneously in Washington, London, Moscow, Chungking, Ottawa, Rio de Janeiro, Mexico City and Havana.[9] By the time they arrived at the United Nations Monetary and Financial Conference in July 1944, the 169 official delegates – 168 men and a lone woman* – were well prepared to offer the world a new set of stable financial arrangements.

The International Monetary Fund had a surfeit of fairy godfathers hovering over its cradle at Bretton Woods. Everyone agreed it would be *the* key postwar institution, charged with ensuring the unimpeded flow of trade through timely financing. Nearly everyone concurred, too, with the *modus operandi* proposed by its American and British architects. The Fund was a sure thing.

Not so an 'international investment bank'. Even the formal invitations to Bretton Woods described the conference's object as the formulation of definite proposals for an international monetary fund and 'possibly' for a bank.[10] In fact, it was only thanks to the preparations undertaken by the British, which is to say by Lord Keynes, and to Keynes's own tenacity, that such a bank was considered by the conference at all.

A sense of high purpose permeated the atmosphere of Bretton Woods. Crass economic and political interests were, if not forgotten, at least momentarily set aside. Besides, the United States was the only serious financial player remaining, and its performance during the war had left other participants favourably disposed. Without American intervention, fascism would already have triumphed worldwide and everybody knew it. The Americans were the crucial combatants – without their troops still in the field the delegates would not even have been around to envisage a different postwar system. From the first plenary onwards, the record of Bretton Woods is suffused with a kind of 'never again' determination.

In his message to the conference, President Roosevelt (who was not present in Bretton Woods) exhorted the delegates to

---

* Miss Mabel Newcomer, a professor of economics at Vassar College.

provide the basis upon which [men and women everywhere] will be able to exchange with one another the natural riches of the earth and the products of their own industry and ingenuity. Commerce is the lifeblood of a free society ... This conference will test our capacity to cooperate in peace as we have in war. I know that you will all approach your task with a high sense of responsibility to those who have sacrificed so much in their hopes for a better world.[11]

In his response to Roosevelt's message, the Chinese delegate stressed the theme of interdependence which alone could 'maintain a high level of prosperity and employment in our respective countries' and reminded his peers that 'the outcome of the Conference will affect the shape of the peace and the welfare of generations to come. We have before us a rare opportunity to serve the common people everywhere.'*

Accepting his nomination as President of the Conference, US Treasury Secretary Henry Morgenthau reminded the delegates (who scarcely needed reminding) of the historical processes that had led to economic and, ultimately, military aggression:

All of us have seen the great economic tragedy of our time. We saw the worldwide depression of the 1930s. We saw currency disorders develop and spread from land to land, destroying the basis for international trade and international investment and even international faith. In their wake, we saw unemployment and wretchedness – idle tools, wasted wealth. We saw their victims fall prey, in places, to demagogues and dictators. We saw bewilderment and bitterness become the breeders of fascism, and, finally, of war.

The task of Bretton Woods was thus no less than to refashion history. Freely flowing and expanding world trade was universally perceived as the means to this end; the newly-minted IMF would be the institution to oil its wheels and finance it. When it came to a bank, however, Morgenthau appeared to be talking about a strictly postwar institution to carry out a precise, technical and, all things considered, short-term task:

---

* The 'common people' and 'ordinary men and women' are much in evidence in the rhetoric of Bretton Woods. They were later to be held in rather low esteem by the Institutions which emerged from the conference.

For long-range reconstruction purposes, international loans on a
broad scale will be imperative ... loans to provide capital for economic reconstruction ... The technicians have prepared the outline
of a plan for an International Bank for Postwar Reconstruction which
will investigate the opportunities for loans of this character.

And he concluded, in more ringing words,

Our final responsibility is to [the young men who have been dying
together and those who must now live together] ... As they prosper
or perish, the work which we do here will be judged. The opportunity
before us has been bought with blood. Let us meet it with faith in
one another, with faith in our common future, which these men
fought to make free.

Whereupon everyone rose for 'The Star-Spangled Banner' and
adjourned for dinner. It was still opening day, Saturday, 1 July
1944. Amid the stirring speeches – and those speakers of the war-
torn 1940s did not fear fine rhetoric – no mention of something
called an International Bank for Reconstruction and Development
had yet been made in plenary session. The US Treasury Secretary
had even just studiously called it something else, leaving matters to
the 'technicians' in the most tentative of endorsements. The word
'development' in particular had not been pronounced. 'Postwar
Reconstruction' was what Morgenthau had said and it was what
he meant: the reconstruction certainly of Europe – possibly of China
and Japan as well, but he was looking no further.

At Bretton Woods Keynes immediately and naturally assumed
the chairmanship of the commission established to deal with this
international investment bank, while Harry Dexter White, head of
the American delegation, took the chair of the commission charged
with formulating the Articles of Agreement of the International
Monetary Fund.

The conference lasted three weeks and for most of that time, the
bank remained the poor relation, relegated to the background. The
'first weeks were devoted almost exclusively to the work ... [of
Commission I] on the International Monetary Fund. In fact, a
major portion of the Fund articles were in final form before Commission II on the Bank began to function actively,' says the Preface
of the conference *Proceedings*. That is putting it mildly. In fact,

Commission I on the Fund was endowed with committees and sub-committees and ad hoc committees busily hammering out every detail of its Articles and manner of functioning. Its provisions had all been under discussion for months anyway, if not for years.

In contrast, fully twelve days into the conference, Commission II on the 'possible' bank had got no further than deciding it preferred the words 'Reconstruction and Development' to 'Investment and Guarantee' in its formal title. Commission II wasn't sure whether the new organization 'should be called a "bank", a "corporation" or by some other name'. While a phalanx of committees dealt with the IMF, delegates working to establish the future International Bank for Reconstruction and Development had only a drafting committee. The *Proceedings* makc clear that its draft barely made it to the wire in time for adjournment.

On Monday, 3 July, Keynes opened the first meeting of his commission, now officially called the Second Commission on the Bank for Reconstruction and Development (it is not clear from the *Proceedings* how the change from Morgenthau's formulation was effected – perhaps Keynes just called it what he wanted and that was that). He reminded its members of a huge gap in the postwar strategy of the 'United and Associated Nations'. No plans existed for an institution which could make loans to countries that had 'suffered the devastation of war, to enable them to restore their shattered economies and replace the instruments of production which have been lost or destroyed'.

Although the war was still very much on, Keynes believed that: 'We should be bitterly failing in our duty if we were not ready prepared for the days of liberation ... Any delay, any avoidable time lag will be disastrous to the establishment of good order and good government and *may also postpone the date at which the victorious armies of liberation can return to their homelands'* (emphasis added).

The threat of keeping troops away from home a moment longer than necessary would have been enough to prod even the most recalcitrant politician into action. But, for his Bank, Keynes had more than postwar reconstruction in mind. He is famous for having said, 'In the long run we are all dead', but his own vision was a remarkably clear and long-run one, based on the whole world, including the colonies, not just the great powers. For this founding father, the less developed countries, as he called them even then, were to be a central part of the Bank's mandate from the very beginning. As he declared to the members of his commission:

> the field of reconstruction from the consequences of war will mainly occupy the proposed Bank in its early days. But as soon as possible, and with increasing emphasis as time goes on, there is a second primary duty laid upon it, *namely to develop the resources and productive capacity of the world, with special attention to the less developed countries, to raising the standard of life and the conditions of labour everywhere, to make the resources of the world more fully available to all mankind* (emphasis added).

The problem Keynes had to resolve was complex. Immediately after the war, no major country aside from the United States would have any spare cash to lend. Potential borrowers, on the other hand, would be legion, impoverished, and utterly lacking in capital equipment which the war had damaged or destroyed. If everyone insisted on playing by normal banking rules, it would be impossible to undertake reconstruction at all. Lenders would be required to assume huge risks. No sane investor – and the Bank was intended from the start to use mostly *investors'* money, not government funds – would accept such a proposition unless the borrower paid a heavy risk premium which, by definition, he would be too poor to afford.

Nor could individual, destitute governments raise their own money by issuing bonds – who in his right mind would buy such shaky securities on which default would be only too likely? The novelty of Keynes's proposal was to provide a mechanism whereby everyone could share the benefits without sharing the costs, while incurring virtually non-existent risks. Magic.

His win/win scenario called upon all governments to pay, in proportion to their capacity, a subscription to the Bank in gold or 'free exchange' (i.e. currency convertible to gold). These subscriptions would serve as the guarantee for bond issues on regular financial markets which, in turn, would provide most of the loanable capital. The bonds would be gilt-edged, AAA investments because investors would find them credible and profitable. In the first place, the Bank's gold and convertible currency resources would back them up. Furthermore,

> the proceeds will be expended only for proper purposes and in proper ways, after due enquiry by experts and technicians, so that there will be safeguards against squandering and waste and extravagance, which were not present with many of the ill-fated loans made between the wars.

And if these iron-clad guarantees were not enough, investors could be reminded that no borrower would be likely to default on such loans because, as Keynes explained, it 'would be under an overwhelming motive to do its best and play fair, for the consequences of improper action and avoidable default to so great an institution will not be lightly incurred'.

In other words, Lord Keynes had invented the pooling of credit insurance among nations. He saw it as a fundamental contribution to the overwhelming task ahead, 'to rebuild the world when a final victory over the forces of evil opens the way to a new age of peace and progress after great afflictions'.

Turning Keynes's vision into legal texts and political reality was another matter. The birth of such an institution at Bretton Woods must at times have appeared to delegates as problematic, not to say touch-and-go.*

---

* Proof that without Keynes's prestige and determination the International Bank for Reconstruction and Development could well have failed to see the light of day, is provided by the lamentable fate of the now-forgotten Commission III. Several delegations, especially from Latin America, were attempting to put other economic issues on the postwar agenda, including the use of silver as an international financial instrument and the never-ending, still unsatisfied quest for an International Stabilization Fund guaranteeing fair and stable prices for raw materials to consumers and producers alike. Although Commission III also had a prestigious Chair (Judge Fred Vinson, later Chief Justice of the US Supreme Court), held about as many meetings as Commission II on the Bank and submitted several final Recommendations to the Conference, no action was taken. One of its Recommendations, adopted by the Final Act of the Conference, called for 'The liquidation of the Bank for International Settlements at the earliest possible moment'. When last heard from in 1993, the BIS was alive, well and still living happily ever after in Basle, Switzerland. See *Proceedings*, pp. 1082–4.

A week into the conference, Commission II's drafting committee, chaired by Dean Acheson, supplied its initial text. Two weeks into the conference, delegations had duly come up with various alternatives and amendments. Four days before the end of the conference, the drafting committee submitted its fifth report. The same day, in sharp contrast, Commission I produced the final Articles of Agreement of the International Monetary Fund, with completed Annexes and Schedules, polished down to the last comma.

As for Commission II, three days before the end of the conference, new versions of various Articles for the Bank were still being approved or rejected. The same day, Acheson, on behalf of his drafting committee, explained that since various matters had just been referred to the drafting committee or were currently under consideration, 'it was hardly worth the Commission's time to consider them *at this stage*'. On Thursday, 20 July, the drafting committee's final working day, the delegation of the USSR proposed major amendments and deletions to five Articles.*

At six p.m. on the final working day of the conference, the full commission was still hastily passing amendments. The leader of the French delegation, future Prime Minister Pierre Mendès France, asked, and was granted, that the wording 'French Committee of National Liberation' be changed throughout to 'France'. Finally, at seven p.m., two hours behind schedule, the Reporting Delegate of Commission II was ready to speak to his colleagues. He reminded them that:

> The creation of the Bank was an entirely new venture. Never, during
> the numerous international meetings which over a period of twenty-

---

* At Keynes's express request, several countries withdrew their reservations at the last possible moment, but not the USSR. None the less, on Saturday 22 July, a few moments before the formal Final Plenary Session, the Soviet delegation informed Conference President Morgenthau that their government intended to increase its subscription to the Bank from $900 million to $1.2 billion. Though Morgenthau announced this development to the Final Plenary as 'fraught with more significance and more hopeful meaning for the future of the world than any which those of us here have heard so far', the USSR in the end refused to join the Bank, seeing it as an American creature. Decades later, after the Soviet Union had ceased to exist, most of its former republics became Bank members separately in 1992–3.

five years have studied all sorts of economic problems, was any thought given to an organization so considerable in its scope and so novel in its conception as that which has been the subject of your deliberations. So novel was it that no adequate name could be found for it . . . However, it was accidentally born with the name Bank, and Bank it remains, mainly because no satisfactory name could be found in the dictionary for this unprecedented institution.

In a remarkably short time, and in largely uncharted territory, the commission had reached 'agreement on the principles which are to govern the activity of the Bank', an 'achievement [which] would have been impossible without . . . the brilliant chairmanship of Lord Keynes'.

The Fund was conceived to provide short-term balance of payments support to its members and thus facilitate the free flow of commerce. The Bank was to work both for 'the reconstruction *and for the development of member countries, and these two objectives are to be pursued on a footing of equality*' (emphasis added).[12]

The interests of private capital, high on the American list of priorities, were not forgotten. A clause declared that the Bank's medium- or long-term capital 'promotes or supplements private investments either by means of guarantees and participations in private loans or by providing funds out of its own resources'. The resources in question were astronomical for the period – fully $10 billion, even though most of this sum would never be paid in but simply be on call.

Once the Executive Plenary had approved the Bank's Articles of Agreement, all was in readiness for the black-tie Final Plenary on Saturday night, 22 July 1944. At the close of the farewell dinner, Conference President Morgenthau called upon Lord Keynes to move the acceptance of the Final Act. Keynes, 'upon arising was accorded an ovation, everyone present standing'. He himself rose to the occasion with characteristic eloquence and wit. Recalling the hurdles of the previous three weeks, he said:

> We have had to perform at one and the same time the tasks appropriate to the economist, to the financier, to the politician, to the journalist, to the propagandist, to the lawyer, to the statesman – even, I think, to the prophet and to the soothsayer.

He praised the teamwork, and paid special tribute 'to our lawyers',

> all the more so because I have to confess that, generally speaking, I do not like lawyers. I have been known to complain that to judge from the results in this lawyer-ridden land, the *Mayflower*, when she sailed from Plymouth, must have been entirely filled with lawyers.

Keynes wanted a lawyer not to do his thinking for him, but to 'tell me how to do what *I* think sensible and, above all, to devise means by which it will be lawful for me to go on being sensible in unforeseen conditions some years hence'.

> Too often lawyers are men who turn poetry into prose and prose into jargon. Not so our lawyers here in Bretton Woods. On the contrary, they have turned our jargon into prose and our prose into poetry.

This poetic breed seems to have become extinct since Bretton Woods. Keynes went on to praise another professional category to which the Bank's staff still often appears to belong:

> We have reached this evening a decisive point. But it is only a beginning. We have to go out from here as missionaries, inspired by zeal and faith.

Keynes recalled too that few believed forty-four such disparate nations could work together, but

> we have done so in amity and unbroken concord. If we can continue ... there is hope for the world ... If we can so continue, this nightmare in which most of us here present have spent too much of our lives, will be over. The brotherhood of man will have become more than a phrase. Mr President, I move to accept the Final Act.

This was Keynes's formal, diplomatic persona and it is not a false one: under the circumstances of the not-yet-postwar world he had undoubtedly obtained as much as it was humanly and politically possible to do. Later, he wrote of the US railroading through its views on issue after issue; evidence exists as well that he was worried about the capacity of these supranational institutions to outweigh national sovereignty. This, indeed, was one of the main outcomes of what he later called the 'monkey-house' of Bretton Woods.[13]

Thus was Keynes's child, the World Bank, conceived and born. It was a hybrid from the beginning. Its own founders declared that this Bank, even if it was a bank, was one in which

> the type of shareholders, the nature of subscriptions, the exclusion of all deposits and of short-term loans, *the non-profit basis* are *quite foreign to the accepted nature of a Bank* (emphasis added).[14]

Keynes, at least in his public statements, never ceased to claim that this unprecedented Bank could do no less than help to remake the world in a finer image and contribute to the brotherhood of man. Throughout the conference that led to its birth, he was honoured as the Bank's undisputed ancestor – Harry Dexter White, along with many others, received polite acknowledgement but no standing ovations. For this institution, Keynes was the founding father.

At the time of Bretton Woods, he was sixty-one; two years later he was dead, officially from a heart attack, in fact from exhaustion. The institution born of his genius and his unflagging work has now reached middle-age. One might expect to see Keynes's portrait proudly and prominently displayed at the Bank's headquarters. Not only is there no picture but his name has absolutely and utterly disappeared from the Bank's canon. He is never referred to, his work is never mentioned; he has vanished down a kind of Orwellian memory hole.

If an ancestor is, according to an irreverent definition, an extremely successful dead person, then Keynes is – at least at the Bank – a miserable failure. The institution he founded has a case of collective amnesia and has consigned him to oblivion. How would John Maynard Keynes judge his offspring today if he were to return, as ancestors sometimes do?

The Bank's Articles of Agreement were ratified by member governments in the course of 1945 and entered into force on 27 December

1945. The inaugural meeting of the Boards of Governors of both the International Monetary Fund and the International Bank for Reconstruction and Development took place in Savannah, Georgia, on 8 March 1946. The Bank made its first loans in 1947.

Chapter II

The Other Ancestor

For better and many would say for worse, Robert Strange McNamara impressed his stamp on the World Bank and transformed its
culture. His presidency lasted from 1 April 1968 until 30 June
1981; he was reappointed twice although he did not complete his
third five-year term. When he came to the Bank after serving as
United States Defense Secretary from 1961 to 1968, he left behind
him not only the Pentagon but also a full-scale war in Vietnam
which was rending the country.

Until McNamara assumed the Bank's presidency, the place wasn't
exactly a backwater but it wasn't an especially exciting institution
either. It had had four presidents: the first, Eugene Meyer, stayed
six months and left because he thought his board and especially his
American executive director second-guessed him and interfered too
much. The second, John J. McCloy, remained for two years and left
in mid-1949 to become the US High Commissioner in Germany.
The third, Eugene Black, a courtly investment banker previously
with Chase National Bank of New York and who had also served
on the Bank's board, was hand-picked by McCloy to succeed him.
He settled in for thirteen years (1949–62). His successor, George
Woods, was less tactful than Black, raised a few hackles and served
only one term, from 1963 to 1968.

Together, over twenty years, these gentlemen lent a grand total
of $10.7 billion (not counting IDA credits which, from 1961 to
1967, added a further $1.7 billion to the portfolio). In only one
year, 1965, did IBRD commitments top the billion dollar mark.[1]

Our purpose here is not to survey or to evaluate the Bank's
project lending. Doubtless during these first two decades, the Bank
made some loans that turned out to be environmental and human
disasters; others were quite blatantly tied to aiding and abetting
transnational corporations to set up shop in the developing world.[2]

Our point is, rather, that in its earlier pre-McNamara days, the Bank was mostly a place full of technical specialists designing investment projects. More often than not, these concerned basic infrastructure and they did, more or less, contribute to development as then conceived. The Bank's presidents were bankers and business-men doing business with sovereign governments – both borrowers and lenders. They and their Bank had no particular concern for or interest in poverty, much less in the poor.

Robert McNamara changed all that. Where the Bank was con-cerned, he even 'invented' the poor. To flash forward for a moment, it is clear that McNamara's indelible mark on the Bank is also a benchmark. When, in 1992, Bank President Lewis Preston an-nounced, after a decade of structural adjustment lending and auster-ity, that 'the overarching goal of the Bank is the sustainable reduction of poverty', he was echoing almost twenty years later McNamara's own mission statement to the 1973 meeting of the Bank's board of governors in Nairobi. Everyone remembers that speech as a watershed, the one in which McNamara launched the concept of 'absolute poverty':

> a condition of life so degraded by disease, illiteracy, malnutrition and squalor as to deny its victims basic human necessities . . . a condition of life so limited as to prevent realization of the potential of the genes with which one is born; a condition of life so degrading as to insult human dignity – and yet a condition of life so common as to be the lot of some 40% of the peoples of the developing countries.[3]

McNamara approached the scourge of absolute poverty as a missionary and it is he who lastingly changed (some would say confused) the Bank's mission. At the end of his speech he invoked 'All of the great religions [which] teach the value of each human life. In a way that was never true in the past, we now have the power to create a decent life for all men and women . . . the extremes of privilege and deprivation are simply no longer accept-able. It is development's task to deal with them'.

Never before had the Bank conceived 'development's task' as relieving the poverty of severely deprived men and women, individu-ally or *en masse*. Development's task had always been making sure that states had sufficient electrical power, transport, communica-tions, et cetera, to become 'modern' and more like the already industrialized countries. The Nairobi speech was a departure and also a kind of apotheosis for McNamara who was just embarking on his second term as Bank President. Throughout his tenure, everyone at the Bank experienced his 'driving sense of mission', to quote his close associate William Clark.[4]

McNamara's predecessors at the Bank had been patrician, establishment figures, at home in the East Coast investment banking world. McNamara was a small-town California boy of stern Scottish–Irish stock whose father had never been able to complete his schooling past the eighth grade. Raised as a frugal, hard-working Presbyterian, McNamara experienced the Great Depression as a young man. He brought to the Bank, as to all his tasks, a fierce competitiveness, a profound sense of vocation and an unaccustomed moral fervour.

When he told the Bank's board of governors in Nairobi that the extremes of privilege and deprivation were 'simply no longer acceptable', he meant it: these extremes were unacceptable to Robert McNamara, and he expected others to cooperate with him or get out of his way and let him get on with stamping them out. If, as one Oxford dictionary definition has it, a Messiah is a 'would-be liberator of an oppressed people or country', then McNamara certainly qualifies.

McNamara's motives were doubtless moral but they were also political. William Clark tells how, while still Defense Secretary, McNamara had informed President Lyndon Johnson that he wanted to devote the next years of his life to the economic development of the poorer nations. Indifference to their plight, he said, would yield results as tragic as those produced by a century of neglect of American blacks after the Civil War.

This zealous, crusading, 'hot' side of McNamara's nature was fused with a far colder one of rational calculation and logic. In her masterly, definitive biography of McNamara, Deborah Shapley stresses his lifelong reliance on – indeed obsession with – numbers. 'Numbers are a language for me,' this latter-day Pythagorean has remarked. They also seem to represent for him the only true basis of knowledge and the sole criteria for measuring professional or personal achievement. Fresh out of college, he declared to a friend who was going on to medical school that he, McNamara, would never choose to be a doctor because that way you could 'only help one person at a time'. McNamara's self-declared ambition was to help the 'greatest number' of people.[5]

Through numbers he sought not just to measure but to analyse and to assimilate reality; he was also clearly haunted by the ideas of manipulation and control, including self-control. By many accounts, he could be a terrifying man to work with – or rather for, as the notion of team-work was quite foreign to him. RSM was in charge, full stop. And what he frequently wanted from his staff were numbers, to the point that they were sometimes virtually forced to invent the desired figures rather than risk the President's wrath.[6] At the Bank one still hears the story of McNamara calling a staffer back to Washington from his holiday in order to supply a single figure.

So good was he at numbers that he served as a kind of human computer during the Second World War. As a young lieutenant colonel in the statistical control unit which planned the most logical deployment of men and material, he undoubtedly played a major role in the victory of the Allies. McNamara then went with his entire stat. control unit to the Ford Motor Company where his skills helped to save Ford from otherwise certain bankruptcy. Later, when RSM became President Kennedy's Secretary of Defense, Senator Barry Goldwater called him 'an IBM machine with legs'. McNamara was also the hardest of hard workers whose 'greater zeal and self-righteousness set him apart from the other Whiz Kids', according to his biographer.[7]

True to his fixation with numbers, McNamara made the phrase 'body-count' part of the standard vocabulary of the Vietnam war era. He fostered the 'electronic battlefield' – 'people-sniffers', infrared sensors, cluster bombs, land mines packed with shrapnel undetectable by medical X-ray, and similar weapons, accompanied by intensive chemical defoliation of the terrain in order to expose the enemy. This modern arsenal was supposed to allow round-the-clock, closely monitored killing and maiming of Vietnamese combatants and civilians alike and to create an uncrossable barrier preventing the Vietnamese from infiltrating what was, in their view, their own country.

McNamara publicly praised the Dow Chemical Company for its 'service to the free world' in manufacturing napalm, the burning substance which adheres to and dissolves the skin.[8] Above all, he was convinced that once some quantifiable threshold of US-inflicted pain was reached, the Vietnamese would give up. The military and strategic problem to which he diligently applied himself was to determine and to attain that level.

Many people in the anti-Vietnam war movement regarded McNamara as a war criminal. But he remained oblivious to the loathing he aroused and reacted with surprise and anger when confronted by protesters in the United States. In 1970, after he had already left the Pentagon for the Bank, McNamara attended a conference at Columbia University, the scene of some of the most powerful anti-war demonstrations of the period. Students at such protests had routinely denounced McNamara as 'the Butcher of Vietnam', yet after the conference, according to William Clark, RSM proposed to 'have a look around the campus'. It simply didn't occur to him that he could not stroll around Columbia unnoticed, unprotected and unmolested. Clark and the conference organizers were deeply relieved when they finally manoeuvred McNamara into a taxi to the airport.

When he assumed the task of running the Bank in 1968, McNamara unquestionably brought a capacity for hard work, zeal, self-righteousness, discipline and a commitment to helping the poor and downtrodden. Because he had been for so long at the eye of the storm over Vietnam which divided the nation with a bitterness it had not known for a hundred years, McNamara's central role in prosecuting that war may have caused him to feel partly responsible for the national trauma. Whether this deeply moral – on his own terms – man brought with him to the Bank a tragic sense of failure and a need for redemption are matters of individual conscience and thus of speculation.

Whatever his motives, true to form, McNamara hit the ground running. He spent his first week at 1818 H Street immersing himself in Bank statistics. He then called his first meeting of the most senior staff to grill them. Why had there been no recent loans to important, strategically significant countries like Indonesia or Egypt? Why was Africa largely left out? Why did the Bank's loans total less than a billion dollars a year in spite of the obvious needs of the 'greatest number'? The staff had ready answers, none of which satisfied their visibly impatient new boss.

As Clark describes it, the mood of the meeting became gloomy and the sky itself turned eerily dark although it was mid-afternoon. RSM cut off the proceedings abruptly, announcing that: 'I am going to ask you all to give me very shortly a list of all the projects or programs that you would wish to see the Bank carry out if there were no financial constraints'. The new President's top management filed out 'in a state of shock', a shock doubtless compounded by the news that the blackened sky resulted from large areas of Washington being burnt down by rioters, expressing their grief and rage over the assassination of Martin Luther King.[9]

McNamara demanded a development plan for every Bank borrowing country which would tell him how much the Bank could invest there if 'the only limit on our activities were the capacity of our member countries to use our assistance effectively and to repay our loans', as he later put it to the board of governors.[10]

For the next several months, Bank staff dredged from bottom drawers and dusty filing cabinets old, forgotten or rejected projects; they cobbled together standard Bank-type infrastructure projects for countries which had hitherto been judged too backward to handle them.

Meanwhile, McNamara was figuring out how to get around Wall Street. One of his staff's main arguments for keeping the billion dollar a year ceiling on loans was the Bank's supposed incapacity to borrow any more on the US bond market. RSM's view was that if New York couldn't or wouldn't supply the necessary capital, then Frankfurt, Tokyo, Zurich, or for that matter Kuwait, could and would. By the time of the annual general meeting in September 1968, a mere five months into the job, McNamara told his board of governors that in the previous ninety days the Bank had borrowed more funds on capital markets than in any calendar year of its history.

He then proceeded to expand Bank staff by 120 per cent (making it much more internationally diverse in the process) and to double Bank lending in real terms compared to the previous five-year period. In its entire twenty-two years of pre-McNamarian existence, from 1947 to 1968, the IBRD had financed 708 projects at a total cost of $10.7 billion. In his first term alone, from 1968 to 1973, McNamara's Bank undertook 760 new projects costing $13.4 billion.

The advantages and disadvantages of those projects for the countries concerned were hardly uppermost in his staff's mind – they well knew they would be rewarded for 'pushing money out the door', as the practice has been known in-house ever since. Nor could staff stop to consider which social groups would benefit and which ones would be harmed by a given Bank intervention.*

McNamara made clear that the larger an officer's portfolio, the more massive and expensive the projects he could 'get past the board', the more brilliant his career prospects. This quantitative mind-set is one for which the Bank is still paying; it might even prove to be its downfall, but McNamara absolutely insisted on such an approach. (Only in 1993 were there timid signs that the qualitative might enhance careers as much as or more than the quantitative.)

Because of this insistence, and the pressure on staff to design and sell projects to governments, Bank borrowers were encouraged to take on more debt than they could safely handle. As of 1992, multilateral debt (owed to multilateral development banks – MDBs – with the World Bank by far the largest creditor among them) represented $272 billion, almost a quarter of the total outstanding long-term debt burden of all developing countries. A decade earlier, these same countries had owed the MDBs only twelve per cent of a much smaller overall debt.[11] For the top twelve country recipients of IBRD loans, the average weight of multilateral debt in their total long-term debt burden was thirty-one per cent.

Under McNamara, project lending also blossomed into multi-project, integrated programmes with many components and complex interactions. Theoretically, the Bank was supposed to finance projects requested by a borrowing government. In practice, the Bank sent out its own flying squads to find bankable projects. The government – apprised of the possibility of a project thus identified and designed by the Bank – would then ask the Bank to kindly study the financing.

* Lending to agriculture was also vastly increased under McNamara, particularly to entrench the so-called Green Revolution in the Bank's major borrowing countries. This system of farming with high-cost inputs (irrigation, chemical fertilizers and pesticides, et cetera) increased overall cereals output but did so at the expense of smaller producers who could not afford to use it and who were frequently dispossessed by larger landholders. The Green Revolution increased income disparities, worsened nutritional levels and wiped out the irreplaceable genetic wealth of thousands of local cereal varieties. See Susan George, *How the Other Half Dies*, (Harmondsworth, Penguin, 1976, and subsequent editions), Chapter 5 and, for the Bank's involvement in this and other technocratic, productivist schemes, Chapter 10, 'IBRD, or, Is the Bank Really a Developer?'.

Governments rarely worried about how they would repay the loans; even more rarely did they refuse money which turned up with next to no exertion on their part. The Bank defined the location, content, organization and priorities of the project. Because the government was only marginally involved in the design, it remained more or less aloof from the project's implementation as well. As Susan George said elsewhere, the integrated rural development projects, a McNamara speciality, were a technocrat's dream:

> The technocrat has a whole area to play with, he has created a zone fenced off from the country at large; an enclave in which he may be able to accomplish 'rural progress' *which is absolutely beyond the reach of, and not necessarily related to, the country as a whole*'.[12]

Furthermore, from the government's point of view, a loan – or better still a *lot* of loans – from the World Bank sent signals to other lenders that they had nothing to fear. Other public donors and commercial banks tended to follow the lead of the Bank and it is not surprising that the Bank's all-time largest borrowers and the countries that held the most IBRD loans as of 1993 should also be the world's top debtors.*

* Comparisons are as follows:

Biggest All-time Bank Borrowers Including IDA	Most IBRD Outstanding Loans 1993	Highest Outstanding Debt 1992
India	Mexico	Mexico
Mexico	Indonesia	Brazil
Brazil	India	Indonesia
Indonesia	Brazil	India
Turkey	Turkey	China
China	Philippines	Argentina
Argentina	Argentina	Korea
Korea	Colombia	Turkey
Nigeria	Nigeria	Egypt
Morocco		Nigeria
		Algeria
		Philippines
		Pakistan

Source: OECD, *Financing and External Debt of Developing Countries, 1992 Survey* (Paris, OECD, 1993), and World Bank, *Annual Report 1993*.

These are not trivial points. Because McNamara equated more and costlier Bank projects – and thus higher levels of borrowing – with the greatest welfare for the greatest number, he paved the way for the structural adjustment programmes that have since devastated the lives of the poor. A dollar disbursed by the Bank, which became a dollar owed by the borrower, was automatically for RSM a dollar somehow doing good somewhere for someone.

This was a false assumption. Bank projects have frequently aggravated existing social cleavages and ills or created new ones.* Many of the Bank's major borrowers are in grave financial and social trouble today and the number of the absolute poor is higher, exacerbated by debt and structural adjustment. Even IDA credits did not necessarily reach those in need: all the African countries which received more than $1.5 billion of these so-called soft loans are undergoing structural adjustment and some of them, like Zaïre, are basket-cases.

Because of the incentive to loan as much as the traffic would bear – indeed, more – the Bank, through wishful thinking or by design, could not, or at least did not, reliably forecast third world debt. As late as 1978, the Bank was still making wildly inaccurate predictions concerning the debt these countries could expect to hold in 1985. Alas, by 1985 their total debt was almost twice as large as the Bank had said it would be and their official (bilateral and multilateral) debt was more than three times what it had expected. (We elaborate on the Bank's unimpressive forecasting record in Chapter IV.)

The Bank's dogged underestimates of debt are all the harder to understand since McNamara was just as doggedly orchestrating its increase. His reasoning, at least in retrospect, is exceedingly odd.

In 1976 he explained to his board of governors that debt service

---

* Pieter Smit, a doctoral candidate at the University of Amsterdam, has collected primary evidence suggesting that one Bank project in Kenya directly resulted in the deaths of hundreds of settlers; another in Mauritania appears to have reinforced traditional slave-labour patterns. Smit presented some initial conclusions in 'The Development of Feudalism', African Studies Centre, Leiden, 15 October 1992.

payments would bunch up towards the beginning of the 1980s. Borrowing countries would need to continue running substantial deficits (i.e. import more than they exported) in order to generate the high growth rates which are 'the very foundation for their credit-worthiness'. To cover these deficits and their debt service payments, they would need to keep on borrowing heavily from private sources: 'If this flow continues it will help to maintain and even accelerate the pace of development'.

> But can we really expect extraordinary efforts from the international commercial banking community if the official lenders themselves do not try to improve their own performance? ... I have discussed this matter with several bankers heavily involved in lending to middle-income countries ... the confidence of the commercial banking community would be substantially increased were it possible to restore the balance between private lending and official long-term lending to the developing nations.[13]

Whereupon he asks for a large capital increase for the Bank and a quick replenishment for the IDA so that they can take the lead in restoring the balance and thus increase the confidence of the international banking community. Private lending justifies official lending which justifies private lending, *ad infinitum*, or at least until the bubble bursts.

In such a context it is not difficult to understand why no one on the Bank's staff would have dreamed of questioning McNamara's 'more is better' model: it would have been asking for the boot. In any event, the staff's opinions were not solicited. McNamara was unenthusiastic about 'participation' inside the Bank (see Chapter VI) and would have considered it ludicrous in the field where project spending necessarily and by definition created benefits for all and sundry. Money could not conceivably worsen a situation.

Non-governmental organizations (NGOs) demand that the Bank slow down and involve local people in the design and implementation of projects which will affect their lives. They may not measure the cultural leap that the Bank would need to take in order to do so more than a dozen years after McNamara's departure. He knew how to help people, particularly the absolute poor: nothing further was required.

As McNamara expanded staff, gave orders, raised fresh lending capital on international bond markets with one hand and pushed it out the door with the other; all the while he preached to his directors and his staff that money wasn't really the point at all: '[I]n my view the fundamental case for development assistance is the moral one ... the rich and the powerful have a moral obligation to assist the poor and the weak'.[14]

McNamara was and remains a complex and driven man who in his professional lifetime probably hurt far more people than he helped if one wants to reason in the same quantitative terms he endorses. Taking at face value, however, his dictum about the moral duty of the rich and powerful, accepting further that McNamara, ex-Whiz Kid, himself now occupied the most powerful position in the world's development establishment and had more money at his disposal for the purpose of discharging that moral duty than any other person at any other time in history, how precisely did he propose to assist the poor and the weak?

Typically, he saw the problem of underdevelopment as a problem of undermanagement. Logic and rationality should be applied in large doses. While still running the Pentagon, McNamara was already thinking about the less developed, poor countries in quantitative and managerial terms. In a quasi-philosophical text he wrote that:

> Management is the gate through which social, political, economic, technical change ... is rationally spread through society ... To undermanage reality is not to keep it free. It is simply to let some force other than reason shape reality.[15]

Dealing with several hundred million poor people was not that daunting a prospect for a man who in 1962 had explained to an interviewer that 'running the Department of Defense is not different from running Ford Motor Company or the Catholic Church, for that matter. Once you get to a certain scale, it's all the same'.[16] Given his own style, the nature of that management could only be analytical, top-down, and numbers-oriented. For McNamara,

> Not to quantify what can be quantified is only to be content with
> something less than the full range of reason ... to argue that some
> phenomena transcend precise measurement – which is true enough
> – is no excuse for neglecting the arduous task of carefully analyzing
> what *can* be measured.[17]

Otherwise, irrational forces like 'unbridled emotion, greed, aggres-
siveness, hatred, ignorance, inertia' would take over and do the
managing for you.[18]

So he turned his formidable energies and his messianic fervour to
the measuring and the managing of the poor and the weak. And
yet, in so doing, this man who got top grades in logic in college and
who prided himself above all things on his rationality proceeded not
merely to make mistakes like an ordinary mortal but to fall into
fundamental logical fallacies.

These breaches of logic can be illustrated from one of McNamara's
best known texts, the title essay of his 1968 book called *The Essence
of Security*. The essay was first delivered as a speech to the American
Society of Newspaper Editors in 1966 while he was still running
the Pentagon. In it, he conveys his perspective on the lives of
millions of poor people and outlines the development model needed
for changing them; he reveals as well the implicit ideological and
political context in which he operated.

McNamara, like all other US officials at the time, was obsessed by
the Communist (always given a capital C in the literature of the
period) threat to the stability and power of the United States.
Revolution any place on earth, no matter how poverty-stricken and
obscure the country, imperilled the free world. In testimony before
the US Congress McNamara noted approvingly that

> the death of Ernesto Che Guevara in Bolivia in the fall of 1967 dealt
> a severe blow to the hopes of the Castroite revolutionaries. *But
> counterinsurgency alone is an inadequate response to this problem. Re-
> moval of the causes of human suffering and deprivation is essential if
> stable political institutions are to flourish free of the threat of violent
> revolution* (emphasis added).[19]

In other words, suffering and deprivation cause revolutions – not
an especially original or startling deduction, but one to which RSM
firmly adhered. Well before the Secretary of Defense had an inkling

he might one day be in a position at the Bank to act upon the 'causes of human suffering and deprivation', he had traced his own blueprint for dealing with them. In *The Essence of Security*, McNamara explains that 'a nation can reach the point at which it does not buy more security for itself simply by buying more military hardware and we are at that point'. The threat to the United States and its allies comes from those 'traditionally listless areas of the world [which have become] seething cauldrons of change'. In dealing with them, sophisticated weapons and more defence dollars will get you nowhere.

McNamara characteristically hammers home his point with numbers, citing the '164 internationally significant outbreaks of violence' in the previous eight years (1958–66), 'each of them specifically designed as a serious challenge to the authority or the very existence of the government in question'. None of these 164 instances was a formally declared war; only fifteen of them involved conflict between two states. These outbreaks of violence are not classical, cross-border wars but large-scale, internal, civil insurgencies. What worries McNamara most is the insurgents' challenge to 'eighty-two different governments'.

Furthermore, he notes that this anti-establishment violence is growing. Whereas twenty-three 'prolonged insurgencies' existed in 1958, by the time of his speech in 1966 this number had increased to forty. There was a seventy per cent increase in serious new outbreaks of violence during the same period.

Let us note here what goes unmentioned by McNamara but is surely obvious to his audience and uppermost in his own mind: the 'eighty-two different governments' under threat are, to one degree or another, allies and supporters of the United States. The challenge they face is not occupation or conquest by rival powers but violent overthrow by significant numbers of their own people who, presumably because of suffering and deprivation, have decided to stop being docile.

Clearly the fires under these 'seething cauldrons of change' must be quenched because 'violence anywhere in a taut world threatens the security and stability of nations half a globe away'. 'Half a globe', as far as Robert McNamara is concerned, and whether you slice it north–south or east–west, means the USA. He later testified at hearings of the US Congress on the 1969–73 defence budget that:

> We could find ourselves literally isolated, a 'fortress America' still relatively prosperous, but surrounded by a sea of struggling, envious and unfriendly nations – a situation hardly likely to strengthen our own state of peace and security ... We must create conditions for economic and social progress in the less developed areas of the world.[20]

What to do? First of all, recognize the importance of some further numbers which confirm that:

> There is a direct and constant relationship between the incidence of violence and the economic status of the countries afflicted ... since 1958, 87 per cent of the very poor nations, 69 per cent of the poor nations and 48 per cent of the middle-income nations suffered serious violence ... there is a relationship between violence and economic backwardness and the trend of such violence is up, not down.[21]

Furthermore, the rich–poor gap is widening and the southern hemisphere's population is young, mostly uneducated and increasingly frustrated. McNamara's 1966 description neatly fits the circumstances of the 1990s, except that thirty years previously one-half the world's population had access to one-sixth of the world's output; whereas in the 1990s fully four-fifths of humanity live in poor countries with access to only a fifth of global goods and services. Mathematically speaking, the South is twenty per cent worse off than it was when McNamara spoke.

Having thus defined the problem by quantifying it within an inch of its life, McNamara turns his attention to solutions – and thereupon faces, but fails to resolve, serious contradictions. Whatever the perils, the US Secretary of Defense affirms that the United States will refuse to act as 'the Global Gendarme ... [it] has no mandate from on high to police the world and no inclination to do so'. Still, 'the irreducible fact remains that [US] security is related directly to the security of the newly developing world ... In a modernizing society security means development ... and without development there can be no security.'[22]

So while the US government and its military should not play Global Gendarme, they should still be prepared to 'help protect those developing countries which genuinely need and request our help'; they should also 'help the developing nations with such training and equipment as are necessary to maintain the protective shield behind which development can go forward'. To that end, the US should encourage and train local military forces in poor countries to undertake 'civic action' – building roads, schools, bridges and the like.

McNamara thus presents the military – whether that of the US donor or the armed forces of the recipient – as uniformly protective, benign, solicitous of the people's welfare – even economically productive. At the time he made these observations, the United States had quite recently invaded the Dominican Republic and the Indonesian army's savage pogrom against some five hundred thousand real or imagined Communists was not even a year old. Smaller-scale massacres by various third world armies were common currency, but McNamara is undeterred. Armies, when their governments ask politely, should receive from their more powerful allies 'training and equipment' so as to 'maintain the protective shield for development'.

McNamara's notion of development is also curious. His census of conflicts has already revealed not just 164 'internationally significant outbreaks of violence' but identified '82 [southern hemisphere] governments directly involved' as the *targets* of that violence. McNamara thus apparently assumes that development can be brought about through outside intervention and by cooperating with precisely those governments whose authority is being repeatedly, severely and violently challenged by significant numbers of their own people.

We are not told how development can be channelled through contested governments and their armed forces and still reach and benefit millions of people who are destitute and desperate enough, in spite of tremendous odds and grave dangers, to rise up and resist them. The same governments (or others much like them) and the same armies have in the past always managed to prevent the advantages of development, like the benefits of land reform, labour laws, human rights and so on, from reaching such people.

Thus if one's goal is genuinely to reduce the incidence of conflict and to help the destitute and the desperate, logical consistency ought normally to require that one not take the side of the rich and powerful who have consistently oppressed the poor and the weak. One ought, rather, to make sure that development goes directly to the latter. This would be the only effective strategic option since, as McNamara's own analysis shows, it is only when such people become *less* destitute and desperate that order, stability and real security for the North and the South can prevail.

Naturally, such a strategy would also entail curtailing or ending altogether support for those governments against which the violence and subversion of the poor are occurring. However, since these governments, governing on behalf of the rich and the powerful, also happen to be US supporters and anti-Communist, such a course cannot be contemplated. Development will have to be channelled through them or not at all.

Does McNamara feel hemmed in by these contradictions? If so, he keeps it to himself. He asks, rather, for more resources so as to make more loans to the same clients. Presumably the contested governments will leave off depriving and repressing their own people long enough to shower upon them all kinds of development benefits. Quite possibly they have no class interests and no desire to retain their wealth and privileges but are, rather, like McNamara himself, motivated by their moral obligations.

Similarly, when McNamara affirms the need to 'help protect those developing countries which genuinely need and request our help' he clearly does not mean protection against outside attack: he has already explained that virtually none have suffered aggression. The developing countries McNamara wants to help protect are not in fact countries at all but once again governments ruling against large numbers of their own people. During the period McNamara spent at the Pentagon and the Bank, such governments had only to raise the spectre of 'Communist subversion' to obtain 'protection' and simultaneously to corner the benefits of development for themselves.

We are now confronted with three possible hypotheses:

1. McNamara saw these contradictions perfectly well but made a conscious choice in favour of the oppressors. One could also posit

that Cold War necessities superseded the claims of logic and morality. But McNamara, a certified Cold Warrior, himself says that while Communists are 'capable of subverting, manipulating and finally directing . . . the wholly legitimate grievances of a developing society' it would still be 'a gross oversimplification to regard Communism as the central factor in every conflict throughout the underdeveloped world'. Faithful to the numerical approach, he asserts that of '149 serious internal insurgencies . . . Communists were involved in only 58 of them, 38 per cent of the total.'[23] The anti-Communist crusade alone cannot explain his behaviour.

2. McNamara saw these contradictions perfectly well but believed that he, RSM, could surmount them single-handed and make the recipient governments opt for their moral obligations instead of their material and political interests. In this scenario, the Lone Ranger rides to the rescue; the mild-mannered Clark Kent changes into his Superman suit in the World Bank's twelfth-floor executive lavatory and saves the day – revealing a McNamara who means well but is devoid of a sense of history and of politics. This 'Messiah' hypothesis would fit well with his top-down view of management – perhaps he thought he could manage, indeed cow, third world political leaders as easily as his own staff.

3. McNamara did not see these contradictions and is not the cool master of logic and rationality he's cracked up to be. He genuinely believed that his eighty-two third world governments – despite repeated proof to the contrary – could be counted upon to act on ethical grounds and subscribe to the proposition that 'extremes of wealth and deprivation are simply unacceptable'. In this case, aside from anything else, it is retrospectively chilling that the armed forces and the nuclear arsenal of the world's greatest military power should have been left for seven years under the direction of a man of such stunning naïveté.

Over the last half-century, policy makers and practitioners of the dominant development paradigm have repeatedly confronted the same contradictions. Rarely have they resolved them in favour of the poor whatever the presence of the poor in their discourse. The Cold War context and the need to keep the resources of poor countries ready to hand, ensured that nearly all cases of political and social change in the southern hemisphere which might have resulted in genuine transfers of wealth and power, would be fought and, whenever possible, destroyed; whereas nearly all changes having the opposite effect would be rewarded with increased aid and more development projects.

If the absolute poor in the end got nothing from McNamara except more exploitation and repression from the governments he helped to reinforce, McNamara got a good deal from the absolute poor. They allowed him to more than double the size of his Bank and to become one of the most powerful men on earth. In contrast, Salvador Allende's Popular Unity government in Chile, which actually tried to improve the living conditions of the poor, received no loans from McNamara's Bank.

McNamara's legacy to the Bank is very much alive in other respects. One is management. The methods he imposed during his thirteen-year tenure were completely at odds with the collegial, 'California' style of his successor, Alden (Tom) Clausen who took over in 1981. Clausen had to battle entrenched baronies created by McNamara, a dense layer of golden boys who had been fast-tracked to the top. One of Clausen's closest aides says that during the McNamara period, if the boss liked you,

> you could be a loan officer one year, senior loan officer the next, division chief two years later and assistant director two years after that. Those he considered the brightest and best got enormously fast promotion, so naturally those people were convinced that his system of management was the right one. In that style of management you didn't need to tell people down the track 'this is what's going on, this is what management's thinking, these are the directions we're going to take'. No. No, you needed in typical McNamara fashion to analyze and study everything to the nth degree, plan it all in secret, get the boss to sign on to it and then implement. People would find out what was happening when the orders came down.[24]

The Reagan administration found Clausen insufficiently tough in disciplining the third world. He served a single term before heading back to the Bank of America, whose fortunes he proceeded to turn around. His managerial competence is thus not in dispute – still he

was completely at a loss to change the McNamara culture. Barber
Conable was another one-termer. Few of the really senior people at
the Bank have ever worked anywhere else – and almost all those
still at the helm are products of the McNamara years. Perhaps the
only choices for a new President are to bring in his own top team
or to leave the old one in charge and suffer the consequences.

McNamara's final legacy has had rather more sinister consequences. He left the Bank just as the debt crisis, to which his
policies had markedly contributed, was about to break. Before he
left, however, he was able to launch the concept which would
govern the entire post-McNamara period and ensure its initial
implementation in some highly indebted countries. McNamara's
parting gift was the as-yet-unfinished era of structural adjustment.
So-called policy-based lending, meaning loans with inescapable
conditions attached, has increased the Bank's power immensely.

Although McNamara used the words structural adjustment as
early as his 1976 speech to the board of governors, they appear
there in the narrow context of export diversification.[25] Not until
1979 did McNamara elaborate on the purpose of the loans intended
to help or coerce governments to make the transition towards
Bank-approved policies.[26]

One of McNamara's closest collaborators present at the creation
of structural adjustment says that when McNamara first coined the
term it was supposed to mean something like

> a quick fix to adapt to changes in the economic environment.* Once
> done, the hope was to get back to an existing development strategy
> that had been so rudely interrupted by mostly external events. *That,
> of course, always was a fallacy* ... [the previous development strategy
> proves obsolete] and adjustment becomes indeed a process of transi-
> tion from *one set of societal goals to another* ... *Whether we like it or
> not, the process of structural adjustment has become burdened with a
> much more ambitious agenda* (emphasis added).[27]

Thus the notion of structural adjustment as quick fix was from
the outset a fallacy – which the logical McNamara again did not

---

*Particularly the 1979 oil price shock and slower growth in the industrialized
countries.

foresee (or if he did, never admitted it). It soon became a means to transform entire societies, forced to abandon their previous goals. Who fixes the new 'set of societal goals' towards which countries must undertake the transition, who sets structural adjustment's 'much more ambitious agenda'? Clearly it is not the governments or the peoples of the countries concerned.

At the Bank, specific loan design followed McNamara's lead as surely as night follows day. Carrots and sticks quickly made their appearance. The Philippines, always a favourite Bank country, was one of the first beneficiaries of a SAL because the government had 'implemented nearly all the [Bank's] recommendations on export promotion . . . [including] the most important and difficult actions required'.[28] Hundreds of similar loans with countless conditions attached would follow.

The pursuit of structural adjustment in the 1980s and 1990s has, in many countries, entrenched poverty and despair but also a kind of exhaustion of potential opposition forces. At the end of the millennium the 'suffering and deprivation' of McNamara's absolute poor no longer readily cause revolution, only deeper despair.

Cold War rivalries are dead, places which used to be important no longer are and aid is reduced proportionally. Political creations like the Group of 77 or the non-aligned movement are moribund, nor is there much regional 'intrapoor' solidarity – nobody can afford it (although some poor countries have taken in more than their fair share of refugees). If they hope to change their circumstances, the absolute poor of the twenty-first century will have to be ten times more determined and twenty times better organized.

True, anti-austerity riots have occurred in several dozen structurally adjusting countries but a riot is not a political organization with clear strategic goals possessing the social and material means to achieve them. Forty years of development, which we would define as the programmed and violent change through outside intervention in vulnerable and permeable societies, has marginalized people on a scale previously unheard of, while simultaneously undermining their political capacity to fight back.

Thus have the rich and powerful discharged their moral duty to help the poor and weak. Whatever McNamara's proclaimed ethical code, the consequences of his actual, existential choices for such people – first in Vietnam, later in dozens of poor countries – are now manifest. For the moment at least, McNamara's heritage is intact and although he left the Bank more than a dozen years ago, his shade still haunts it.

Chapter III

Structural Salvation

Since Robert McNamara first introduced structural and sectoral adjustment lending in 1979–80, nearly $50 billion has been devoted to it and the literature on its impact has grown exponentially. Libraries will soon need to make a separate catalogue heading for the phenomenon if they haven't already done so. Much of this literature is polemical or at least challenges the opposing point of view. The defenders tend to be long on theoretical models and short on facts while the challengers may be prepared to attribute any and all unpleasant phenomena of the 1980s and 1990s to structural adjustment. It is not a subject on which people are neutral.

A quick reminder: government acceptance of structural adjustment is the condition for receiving financing from the IMF and the Bank, and consequently from other public and private sources. These programmes are supposed to: firstly, improve a country's economic climate and its capacity to attract foreign investment by eliminating trade and investment barriers; secondly, reduce government deficits through spending cuts; and thirdly, boost foreign exchange earnings by promoting exports. The usually unspoken fourth goal, in reality the most important, is to ensure that the country's debt is serviced. Much of the hard-earned foreign exchange is devoted to interest payments.*

Nobody pretends that countries can live beyond their means for ever or avoid 'adjusting' their economies to reality. Individuals and families cannot continually borrow their way out of financial

---

* As noted in the Introduction, standard components of adjustment packages include currency devaluation, trade liberalization, privatization, a reduced role for government and lower social spending, higher interest rates and severe compression of real wages.

trouble and neither can nations. Days of reckoning come to pass in one form or another. The Bank's standard argument – not to adjust is more painful than adjusting – is not without merit although it leaves unanswered such questions as why countries lived beyond their means, who encouraged them to do so, which political and social interests inside the country took advantage of the easy money while it lasted, and who now pays the costs of adjustment.

So is adjustment good or bad? The question is the wrong one, or in French, the quintessential *question mal posée*, because the answer depends so strongly on who is asking and who is answering. The battle lines between the pros and the antis have been so clearly and so predictably drawn that arguments about adjustment are boring in an intellectual sense as well: one knows more or less what most protagonists will say before they say it.

Aside from the Bank's own in-house defenders, for example, USAID announces categorically that 'structural adjustment has not had any general negative impact on the poor ... it seems clear that the most important way to help the poor ... is to push the adjustment process faster and harder'.[1] The OECD also finds that adjustment doesn't necessarily lower growth or aggravate already existing poverty, but states its case with more supporting evidence, finesse and nuance than USAID.[2]

In contrast, virtually everyone affiliated with a non-governmental organization in contact with poorer people or concerned about the environment in adjusting countries says that adjustment is an unmitigated social and ecological disaster. Popular movements in both North and South have been campaigning for years to force the Bank and the IMF to change policies that 'undermine the well-being of families, food producers, workers and the natural environment, as well as the viability of fragile democracies', in the words of one typical NGO publication.[3]

Although we have taken part in this debate in previous work, that is not our purpose here. We are concerned, rather, with how adjustment fits into the overall 'project' of the Bank itself. Just as economists speak of price makers and price takers, one can identify policy makers and policy takers. The Bank makes policy others have little choice but to take in a kind of dialectics of power and acquiescence.[4] We think the policy is based not just on spurious economics but on a threatening and so far successful political programme as well.

First the spurious economics. Consider this criticism of the Bank's adjustment policies from a surprising source, the Japanese government, specifically its Overseas Economic Cooperation Fund (OECF), the official development assistance wing of the foreign ministry. Japan is a major shareholder and financial power in the Bank. By September 1991 it had already contributed 450 billion yen ($4.2 billion or £2.9 billion) to structural adjustment. In its critique, second thoughts clearly prevail.

The OECF, drawing on Japan's own development experience, sharply criticizes the Bank's approach to structural adjustment, citing its heavy reliance on market mechanisms and rejection of state intervention, excessive liberalization of trade and financial institutions and indiscriminate privatization.

The Japanese find the Bank 'too optimistic' when it expects 'that industries that sustain the economy of the next generation will sprout automatically through the activities of the private sector'; the Bank's view of trade is erroneously based on 'static comparative advantage' and, contrary to what the Bank believes, 'it is impossible to achieve an optimum allotment of resources through market principles alone'. Government should provide some subsidies and especially subsidized interest rates for 'socially beneficial activities'. All these recommendations are, needless to say, anathema to the Bank.

The Japanese agency further notes that 'different conditions of individual countries have to be carefully taken into account. Unfortunately, the World Bank focus seems to be almost the same for all countries'. It faults as well the 'idea that the private sector has to be treated in the same manner whether it be national or foreign'. For the OECF, 'the notion of transferring basic industries to foreign capital is an extremely grave and serious affair'. The Bank, however,

> seems to lack a long-term vision of how to develop [export] industries, perhaps because it supposes that the activities of the private sector alone will be enough to reach that goal. This lack of vision is truly lamentable.[5]

For a culture known for its unwillingness to confront and to be negative, these may well qualify as fighting words! Japan retains a keen memory of how it became successful: it did so through policies quite different from those now pushed by the Bank. Could the point possibly be that others should not be allowed an opportunity to become successful?

Between the various official positions on structural adjustment and those of NGOs are the views of reputable scholars exemplifying various shades of orthodoxy, dubiety or dismay. Again, we are not attempting even a summary of the voluminous research on how adjustment works or has affected this or that country.[6] We prefer to outline the views of a single highly qualified academic, Professor Colin Stoneman of the University of York, an economic statistician who is an expert on Zimbabwe.

Why Stoneman and why Zimbabwe? Because Stoneman knows the country intimately, writes the quarterly reports on it for the *Economist Intelligence Unit*, is the author or editor of numerous scholarly publications and, in association with the auditing firm Coopers & Lybrand, has supplied the Zimbabwean government with a major study on foreign exchange. His impeccable qualifications allow him all the better to make the case that *the Bank's policy recommendations are ideologically driven*. In the case of Zimbabwe, this is perhaps clearer than elsewhere.

Between its independence in 1980 and 1987 Zimbabwe received nine Bank loans plus four IDA credits totalling $646 million. The country was not subjected to structural adjustment because it was not in arrears to any of its creditors and had never had to ask for debt rescheduling.

In the course of the 1980s Zimbabwe was hard-hit by many factors beyond its control, including drought and South-African-sponsored violence that nearly destroyed the tourist industry and forced the government to increase defence spending. In spite of all this, Zimbabwe was doing remarkably well among African countries, applying policies which were if not socialist as the authorities often claimed, at least nationalist.

Here was a non-adjusting country measurably more successful than the adjusters. How embarrassing that a country which protected its infant industries and local suppliers, which was self-

sufficient in food, which had even managed to diversify into manufactured exports should prosper! Zimbabwe even contrived to sell
wine to Europe. It was growing at two or three times the average
rate elsewhere in Africa, while at the same time employing
policy measures like trade controls, subsidies and high government
spending on health and education.

By 1987 people at lower levels of the Bank who were genuinely
committed to the country's success had almost completed arrangements for a loan to promote the export of manufactured goods. It
would follow a previous, similar loan which Zimbabwe had used to
extremely good effect. Then,

> after a long delay in Washington, without any technical problems
> being raised, nor any doubts being cast on the potential of Zimbabwe
> to benefit from the loan, it was finally vetoed for ideological reasons
> at the highest levels of the Bank. The last thing the Bank wanted to
> happen was for Zimbabwe to succeed with 'the wrong policies'.[7]

Stoneman has been following the Bank's activities in Zimbabwe
since independence. He sees it as an institution

> whose overall intention, and increasingly effect, is to promote the
> construction of a single world market, *substantially on the basis of the
> present world division of labour* ... [a] role mediated through an
> ideology that is claimed to be a value-free science (emphasis added).[8]

Take the Bank's preoccupation, not to say obsession, with comparative advantage. One of the Bank's favourite instruments is
known as the DRC, which is not a surgical procedure but an
economic measuring technique called the domestic resource cost.
According to the Bank, the DRC approach provides a reliable guide
to the economic areas in which a given country can reasonably
expect to succeed, the ones it presently engages in but should
abandon, and those it should not even contemplate entering.

The DRC is simply a measure of the cost in domestic resources of
earning or saving a unit of foreign exchange by the local production of
a good. In other words, the world market becomes the ultimate
reference for the way a country's internal economy should – indeed
must – be structured. The yardstick, the scale of values, are external

and thus the cost of using a domestic resource is unrelated to such goals as equity or the long-term well-being of the population.

The Bank, with its phalanxes of highly paid economists, should be in possession of the most finely honed analytical instruments, but as Stoneman demonstrates in detail, the DRC approach is unsophisticated, indeed crude. It simply takes a snapshot of the status quo, of *present* world market conditions in order to determine what a given country's behaviour ought to be so that it can earn or save a dollar of foreign exchange *today*; which as we have seen is the only criterion for using, or not using, a domestic resource. This in turn implies accepting as givens whatever prices the world market says are the prices right now. In this way the past (including past investment) is wiped out and, economically speaking, the future is assumed to be no different from the present, the only temporal dimension in which the country's economic choices are to be situated.

Domestic resource cost analysis neither asks why a country is poor, nor if it might emerge from that poverty through a significant departure from the status quo, nor if state policies could make a difference. By definition, the country's poverty and problems cannot in any way have been *caused* or aggravated by reliance on and integration into the international market. The DRC approach ensures that the outcome will be to tell Zimbabwe, or whomever, to stay just about where it is in the present world division of labour.

As Colin Stoneman puts it, using the DRC and comparative advantage to the exclusion of other methods plays an

> ideological role in the hands of the World Bank ... [it] derives in part from a successful confusion between the correct argument which tells us not to try to grow bananas in Britain, and the incorrect one that tells us not to try to make steel in Zimbabwe.[9]

Maybe today Zimbabwe would have little comparative advantage in steel-making because it lacks the proper infrastructure, skills, suppliers upstream and customers downstream, et cetera. But what is this truism, asks Stoneman, if not simply a *'restatement of the problem of development'*? The comparative advantage argument is circular: 'Zimbabwe is underdeveloped so it has a comparative disadvantage in developed activities and so should avoid them!' (his emphasis).

The economists who were the Bank's eyes and ears in Zimbabwe produced various reports and recommendations. Stoneman remarks fatalistically that, 'All World Bank or IMF reports in the end turn what evidence they have to recommending the standard free market package', which invariably includes currency devaluation, removal of foreign exchange controls and import restrictions, cutbacks or removal of subsidies, adaptation of relative price structures to the world market, and reduction of the state's role in the economy.

A matter like currency devaluation, for example, is not just a technical measure. The Bank uses the DRC to tell governments which industries or firms to keep and which ones to junk but the DRC varies wildly according to the exchange rate used. If the Bank's economist estimates, for instance, that the currency is overvalued by twenty per cent, the DRC will be raised by an equivalent amount.* On this basis, whole industrial areas may be defined as inefficient and therefore candidates for the scrap heap.[10]

One Bank report on Zimbabwe went ideologically overboard even for the Bank, stating that all market imperfections were 'considered to be entirely the result of government policy'. According to Stoneman, its prescriptions for the totality of Zimbabwean industry were based on an analysis covering only one-half of one per cent of the items then listed in *Products of Zimbabwean Industries*.

A further failing of the DRC method is its assumption that a static measurement – the snapshot of the economic status quo – is an adequate instrument for deciding moves in areas which necessarily involve long-term endeavours. A high DRC is the signal of a firm's inefficiency. But maybe it's in a learning phase, or is just beginning to gain benefits from a new technology, or maybe it's affected by a worldwide slump which does not justify dismantling part of the industrial infrastructure of a fledgling nation. In any case, industry can't switch investments around all the time like a farmer planting potatoes one season and corn the next. The DRC

---

* Please see endnote 10 to this chapter for an example generously provided by Colin Stoneman showing the arbitrary nature and the disadvantages of this method for the country concerned.

method is an important weapon in the Bank's ideological arsenal but economically speaking it is a blunt instrument.

Another Bank report on Zimbabwe analysed by Stoneman provides recommendations which 'are in all respects exactly those which someone with no knowledge of Zimbabwe, but familiarity with the World Bank, would have predicted'.[11] This report does acknowledge – the evidence is too strong not to – that so far, Zimbabwe has made progress by using precisely those policies the Bank wants to abolish. The Bank's author reacts by saying that this is surprising. (The Bank is always surprised, too, by the failure of those who apply its policies to the letter.)

The Bank may, in other contexts, point to the spectacular growth of the Asian dragons' economies but it generally neglects to mention that countries like Korea or Taiwan got their start in the 1960s in a context of no-nonsense protectionism and subsidies for the industries they chose to favour. Such strategies being long-term, they do not fit the present free-market canon and are consequently now off-limits.*

The analytical tools whose use the Bank allows in politically weak, policy-taker countries, if based on scrupulously collected data, could perhaps give an accurate picture of a given country's *static* comparative advantage and thus point to some measures to improve *short-term* efficiency. But as Stoneman shows, the Bank denies itself any grasp of *dynamic* comparative advantage: it cannot plan for a future in which world markets might change, or industries might realize economies of scale, improve their technology or simply go out and find more customers.

On the surface, structural adjustment may appear to be a package of technical measures and this is what the Bank always claims. A closer look at both the analytical techniques and the recommendations that follow from them shows, however, that they result in freezing countries in existing patterns of production which are, on

---

* In late 1993 the Bank published *The East Asian Miracle*, a 400-page study on eight East Asian economies. We have not been able to incorporate the findings here, but the Bank's *Publications Update* blurb says that the book 'explains why most countries should *not* [their emphasis] use government interventions in today's changing global economy'.

the whole, the ones left over from colonialism. This is an extremely serious *political* consequence which should not be glossed over just because it is a consequence of 'sound' (one of the Bank's favourite words) economic policy.

The imposition of structural adjustment worldwide is a profoundly ideological choice, not only because it harms nature and the poor as the NGOs claim, but also because it casts the New World Order in stone. This New World Order turns out to look uncommonly like the old one and has been instated in little over a decade without firing a shot. The only troops deployed have been the battalions of uniformed economists.

To return to Zimbabwe, by 1990–91, a real, Bank-inspired Economic Structural Adjustment Programme was introduced by a finance minister who travels in all the right international circles and who is a darling of the Bank. In 1988, his daughter – in what was seen in Zimbabwe as a highly symbolic event – married the son of the Bank's resident representative in Harare. Robert Mugabe, the President who symbolized Zimbabwe's nationalist policies, has not been overthrown but he has certainly been marginalized. The standard economic package is in place, including further currency devaluation, an end to price controls, elimination of the minimum wage and the introduction of cost-sharing (i.e. fees) in health and education. Slum residents in Harare immediately christened the ESAP 'Extreme Suffering for African People'.

Meanwhile, during the six years from 1986 to 1991, Zimbabwe remitted over $2.6 billion to its creditors in debt service. This ongoing drain amounted to about $1,200,000 a day, or approximately $50,000 exiting Zimbabwe every hour to pay its foreign creditors. Although the finance minister exhibits a 'determination to repay debts',[12] these efforts have not improved the country's external financial position, quite the contrary. Zimbabwe's debt grew during the same six-year period by nearly a quarter.[13]

The $50,000 an hour in gross interest payments might come in handy for importing technology, or constructing roads, hospitals and schools but one can't have everything. At the Bank's behest, Zimbabwe has also turned one of Africa's best health and education records into a virtual shambles.

Many women can no longer afford hospital births and children are leaving school. When families cannot pay to educate all their children, girls are the first to be withdrawn. In one poor district the British charity CamFed (Cambridge Female Education Trust) has found that 'if girls are short of food or examination fees, the immediacy of their material needs can override the possibility of AIDS or pregnancy and they may offer sex in exchange for cash or food'.

> Sex can become the only commodity left to sell, not only for girls but for their mothers as well. In the town of — in the — district, I have spoken to women working as prostitutes and they have cited their children's school fees as a primary reason for selling sex. They are well aware of the risks to their health but see little choice and buy security for their children by selling their own. [Most of the clients are migrant workers whose access to their own wives and families has been] hopelessly diminished by distance and practical considerations like bus fares which have increased dramatically since the introduction of ESAP . . . I would really like the Bank to confront the enormity of misery downline from its policies.[14]

Colin Stoneman explains that de-industrialization is likely to be the major long-term consequence of structural adjustment but serious food shortages were the initial price to pay. The Zimbabwe Grain Marketing Board used to have maize stocks of nearly two million tons but since structural adjustment requires 'inefficient' state enterprises to break even, it sold off its stockpile at a low price, just before serious and prolonged drought descended on the country. The Grain Marketing Board has also stopped building storage facilities in remote districts and Zimbabwe, previously self-sufficient, has had to import food.[15]

That Zimbabwe should sell maize cheap and buy it dear from the world market because it no longer has any stocks is a logical consequence of adjustment. The whole point of policy-based lending is to tie the borrower's economy to the global one and to apply the same strategy worldwide, with no exceptions tolerated. The Bank reorganized itself in 1987 around this principle (see Chapter vi) and the steering committee overseeing the Reorganization called this process the 'integration of the domestic economy with the international trading and financial system'.

Note, however, that responsibility for 'integrating the domestic economy into the international trading and financial system' rests squarely with the domestic economy. Nothing whatever is required of the 'international trading and financial system'. That structural adjustment is necessarily beneficial to the country is an article of faith. Contrary evidence is suppressed or ignored or simply declared theoretically impossible.

A particularly telling example of this article of faith is the following report from a European Community official. At the beginning of April 1992, a high-level seminar on 'Employment and Training Dimensions of Adjustments in Central and Eastern Europe' was held in Turin. Ostensibly hosted by the International Labour Organization (ILO), it was actually 'a World Bank-managed affair fronted by the ILO', to quote the EC participant, one of about 120 people attending. Other participants included ministers and secretaries of state from Central and Eastern European countries. The Bank's representatives, Messrs F. and H., sat beside the ILO chairman throughout the proceedings, part of which the EC representative describes as follows in an internal memo:

The opening session was the most extraordinary ... I, like the others, spoke for 5 to 10 minutes. We were then followed by Mr H.,* who spoke for 25 minutes. He offered us a 'hypothesis to be considered': whether we should not judge our success in achieving adjustments in Central and Eastern Europe by the extent to which unemployment *rises* rather than by the extent to which we were able to keep unemployment down. A figure of 20% was referred to in later discussion. In other words, it was the 'it's not working if it's not hurting' approach. In the same discussion, he referred to the changes in Central and Eastern Europe as being a massive 'experiment' for which we had no previous experience to guide us.

The insensitivity and arrogance of H. and F. has to be experienced to be believed. They behave like a mixture of missionaries and insurance salesmen – a frankly rather repulsive sight.

The consequences of the World Bank approach could be very serious, economically, socially and politically, not only for the coun-

* Chief of the World Bank's Human Resources Operations Division for Eastern Europe.

tries of Central and Eastern Europe, but also for the Community. It will be the Community countries, not those of North America, which will be the first to face the consequences of rising unemployment, social tensions and migratory pressures in Central and Eastern Europe if such World Bank policies are followed.

The ILO is clearly being lined up behind the World Bank [this may reflect the ILO's financial weakness]. Overall, however, it is an extraordinary situation when a top ILO official presides a conference at which one of the principal participants' aims is to increase unemployment as far and as fast as possible (emphasis in the original).[16]

Why should the Bank's Mr H. want unemployment to *rise*? Because this would be proof of success in stripping down bloated state-run enterprises and turning them into lean, mean units able to compete on global markets. The Eastern bloc countries used to trade mostly with each other – now, like all other structural adjusters, they have to face the music and become economically 'efficient' so as to compete in the global marketplace. That means as few workers on the payroll as can possibly be achieved.

In this case, quite explicitly, the Bank's yardstick of success is the degree of suffering which must be accepted and surmounted in order to be saved. There are no particular *economic* grounds for setting a level of twenty per cent unemployment as a measure of success – Mr H. says himself that the whole undertaking of structural adjustment in Central and Eastern Europe is a vast 'experiment' – a euphemism for 'we don't actually know what we're doing'. He seems, however, quite comfortable with the idea that many, many people must be put out of work for this massive societal transformation to work.

The many academics and activists who have devoted their skills and energies to documenting the effects of structural adjustment have not, certainly, been wasting their time – such knowledge is always valuable – but they have been engaged, we think, in a futile debate. If I believe that the earth is flat (or that structural adjustment is a great thing) and you believe that it is round (or that structural adjustment is a disaster), if neither of us can persuade the other of our own premises, we are destined to argue for ever.

A hundred case studies showing that the earth is round, or that structural adjustment is an environmental catastrophe, a terrible ordeal for the poor and a social tragedy will not convince me, because I know that the earth is flat and that structural adjustment, given time, will bring about 'the transition of an economy to a new, sustainable and poverty-reducing growth path', in the words of an authoritative Bank document.[17]

Some truths are not disputable – they are just there, like Natural Law for the Church. Or, as we have heard high African officials actually say, 'TINA', which is short for There Is No Alternative. In practical terms, these officials are right in so far as they are speaking for any country in need of Bank financing. Many if not most leaders have learned their lesson and have internalized the Bank's own doctrine. Since these members of the élite rarely pay the human costs of adjustment themselves, they are often among its more fervid supporters.

At some point one must ask whether this insistence on neo-classical orthodox remedies derives from sheer ideological pigheadedness or whether it represents a carefully determined *political*, as opposed to economic world-view. The second hypothesis in no way requires subscribing to conspiracy theory. As three keen observers of the Bank's behaviour have remarked, structural adjustment demands above all 'the roll-back of the state' through privatization, deregulation and letting the market work its magic.[18] Weakening existing states is what rival powers have always tried to do.

Three other, equally keen, observers note that for Northern (particularly US) foreign policy – which they believe the Bank faithfully reflects – rollback is to the South what containment was to the East in the days of the Iron Curtain and the Berlin Wall.[19]

We would go even further. The Bank does not, in the mid-1990s, necessarily reflect anything but itself. In the United States, the Clinton presidency, after a year in office, had not formulated any particular policy towards the Bank's borrowing countries, unless they erupted into civil strife or otherwise threatened to get in the way. Europe, aside from the limited scope of the Lomé Convention, has established no policy either. Although individual European Union countries have more or less privileged relationships with various countries in the South – usually ex-colonies – there is nothing resembling a European vision of how North–South relations should evolve, nor what role, if any, the Bank should play in a grand design.

Help for the battered South to recover from the 'lost decade' of the 1980s, as UNICEF has called it, has not been forthcoming. Debt continues, on the whole, to be serviced: that is enough. When a crisis looms here or there, it is usually dealt with through short-term confrontation. Compromise, much less cooperation, is not on the agenda; at best Northern policy consists in benign neglect.

Since the North no longer even seems to be bothering to articulate a policy towards the South, the Bank's own policies are filling the void. No effort is made to understand why so much of the southern hemisphere remains mired in poverty. Whatever woes a country or a region suffers are supposed to be its own fault. Nothing is ever the international system's fault, the North's fault, nor, of course, the Bank's. Policy makers and policy takers are, literally, worlds apart.

The Bank, unlike the North, does have a grand design and a single unified strategy, the policy of structural adjustment. Logically speaking, there are only two possibilities: the Bank wants this strategy to 'succeed' or to 'fail' in the South and, now, the East. We take both these words at face value, assuming success means a better standard of living for the population and a less poverty-stricken, peripheral existence for their nations whereas failure means stasis or regression.

Through instruments like the DRC and static comparative advantage analysis, the Bank policy makers require the policy takers to produce what they can best produce *today* which, unsurprisingly, is generally what they best produced yesterday. Although there are no mother countries left, there is a kind of mother world, which has benefited from some of the lowest commodity prices ever recorded and which receives an ongoing tribute in debt service. The countries of the South, in individual and collective disarray, the state weakened by a decade or more of structural adjustment, pose no credible political threat.

In economic terms, this may be failure, but if political criteria are applied and North–South rivalry or hostility is assumed, in Machiavellian terms it is a decided success. In this hypothesis, the Bank must be assumed to be acting as an agent of the G-7 or the OECD countries, deliberately enfeebling a potential adversary. Many external signs point to such a project and objectively justify what some commentators call neo-imperialism or re-colonization.

The Bank's project can also be analysed, however, as a religious utopia. Structural adjustment does not *set out* to make countries fail. But nor can these countries be allowed to succeed with the 'wrong' policies as the case of Zimbabwe shows. The Bank must, again and again, affirm the rightness of its teachings, in the teeth of all the evidence.

The Bank did not invent neo-classical economics, liberalism, free market orthodoxy, or whatever one cares to call this doctrine. It did not even invent the notion that the doctrine works in all places and at all times, regardless of the historical and social context and the relationships and inequalities between nations. The formalist school of economic anthropology has claimed the same thing for half a century.[20] The Bank was, however, the first (along with the IMF) to put this doctrine into practice and to convince most of its contemporaries that the greatest good for the greatest number will necessarily emerge from its adoption, voluntarily if possible; if not, then under duress.

The salvation of the people and of the nations shall come about through binding them ever more tightly to the international market, equated with the world community. There, the poor shall partake of the same substance as the rich. Like any universal truth, adjustment is a purely abstract notion even if its application causes concrete pain. The available choices are reduced to one, There Is No Alternative; we are all bound by a single, compulsory, truth which shall be recognized. Then shall the wayward nations be freed from their errors.

The Savage Mind

What I'm suggesting is that there really is a cargo mystery and that the natives are justified in trying to solve it ... Big men ... must redistribute their wealth. The natives believe that there is nothing worse than a stingy big man ... To get these strange big men to share more of their wealth and to moderate their appetite for land and labor, the natives tried to learn their language and penetrate their secrets ... They insisted on making the Europeans act like true big men; they insisted that those who possessed wealth were under the obligation to give it away ... The more [the New Guinean cargo-cult prophet] Yali learned about how Europeans produced wealth, the less was he prepared to accept their explanation of why he and his people were unable to share in it ... But Yali always had the good sense to dismiss the standard European explanation, 'hard work', as a calculated deception.

Marvin Harris, 'Phantom Cargo', in *Cows, Pigs, Wars and Witches* (New York, Random House, 1974)

Yali, a true primitive and as noble a savage as one might hope to meet, is still seeking to penetrate the secret of cargo. His life's ambition is to understand why some societies are rich beyond measure, with motorcycles and matches, tinned meats and wrist-watches, rice in bags and steel tools, whereas he and his fellow tribespeople are deprived of all these things. He remains confident that one day the ancestors, piloting jet planes, will land and unload for him and his people the cargo of all these goods and much, much more, thus inaugurating the age of heaven on earth when no one will ever again want for anything. Meanwhile, Yali keeps trying to learn as much as he can about those who *do* have cargo.

We had the good luck to meet him last summer in Washington,

D.C. He wore a richly patterned shirt and bright red shorts, a few feathers and a handsome nose ornament, so as not to stand out from the rest of the crowd in Dupont Circle. When we asked how he came to be in town, he explained that his followers, who themselves had every interest in uncovering the secrets of cargo, had put up the money for the trip. We quickly discovered that the object of his research was closely related to our own and we were privileged to exchange views with him at length.

Yali's English is excellent. He learned it at the mission school (in that far-off time when he had believed the missionaries held the secret of cargo) and later perfected his language skills in Australia. His most cherished possession is a transistor radio which was, in a way, the proximate cause of his visit to Washington. The radio people are very odd, he told us. They almost never speak about the most important things in life – family, yams, pigs, ancestors or indeed cargo – but when they aren't talking about wars or the weather, they go on and on about money and the places it's kept, some called stock markets and others called banks.

He had reached the conclusion that these were surely the places the cargo is kept. One day he heard about a 'World' Bank in Washington. With a name like that, this clearly had to be the most important, richest and most powerful bank of all. Yali had immediately decided not to waste any time on places with strange names like Manufacturers Hanover but to go straight to the top.

Furthermore, he told us, he had learned that Big Men from many tribes believed that this World Bank really did know why some societies are desperately lacking in motorcycles, wristwatches and steel tools and – much more important – that it knew how to make everybody rich. Yali was sure that finally – after all the false starts and time wasted with missionaries, soldiers, bureaucrats and anthropologists – he had located the ultimate repository of cargo.

What had he learned so far? we asked. Yali was a gentleman and a scholar, quite willing to share his findings. 'The World Bank has great and powerful ancestors,' he said. 'They have handed down an initiation rite which can make poor and primitive people modern and rich. This rite is very difficult to learn, it causes the people much pain and suffering and it must be practised for many years with great discipline before taking effect, but the Bank teaches that those who persevere will, in the end, get cargo.

'The Bank's word for cargo is "development". The long rite of passage, which is the gateway and the path to development, they call "structural adjustment". This is what I have understood up to now, but I do not yet know much about this rite nor how it fulfils the great and noble purpose of the Bank's ancestors.'

Yali was clearly on the right track and we suggested that we should henceforward work together, a proposal he welcomed with enthusiasm. Yali had the temperament of a true researcher. He understood that his task was not to be content with appearances but to seek what was hidden beneath the surface. He never stopped digging until he had uncovered to his own satisfaction the real significance of any phenomenon. He taught us a great deal, but at the beginning we had some serious problems communicating. Sometimes it was awfully hard to get across to him our own understanding of how the Bank actually worked – something we felt, perhaps wrongly, our own Western culture should have equipped us to do.

For example, as he tried to understand the meaning of this rite of passage called structural adjustment, Yali asked us what, exactly, was supposed to be adjusted and what it was supposed to be adjusted *to*. As he understood it, an adjustment was needed when something was out of whack. The idea was then to make whatever it was new and right again, like tuning up a sputtering motorcycle or making a door fit its frame. Sometimes, on dire occasions, things could even be maladjusted in the universe, for example if the people disobeyed the ancestors and consequently had a bad harvest and needed to get back into their good graces with ceremonies, sacrifices and offerings.

'That's exactly it,' we said, pursuing his own example. 'In a country that needs structural adjustment, the economy is out of whack and the leaders have disobeyed. They have slaughtered their pigs and neglected their gardens, they have squandered their people's wealth on fancy spears and paint and parties; some of them have even looted the common stores in order to become Big Men and then hidden their stolen wealth beyond the seas. They have borrowed so many cowrie shells just to live on from day to day that nobody will lend to them any more.

'But the World Bank is much, much bigger than these Big Men. With its sister (her name is IMF and we'll explain about her another time) the Bank has proclaimed to these foolish, profligate and improvident leaders that it will lend them enough cowrie shells to get them out of their mess. But in exchange they have to pay back everything they borrowed before and from now on they have to do as they're told – in other words, they must do exactly as the *Bank* tells them.'

'That sounds just like home,' said Yali. 'The Big Men give the orders and the others obey so as to get favours and be invited to the feasts. But what orders do these Bank Big Men give that the tribal leaders have to obey?'

'For one thing, they always have to make the money cheaper.' Yali looked at us blankly, so we tried another tack. 'You see this dollar? How many cowrie shells could we buy in your country with this dollar?'

'Ten,' said Yali.

'Well, if your Big Men had to obey the Bank, we would be able to buy twenty or thirty cowrie shells with this same dollar. That means we could buy twice or three times as many pigs or yams today as we could yesterday, without having to work any harder. For us it's still the same dollar, but you have to give us more pigs or yams to get it.'

'Well, then I don't want your dollar,' replied Yali. 'Anyone can see that's a stupid bargain.'

'Maybe so, but remember that you have to obey and you have to pay back everything you borrowed before. The people you borrowed from won't take cowrie shells. They want dollars, so if we have a dollar, you have to give us twice as many pigs for it whether you like it or not because you need it so as not to displease the Bank's Big Men. This is called "devaluation". It means making your money – and therefore your pigs and yams – cheaper so that outsiders will buy more of them and then you will have more dollars you can give to other outsiders.'

'Whoever got his tribe into that kind of a mess should go to the shaman to be purified and get his head fixed,' said Yali.

'Another rule,' we explained, 'is that the tribespeople have to work harder and longer every day, but they get fewer cowrie shells for their work. Why? Because if you let them keep too many cowrie shells, they could buy all the pigs and yams and paint and copper bracelets for themselves, their husbands and wives, their children and their friends. If the tribespeople bought up everything there was to buy themselves, there would be nothing left over to send across the sea in ships and airplanes to sell for dollars. The Bank Big Men say you have to save the best things and your hardest work for selling to people beyond the seas. This is called "export orientation". Keeping the local people's stocks of cowrie shells as low as possible is called "demand management".'

'Are you telling me,' exclaimed Yali, wide-eyed, 'that not only do we not get cargo but we have to send what little cargo we have to other people, people beyond the seas? And they pay us with dollars we can't even keep but have to send right back to other people beyond the seas?'

'Exactly right,' we said. 'And there are still other rules that must be obeyed. Anyone, no matter what his tribe, who wants to sell his own pigs, yams, paint or bracelets in your country must be allowed to sell them. Even if dozens of foreign pigs come squealing all at once into your village marketplace, the leaders cannot stop them. If your coppersmiths make beautiful bracelets by hand and one day cheap, shiny bracelets stamped out far away with machines are put on sale in your village by the hundreds, they still can't refuse.

'The value of a pig or a bracelet will drop and drop because there are so many for sale, but the Big Men of the Bank are happy. This great inflow of pigs and bracelets (which they call "import liberalization") pleases them because it creates "competition" between home-bred and foreign pigs, between hand-made and machine-made bracelets. The Bank Big Men say this will make your pig-raisers and your coppersmiths more efficient and better fighters. They will have to fight each other for customers if they want to keep on selling their pigs and bracelets and they will also have to fight against foreign pig-raisers and coppersmiths they don't even know, and will never meet. These battles placate the Bank and, they say, bring the people that much closer to the day they will receive cargo.'

Yali exclaimed that it was like making a raid on another tribe with invisible warriors. He thought that was unfair to the visible ones. There have to be rules.

'Oh, but there are rules,' we replied. 'Just different ones from yours.

We haven't told you half of them yet.' So we continued, 'The Bank Big Men tell the tribe that it's wasting valuable food and huts when it gives them free to shamans who heal the sick and masters who initiate the children. The Bank believes that no one – not even the ancients – should get completely free healing or have a hut built at the expense of the tribe. In fact, there are so many rules we can't explain them all, but there's one more really important one: everyone must pay exactly the right number of cowrie shells for everything, including food.

'The Bank Big Men know that in many tribes, the elders try to make sure that everyone gets at least enough rice and yams, even if they're poor. Maybe a few lazy people get cheap rice and yams that way, but so do the grandfathers and grandmothers who can't work, and the children, and the crippled and the sick; so the elders think it's worth paying part of the cost themselves.

'But the Bank Big Men say they have to stop. The price of rice and yams and everything else has to be decided by laws called the "laws of supply and demand". Remember that people are often working to produce things to send across the sea to earn dollars, so usually there are fewer yams for sale and they cost a lot more. But still everyone has to pay the exact market price for food and some poor or weak people can't buy enough to stay healthy.'

Yali thought this was particularly crazy – the whole point of having Big Men is for them to make sure that everyone has enough, especially enough food. Again and again we explained the idea, but no matter how hard we tried, he couldn't understand what was right about what the Bank called 'getting the prices right' or where the truth was in its 'market truth'.

'OK,' said Yali, a very patient man, 'I know that truth is what the ancestors have passed down to us; we have many truths and they all fit together. They tell us how the earth and the sky and the sea and the creatures in them were made; they tell us who we are, where we come from, why we are here and where we are going.'

'In a way, the Bank is like that too,' we mused. 'Its truths also fit together and tell us who we are and what we must do.' Yali helped us greatly, during the course of our long conversations, to better understand the Bank's reigning myths. Alas, Yali himself left Washington disappointed: when we last heard from him, he still had not discovered the ultimate secret of cargo.

Chapter IV

False Prophecies

If Mr X subscribes to a financial newsletter and as a result of its advice, invests all his worldly savings in Consolidated Widgets; if Consolidated Widgets then proceeds to declare bankruptcy and he loses his shirt, few people are likely to commiserate. 'Tough luck' might be the average comment: he should have sought alternative wisdom and spread his risks. His only consolation is that the newsletter, too, will fail if its advice is consistently poor.

The Bank's advice to its borrowers is different for several reasons. Developing countries are captive subscribers to its 'newsletter' of economic predictions. Right or wrong, the Bank automatically integrates its beliefs into its 'policy dialogue' (the polite phrase for instructions) with client governments. If these governments do not accept the Bank's assumptions and forecasts at face value and implement the policies based upon them, they risk becoming outcasts, losing their financial standing in the international community. They have no recourse if the Bank makes dire mistakes and are the only ones to suffer the consequences, particularly the poorest and weakest among them. They are in this sense subject to an absolutist or hegemonic system.

In contrast, nothing untoward will happen to the Bank. Its *tour de force* has been to maintain and increase its institutional strength and leadership in development thinking and practice despite repeated and fundamental errors of judgement, with some extremely detrimental consequences for its captive subscribers, its clients. However frequent these errors, however poor the Bank's track record, its pronouncements are still quoted as Holy Writ.

Some examples of the Bank's more serious wrong projections follow. Part of the demonstration must be supported with relatively technical information – this cannot be avoided. Oddly enough, no staff, no office inside or outside the Bank seems to be charged with checking systematically the accuracy of its predictions with a view to improving them and learning from mistakes, even though policies affecting millions of people may be based upon them. Odder still, almost no one seems to notice its lapses. Unless it gets caught out in a mistake, the Bank generally just shuts up about it, and why not?

One of the more revealing instances of this behaviour relates to developing-country debt, already briefly referred to in Chapter II. The havoc wrought by the debt crisis and its aftermath throughout the 1980s and 1990s is generally recognized as the development *débâcle* of the century. The grim cycle of over-borrowing, volatile interest rates, unpayable loans, huge deficits and the ensuing austerity of structural adjustment have drastically set dozens of countries back: in particular, they have had to write off the entire 'lost decade' of the 1980s.

The world's foremost development institution might have been expected to keep an eye on these trends, recognize that a crisis was brewing and caution its rich member countries against excessive lending, its less developed members against excessive borrowing. It did neither. The Bank utterly failed to foresee, much less warn against the crisis; it even substantially contributed to it.

Speaking about the dramatic pile-up of African debt, former World Bank economist Percy Mistry observes,

> in these countries the accumulation of such obligations owes at least as much to the miscalculations and imprudence of MDB [Multilateral Development Bank] managements and staff . . . as to the incompetence of borrowing governments. The case in terms of MDB culpability is a strong one; they at least should have known better . . . There was too much pressure on MDB staff to meet annual lending targets in these countries . . . and insufficient prudence was exercised by MDB managements.[1]

The debt crisis was triggered in August 1982 by the Mexican default (at the time euphemistically called a rescheduling).[2] The Bank did not foresee any crisis, as witnessed by the *World Development Report* (*WDR*), its premier publication and the one everybody consults to see what's on the world's agenda as well as the Bank's. In 1981, the *WDR* stated:

While these trends indicate that the developing countries will face more serious debt-management difficulties in the future, they do not signal a generalized debt problem for the developing countries. Balance of payments projections for the 1980s under probable scenarios support this view . . . [G]iven the profitability of lending to developing countries, their exemplary record (with few exceptions) in meeting their obligations and their continuing need for foreign finance, it seems unlikely that financial intermediaries [i.e. banks] will discriminate against developing countries as a group.[3]

Since this prediction appeared a little over a year before the crisis broke, we shall overlook the flawed crystal ball. In 1982, however, the Bank was even more sanguine in the *World Development Report* which came out a scant few weeks before the Mexican bombshell burst, followed by a cascading crisis for many other debtors. Not only did the Bank fail to note that anything might be amiss, it even assured the world that private banks would continue throughout the decade to lend to developing countries the same huge amounts of fresh capital – possibly much more – that they had been lending up to that time. According to the 1982 *World Development Report*, even if the recession in the OECD countries (then fairly severe) continued, the developing countries'

net medium and long term borrowing would average about *$90 billion a year for the rest of the 1980s*. If the industrial countries recover rapidly [from recession] the developing countries' borrowing would increase, underwritten by larger export revenues; their net *annual borrowing* [from commercial sources] *over the decade would average at least $115 billion* (emphasis added).[4]

That was for the 1980s – every year an extra $90 to $115 billion was to enter the coffers of the borrowing countries in the form of new loans. This forecast is accompanied by another one for the year 1990. That year, the Bank expected at worst (the 'low-case scenario') that all developing countries would receive medium- and long-term loans of $44 billion from official sources and $55 billion from private banks. At best (the 'high-case scenario') they could expect $55 billion in public funds and $96.7 billion in private capital in 1990.

Commercial Lending

Billions ($)	Bank Est. WDR 1982	Reality (OECD)	Bank Off By (Minimum)
1983	90–115	35.0	× 2.5
1984	90–115	17.2	× 5.2
1985	90–115	15.2	× 5.9
1986	90–115	7.0	× 12.8
1987	90–115	7.0	× 12.8
1988	90–115	7.8	× 11.5
1989	90–115	10.5	× 8.5
1990	55–96.7	15.0	× 3.6

Source for actual commercial bank loans (including short-term, which the Bank does not include in its projections): OECD, *Financing and External Debt of Developing Countries, 1991* and *1992 Surveys* (Paris, OECD, 1993 and 1992), Tables III.1.

Thus, in the Bank's judgement, expressed a few weeks before the debt house of cards collapsed, the developing countries would, throughout the 1980s, be adding an average of $90 to $115 billion annually to their existing stocks of debt, with an extra $100 to $150 billion (from all sources) thrown in for good measure in 1990 to start the new decade with a bang. Whether in the high- or low-case scenario, the Bank was counting on private commercial banks to provide the bulk of these funds. The borrowers were then supposed to pay interest on these staggering additional sums from larger export revenues.

What actually happened a few weeks later? After the Mexican explosion and the debt crash of 1982, private lending completely dried up. *Even including short-term loans* (which the Bank specifically excluded from its own projections), commercial loans ceased to flow and trickled to the third world at an average $10.8 billion a year from 1984 to 1989. In 1990, the year in which they were supposed to gratify the LDCs with between $55 and $96 billion in fresh money, private banks lent them $15 billion. In 1991 loans to developing countries fell again, this time to a paltry $7 billion – the same amount as in 1986, 1987 and 1988.[5]

In 1983, although the Bank finally and grudgingly admitted that 'the way developing-country debt evolved during the 1970s left most borrowers vulnerable to the pressures of the early 1980s', it was still brushing off the profound and lasting impact of the debt crisis. The 1983 *World Development Report* said:

> While these ... factors help to explain how debt difficulties worsened in the 1980s, those difficulties have affected individual countries rather than whole regions or groups ... In several major countries with debt servicing difficulties, such as Brazil and Mexico, the problem is basically that of liquidity.[6]

Contrary to what the Bank affirmed, within two years of Mexico's default, thirty other major debtors representing half of all developing country debt were failing to service their debts on schedule.[7]

The Bank, moreover, continued to cling to the fiction of a liquidity (cash flow) problem for several years, rather than accept that these debtors were insolvent, i.e. plain broke; that it had not a problem of liquidity but a genuine, structural and long-term crisis on its hands.

In 1992, the Bank's then Chief Economist, Lawrence Summers, in an article written jointly with the Chief of the Debt and International Finance Division in the Bank's International Economics Department, listed in a 'spirit of humility' ten key lessons of the debt crisis. Among them was: 'Treating the debt crisis purely as a liquidity problem [which] delayed the search for a stable and real solution'.[8] The authors do not include their employer among the guilty, simply attributing this mistaken attitude to 'many observers'. What were the consequences?

According to Summers and his colleague,

> This lesson is well learned now, but the cost of delay has been to put development on hold for a decade in many of these countries. A lesson for the future is the importance of acknowledging reality sooner.[9]

Right, we're the world's top development institution but we're a bit slow acknowledging reality, so we may have inadvertently put the development of a few dozen countries on hold for a decade. Actually we were just one among many observers and in any event this lesson is well learned now – we affirm this in a spirit of humility.

As late as 1986, when LDC debt had already shot well past the trillion dollar mark, the Bank, with unrelenting cheerfulness, announced that in the mid-1990s developing-country debt would amount, *at worst*, to $864 billion. At best, these countries would owe within a decade a mere $560 billion to their public and private creditors. In reality, by 1993, their total debt attained an astronomical trillion and a half dollars (more precisely $1,534,000,000,000). By 1993 actual debt was already between in $670 and $974 billion more than the Bank said it would be in the mid-1990s. The Bank's estimate was thus off by a factor of 1.7 to 2.7.[10]

Two years later, in 1988, the Bank was still seriously underestimating future debt burdens (particularly for sub-Saharan Africa) by at least a third. Not until its 1991 *World Development Report* did it finally admit that 'No early end to the debt crisis is in sight – nor is any substantial resumption of North–South capital flows'. (Actually, this prediction may be wrong as well, at least for Latin America: in 1992 and 1993 some countries were beginning to experience substantial inflows of foreign capital as well as repatriation of their own citizens' money previously kept abroad in safe havens. For Africa the forecast is, alas, probably accurate.)

Possibly figuring that someone might notice its hugely inaccurate forecasts, the Bank belatedly included a box in the 1991 *WDR* asking, 'How well did early *World Development Reports* foresee growth in the 1980s?' Even though the authors prudently refrain from mentioning the evidence we have cited above, their reply is still, on the whole, 'not very well'. They also note that 'projections published in *World Development Reports* have become more guarded in recent years'. No wonder![11]

The Bank's 'unguarded' projections, however, seriously affected the debtor countries. Because these countries, according to the Bank, were supposed to be awash in tens of billions of fresh private capital every year and were also supposed to pay the interest on these steadily mounting obligations from export revenues, it followed that these export revenues also had to be optimistically viewed. Trade would come to the rescue.

Here again, the Bank's projections were vastly wide of the mark.

Minerals, petroleum and agricultural raw materials are still the mainstays of most debtor country exports: in 1980 these product groups represented over eighty per cent of the value of both Latin America's and Africa's total exports, a third of Asia's and ninety-five per cent of the Middle East's. Thus for the problem debtors, the Bank was necessarily counting mainly on primary commodities to furnish the hard cash for debt service.[12]

The Bank's International Economics Department (International Trade Division) regularly prepares commodity price projections. These forecasts are usually for internal consumption only but for once were published in late 1981 in a major Bank study on Africa. Here is the way the Bank's 1981 predictions for 1990 raw material prices stacked up with reality (all figures are based on an index of 1980 = 100):[13]

Commodities	Bank-Projected Price Index 1990	Actual Price Index 1990	Bank Off By (%)
Minerals/Metals	127.7	78.8	62
Petroleum	137.0	53.6	156
Fats and Oils	132.9	47.5	180
Beverages	86.0	42.4	103
Timber	135.7	84.7	60
Agr. Non-Food	117.0	59.5	97
Total Food and Bev.	88.8	52.6	69

The size of one's debt, one's prospects for fresh capital and the prices one's commodities are likely to fetch on world markets are vital components in any developing country's economic strategy. It is thus of considerable concern that the Bank, the chief development advisor to these countries and the principal outside agency making crucial economic decisions about their future, should be both so sure it is right and so wrong.

The Bank's 1981 report on Africa can, perhaps, be excused for not foreseeing that in the ensuing years nearly everyone, under instructions from the Bank, would be exporting flat out. The authors of the study, although they espouse all the neo-liberal policies subsequently put into effect in Africa, were not to know how exceptionally successful their recommendations would be; nor how many countries would be undergoing structural adjustment a decade later. Their report did, however, bewail African governments' 'policy bias against exports' and set out to change it.*

A decade later, however, excuses were a good deal harder to come by. By then, it had become all too clear that commodity prices had plummeted to their lowest levels since the Great Depression and the slide seemed destined to continue since no mitigating factors had surfaced. None of this deterred the Bank's International Economics Department from continuing, in 1991, to make optimistic projections which, even in the short space of two years, have once again proven completely unrealistic.

We compared the Bank's 1991 forecasts for 1993 commodity prices with the actual prices, as listed in the *Financial Times* and the *International Herald Tribune* in August 1993 (all in current dollars). We found the real prices catastrophically (for producers) lower than the Bank had said they would be only two years previously. The Bank's 1991 projections were off by 47 per cent on coffee, 56 per cent on cocoa, 74 per cent on sugar, 30 per cent on coconut oil, 35 per cent on rubber, 39 per cent on tin, 34 per cent on aluminium, 52 per cent on lead and 37 per cent on zinc. They got petroleum, copper and silver about right; palm oil, alone among the commodities we were able to check, did better than the Bank said it would, by 15 per cent.[14]

The Bank's forecasters are still wearing their rose-coloured glasses. In their *Global Economic Prospects and the Developing Countries* for 1992, which deals with the coming decade, they continue to claim that commodity prices are headed upwards and that the gross domestic product of developing countries is slated to grow by

---

* We are, of course, aware that factors besides structural adjustment policies have contributed to chronic oversupply of primary commodities, among them increased competition from Asian producers, substitutions (high fructose corn syrup for sugar, optical fibre for copper, et cetera); improved material-saving technologies and the like. These trends have been apparent for over a decade, much scholarly work has been devoted to them and the Bank could have incorporated the relevant research in its own analyses as well as attempting to assess the impact of its own policy advice. For the real prospects for African commodities in particular (which are not encouraging) see Michael Barratt Brown and Pauline Tiffen, *Short Changed: Africa and World Trade* (London, Pluto Press and the Transnational Institute, 1992).

more than five per cent a year for the period 1992–2002. We'll get back to you with the actual outcomes in a decade or so.

The Bank's board of executive directors also seems to have become mildly alarmed by the inaccuracies of the institution's projections upon which so much development advice is based. In late 1989, the Joint Audit Committee (made up of eight executive directors) recommended that 'the Bank should undertake a review to try to improve the quality of agricultural commodity price forecasting'.[15]

Asked if it had taken steps to improve this quality in accordance with the Joint Audit Committee's request, the division that compiles the forecasts replied that since 1990 the division has taken into consideration commodity futures market quotations in its projections – which, strangely enough for such a market-oriented institution, it did not do before. Otherwise, little appears to have changed.[16]

The Bank has also consistently and grossly overestimated growth not just of export *prices* but of export *volumes* as well, always seeing light at the end of the tunnel and prosperity just around the corner. From the late 1970s until 1986, it kept on insisting that developing country exports would grow (as they effectively had done in previous decades) during the 1980s by at least five per cent annually. Alas, between 1981 and 1986, the actual average annual growth rate for these export volumes was a *negative* 0.4 per cent.[17]

Finally, in the early 1990s, export volumes *are* growing, but with what consequences? Twenty-six particularly needy sub-Saharan African countries, all undergoing structural adjustment, are eligible for the Bank's Special Program of Assistance. The Bank's structural adjustment programmes (SAPs) require governments to concentrate their efforts on exports and between 1991 and 1993 these *did* increase, by nearly five per cent a year. This relative success was, however, of little value to the people of these twenty-six poor countries concerned: their per capita consumption during the same period fell by minus 0.3 per cent.*

---

* The Bank, if asked, would doubtless attribute this drop in consumption entirely to population growth, without considering reduced resource allocation to food crops, lack of investment in primary industries or intermediate technology, and the significant drop in real incomes which has been a constant feature of African countries under adjustment.

The Bank claims that countries 'on-track' with adjustment are getting better results than the hesitant and tardy middle group, and much better results than the 'off-track' countries, the really recalcitrant ones (mostly in the French CFA franc zone, against which the Bank has waged a running battle). In fact, 1992 consumption figures for all three groups were negative, according to the Bank's own figures.[18]

In our attempt to understand the Bank's criteria for including or excluding various factors in its economic analyses, we have been forced to conclude that ideological bias (or blindness) is at work. 'World' Bank though it may be, it does not seem to view the world as a unit. For example, it refrains from examining the consequences of obliging many countries at once to devalue their currency and to export.

Although it may seem barely credible, to the best of our knowledge the Bank's army of economists has never thought it relevant or useful to make a general assessment of the impact of the Bank's own structural adjustment policies on market prospects for commodities – or if something of the sort has been undertaken the results are not public. Yet the first and most universal feature of any structural adjustment package is the reorientation of the economy towards maximum production for export. Since dozens of countries are now subject to such packages, since many of them export the same commodities, it does not take a Ph.D. in economics to foresee gluts and declining prices for everyone.

Professor Emeritus of Development Studies Hans Singer, in an article only mildly critical of the Bank's policies in this regard, points out that:

> For instance, if devaluation is recommended to say, Kenya, in order to increase the export of tea, the impact of this on the tea exports of say, Sri Lanka, cannot be disregarded. If Sri Lanka at the same time is induced to devalue its currency to bolster its tea exports, the backlash on Kenya will undo at least some of the intended advantages of Kenya's own devaluation; in the end both countries may be worse off, with the tea importing countries the main beneficiaries.[19]

Now that some ninety countries have adopted similar policies, one would think that the Bank would accord a high priority to addressing their overall impact and, more generally, re-examine the assumptions on which its structural adjustment strategies are based. As far as we know, it is not doing so.[20]

One senses almost a kind of self-hypnosis: our policies are necessarily good, therefore their consequences must also be good, therefore commodity prices will rise, indebtedness will fall and foreign investment will turn up, thus proving that our policies were correct, in an unending, self-gratifying circular argument.

The Bank does suggest that indebted countries should move away from primary commodities, into processed products and manufactures. Of course they should – but using what for investment capital in these capital-strapped times? They are paying out huge percentages of their meagre export revenues in debt service anyway (Algeria and Madagascar seem to be the champions here, with about two-thirds of their export revenues devoted to debt service; the average is about twenty-five per cent). Little is left over for imports of technology, know-how and 'intermediate goods' to bolster production.

The Bank's view is that foreign direct investment (FDI) will reward countries willing to accept the sacrifices imposed by structural adjustment. The usual clichés apply: no pain, no gain, virtue will be rewarded and investors, like opportunity, will knock. Diversification will become more than a pious hope. This is the good news.

The bad news is that once again the Bank's clients, not the Bank, are likely to pay dearly because once again the Bank, with characteristic doctrinal rigidity, is getting it wrong. This time, the subject for serious error is foreign direct investment. Virtue may well have to be its own reward because, in reality, this investment has been highly concentrated in fewer than ten countries. Even there, the profits are infrequently reinvested in the country concerned but are repatriated. Nor does the Bank seem to have grasped the significance of changes in the needs and preferences of transnational capital.

In a report commissioned in 1993 by the European Commission, British economist Stuart Holland argues that the Bank (like its partner, the IMF) designs its policies on the basis of 'outdated paradigms'. He sees the Bretton Woods institutions relying on traditional theories of comparative advantage, believing that cheap labour and low social costs will attract investment. These theories may have worked well enough in the nineteenth and pre-war twentieth centuries; meanwhile the TNCs which are the source of FDI have moved on into the twenty-first. Such firms, according to Holland, are now

> transcending the specialisation implied by both comparative advant-age theory and economies of scale ... they now exploit economies of *scope* ... Comparative advantage now lies mainly with those multinational firms which can prove themselves more flexible and more diversified than others at the global innovation frontier. Global investment, trade and payments are now innovation rather than cost-led (his emphasis).[21]

The TNCs want well-trained, skilled workers who can switch tasks smoothly and quickly; they want to be close to efficient component suppliers who can modify production specifications at short notice. They are prepared to pay for such advantages on the perfectly accurate grounds that increased flexibility and high worker productivity will offset higher salary or benefit costs.

Contrary to the Bank's expectations and to the hopes it holds out to its borrowers, its 3-D strategy of Deflation, Devaluation and Deregulation imposed on all its clients is only rarely followed by significant foreign investment. The strategy isn't working because the economic theory that underpins it is obsolete. Holland says that, indeed, 'Low direct labour costs and lowered indirect social costs' (both guaranteed by structural adjustment) 'are not sufficient – and increasingly are counter-productive – in attracting foreign direct investment'.

The proof of this pudding is found in the *World Investment Report*. It shows that over the decade of the 1980s, most FDI went to the already rich countries while the portion going to developing coun-tries dropped dramatically. Some years ago, less advanced countries were doing relatively well in this department: between 1980 and 1985, the southern hemisphere's share of FDI averaged about twenty-nine per cent of the total.

By 1990, however, they were receiving only seventeen per cent (of a larger aggregate sum, it is true). During this decade, Africa's share of FDI fell from an already insignificant three per cent to a barely perceptible one per cent. In the first half of the 1980s, Latin

America's share of FDI was nearly fourteen per cent. In the early 1990s it had plummeted to a mere five per cent. Only Asia held steady throughout the decade of the 1980s at ten per cent of FDI. Investors overwhelmingly want to put their money, their plants and their services in the richer, more developed countries, where the telephones work.[22]

The implications for most of the Bank's clients are alarming. We now live in a world of *cumulative*, as opposed to comparative, advantage. Or, as the less elegant popular saying goes, 'Them as has, gets'. Those who can promise the highest skills and the greatest flexibility are the winners now.*

In spite of its tragically outdated model, Holland sees some hope for the Bank (although much less for the IMF). He believes that:

> In the World Bank there recently has been very considerable change, not least through the influence of some executive directors who have started to act as a board rather than as clients of the conventional wisdom . . . the US administration used to gather the G7 directors of the Bank, establish the line to be taken at board meetings and then reflect the ideology prevailing in the [US] administration itself. [This is changing and moreover] many individual officials in both the Fund and the Bank do not share assent to the official line taken by either institution.[23]

We wish we could share Stuart Holland's optimism. Yes, there are a few strong executive directors and some heretics inside. But as Holland himself not only recognizes but also documents, the Bank and the Fund apply 'cross-conditionality', requiring that a country have a Fund stabilization package in place before the Bank will make any loans. Genuine change in the Bank's policies towards its adjusting clients would therefore also have to include mass conversion in the Fund, which Holland himself does not think likely. Adjustment is still on the menu, eggs are being broken by the thousands yet the omelettes remain problematical.

The Bank's culture weighs on and inhibits its capacity to change.

---

* Naturally, this does not mean that downward pressure on wages, social benefits, working conditions, environmental standards, et cetera will abate in the industrialized countries, quite the contrary.

Yet change is crucial if the Bank is to avoid continual false prophecies with increasingly grievous consequences for the countries under its tutelage. One of the Bank's problems – at least seen from outside – is that the institution and its personnel are never even made to *define* failure and the steps that might be taken to avoid it, much less take responsibility for it. As Susan George wrote in *A Fate Worse than Debt*:

> They go on getting their comfortable salaries no matter how much human suffering their policies demonstrably cause. They are not subject to ostracism by their peers. They continue to dominate the 'respectable' publications and the institutions where those who will follow in their footsteps are trained. They are not accountable.[24]

We think this bears repeating because principles like accountability are generally regarded as among the more profound achievements of civilized societies. No checks and balances are brought to bear on the Bank (a subject to which we return in Chapters VII and XI). In the real world, when political accountability does not apply, professional codes usually do. Doctors swear the Hippocratic oath, whose first principle, 'Do no harm', would be equally pertinent when the patient is a whole community or society; priests take vows, other professions have established their own ethical standards. The Bank is subject neither to a political jurisdiction nor to recognized deontological practice. Staff are set no particular ethical standards towards which they are expected to strive, even if they cannot always attain them.

In the absence of recognized political or ethical curbs on behaviour, then at least the sanctions of the marketplace ought to apply, particularly to a Bank which never tires of repeating that it is a purely economic institution. But here again the institution is exonerated. If it gives its client countries wrong advice and shapes their policies on the basis of erroneous assumptions, if it continues to make them loans that cannot possibly be repaid out of real export earnings, it suffers no economic consequences.

The Bank's Articles of Agreement do not presently allow for default on the part of any borrower – that is, the Bank cannot now legally cancel its own loans or make their terms less onerous – even if those loans were granted for projects or programmes with negative economic returns and whose failure was the Bank's fault.

None the less former Bank economist Percy Mistry explains that the Bank could, without violating its Articles, still use its own considerable reserves for a significant write-down of its poorest clients' debts. This would justifiably 'inflict a measure of disciplinary pain' on the Bank itself for its poor lending decisions. It should be called upon to cut frills and to rein in its own administrative budget ($1.4 billion for 1994), using the savings for further relief.[25]

Thus far the Bank has succeeded in having its cake and eating it, preaching market theology while constantly misreading the market and avoiding the market consequences of those misreadings. The Bank (with the IMF) automatically stands first in line for all repayments by all countries because their global credit ratings depend on the status of their payments to the Bretton Woods institutions. For this reason, the Bank virtually *cannot* go bankrupt. Because of its political power, it need not fear the market – other lenders may be left holding the bag – never the Bank. Thus the Bank has no market incentive to loan only for viable ideas and projects 'benefiting the greatest number' because it will get its money back, with interest, whatever happens.

Yet the Bank, with all its special, non-market features, is still a bank, and one with a balance sheet any commercial bank would envy. From 1988 to 1991 its surplus consistently topped a billion dollars a year; in 1992 income was $1.645 billion. By 1993, the Bank's overall hoard – or retained earnings – came to a tidy $14 billion.[26] The Bank has discovered the dream formula: Guaranteed Profits, No Risk. We are not sure what this system is called, but it is not capitalism.

Perhaps the Bank is saving for a rainy day. Perhaps it plans at some unspecified future date to use its hoard to treat the poverty and environmental damage its earlier loans have done so much to inflict. In any event, it is not today giving part of this stockpile to UNICEF, nor using it to write off its African loans.

For the moment, at least, rather than answer to anyone for the consequences of its mistaken analyses or failed schemes, the Bank relies on two strategies. The first is a stance of infallibility, as befits the Holy See of development. One just plunges ahead and ignores the past as if everything one had ever said was necessarily true. This system of self-legitimation is also tautological – I'm excellent because I'm excellent. Usually this strategy works.*

When it doesn't, when errors are too egregious to be kept under wraps, strategy number two comes into play. Then the Bank switches to a dialectic of error and learning, mistakes and fresh starts, a modern version of confession and absolution. In a back-handed way, the Bank recognizes that it is immune from market sanctions, as from external political control or internal ethical standards, and in the absence of any countervailing power forcing it to change, casts itself as the Bank-that-is-changing.[27]

From the Bank's point of view, although not as good as silence, admitting errors is clearly preferable to assuming responsibility for them. Sincere and contrite, it concedes that: Yes, we've made mistakes but now we've seen the light and we're turning over a new leaf. Things will be different from now on. Our learning curve is on the upswing.

This attitude parallels the Christian view of sin and redemption: we are born sinful and will doubtless continue to sin throughout our lives; but we can, through contrition, confession and grace, obtain forgiveness. The Bank always seems to leave the confessional with a clear conscience, say three *Paters*, three *Aves*, issue three press releases and go back, shriven and absolved, to business as usual.

Protestants believe that prayer and repentance will win God's forgiveness because his love is infinite. For the Catholic, absolution requires an absolver; the priest, acting as the intermediary of God's grace, is sacramentally empowered to grant it. For the believer *as an individual*, these are spiritually efficacious, healing processes. We know of no one, however, who would argue for a similar mechanism of collective absolution for a worldly institution. Organizations are simply not subject to the same rules as individual consciences.

---

* For example, aside from the 1987 work of John Cavanagh and Robin Broad (see endnote 17) and Nicholas Stern's chapter for the official Bank history (see Chapter IX), we found no other sources that had checked out the Bank's predictions after the fact. We rely here almost entirely on primary sources, mostly from the Bank itself.

Most advanced societies, after centuries of philosophical enquiry and political struggle, have reached the conclusion that law, not religion, is the better organizing principle for the polity. The rule of law and agreed-upon structures to bring about orderly change or to prevent abuses of power are preferable to the dubious prospect of institutional self-amendment and reform. Western societies acknowledge that the realms of the secular and the sacred should be kept rigorously separate.

Promises to learn from our mistakes and to mend our ways are not the same as being held accountable and, possibly, sanctioned for those mistakes. The Bank would certainly react to plausible threats of reduction, suspension or abolition of its funding, power, or privilege.

If the Bank is not obliged to quit the unassailable, non-market, self-legitimated terrain for a secular, legally regulated, market-sanctioned and political one, and if past experience is any guide, it will continue to make false prophecies. Afterwards, rather than taking the consequences itself, it will revert to the familiar mode of confession of error, self-absolution and the pursuit of its chosen policies, at other people's expense.

Chapter V

The Fundamentalist Freedom Fighter

Canadian scholar John Mihevc titles the first chapter of his doctoral dissertation in theology 'The Fundamentalist Theology of the
World Bank'.[1] He means it literally. Mihevc, who wrote his thesis
on the response of churches and social movements in Africa to
World Bank structural adjustment programmes, found striking
similarities between the development vision of the Bank and the
neo-conservative, right-wing fundamentalist religious agenda on
the rise in many Northern countries in the 1980s.

> The manner in which the World Bank has presented, promoted and
> defended structural adjustment against its critics closely parallels
> fundamentalist interpretations of the Bible. The strategies employed
> by the World Bank to guarantee the hegemony of its ideology and to
> deal with dissenters also correspond to those of fundamentalism . . .
> [The Bank] not only denies the legitimacy of alternatives, but has
> actively sought, over the past decade, to ensure that all of the
> options available to developing countries have been narrowed to
> one.[2]

Mihevc is not alone in his views. According to this theological
interpretation, the Bank has contrived to confer on its own doctrines
a status akin to that of divinely ordained natural law. The operations of the free market are assumed to be value-free, efficient in
allocating resources and socially neutral. Because it is value-free, it
would be absurd to judge the market against values: as the Central
American Jesuit theologian and philosopher Franz Hinkelammert
has put it, the market is 'judge over life and death but cannot itself
be judged in terms of the effect it has on the life and death of every
individual'.[3]

Or, as a Protestant thinker explains, 'The laws of the market . . .

come to be seen as transcendent, [undergoing] a process of sociolo-gical sacralisation. Not only are they given a higher status, they actually become untouchable, like the laws of nature.'⁴ The invisible hand, like God himself, moves in mysterious ways. Those who deny it or, worse still, try to get in its way, do so at their peril.

In this modern theological setting, the missionary is replaced by the neo-classical economist; the development expert mediates be-tween the developed and the underdeveloped worlds as the priest mediates between the divine and the secular ones, helping the underdeveloped to tread the long road to salvation. The way is hard and steep; it is not for the faint-hearted.

Debt payments are one offering, a kind of tribute; the structural adjustment measures which ensure that these debts can and will be paid, act as a kind of ritual cleansing through sacrifice. As is the case with fundamentalist religion, only one interpretation of the Word is allowed. Proposals of alternatives to adjustment are dis-missed by its proponents as dangerous, unrealistic, or irrelevant.*

If the invisible hand of the market, like the divinity, is beyond the control of mere mortals, if the road to redemption requires sacrifice and penance, then no human agency, much less any individual, can be considered responsible for the consequences of the market's operations. The Word can only be proclaimed, administered and made manifest; it cannot be changed.

The task of the missionary is to interpret the Word to the Nations but also to do battle for it. An exemplary fighter of this good fight is Lawrence H. Summers. We will introduce him as the protagonist of

---

* A single example: with about fifty African economists, Susan George was to a degree associated with the production of the United Nations Economic Commission for Africa's (ECA) *Alternative African Framework to Structural Adjustment Programmes* (AAF–SAP, ECA, July 1989), under the leadership of Professor Adebayo Adedeji of Nigeria, then the General Secretary of the ECA. This report not only called for alternative economic policies and adjustment measures (land reform, heavy invest-ment in agriculture for food self-sufficiency, closer links between agriculture and industry, reduction of military spending and the like) but also recognized as well that 'political systems will need to evolve to allow for full democracy and participation by all sectors of the society'. Even though this document represented the work of excellent and highly representative African economic thinkers and emanated from a UN agency, the Bank completely ignored it.

a story now widely known, but so revealing that we hope not everyone has heard it and that those who have will not mind our retelling the tale of the Toxic Memo. When Summers wrote it, he was the Bank's Chief Economist and Vice-President for Development Economics, a position he held from December 1990 until he left to join the Clinton administration as Under-Secretary of the Treasury in April 1993.

This job made him the general of the Bank's army of macro-economists. His responsibilities included the production of the Bank's annual, pace-setting *World Development Report* as well as the supervision of other Bank economic publications. Commenting on one of the latter, a draft of *Global Economic Prospects*, he wrote the now-notorious memo to a select list of six highly placed Bank colleagues in the trade or international economics departments.[5]

Some brave soul, doubtless much lower down the pecking order, snaffled a copy and leaked it to the Environmental Defense Fund and to Greenpeace, which in turn alerted the press. The US newspapers sat on it. Then the *Economist* published the juicier bits and all hell broke loose.

Probably because he was writing for a small audience of *intimes*, Summers didn't bother to gild any lilies but expressed the fundamentalist doctrine in its purest form. When the memo was made public, he repudiated it, saying he had merely hoped to 'sharpen analysis'. None the less, the decried passage is intellectually coherent and simply takes the doctrine to its logical, value-free conclusion.

Commenting on a section of the draft dealing with '"Dirty" industries', Summers asked his colleagues:

> Just between you and me, shouldn't the World Bank be encouraging *more* migration of the dirty industries to the LDCs (Less Developed Countries, his emphasis)?

'I can think of three reasons,' he said, elaborating. The first is that:

> The measurement of the costs of health impairing pollution depends on the foregone earnings from increased morbidity and mortality. From this point of view a given amount of health impairing pollution should be done in the country with the lowest cost, which will be the

country with the lowest wages. I think the economic logic behind dumping a load of toxic waste in the lowest wage country is impeccable and we should face up to that.

This passage, quoted in its entirety, perhaps requires explicating for those who, distracted by moral concerns or ordinary human sympathy, may fail to grasp its impeccable logic. If one dumps 'a load of toxic waste' in a rich country, it could cause the illness or death of people who earn high incomes and have long life expectancies. According to World Bank figures in Summers's own *World Development Report*, an American or European represents $20,000 per year in gross national product. Assume this person is forty years old and will go on being productive for another twenty-five years: he or she will thus be worth a further $500,000 to the global economy.

Furthermore, if such a person sustained health damage due to toxic waste, s/he would also be more likely to possess the cultural know-how and financial capacity to sue the companies that dumped it. This could cost them dearly in legal damages, thereby reducing their profits.

In contrast, according to the *WDR*, the average inhabitant of one of the lowest wage countries contributes only $360 annually to GNP and has an average life expectancy of fifty-five years. If this person is also forty, statistically speaking s/he has only another fifteen years to go and is thus worth $5,400, or ninety-two times less than the value of the person who lives in an OECD country. This financial midget is also a legal cipher who is unlikely to worry the company much in case of toxic disaster, as the victims of Union Carbide's plant in Bhopal can readily testify. As of this writing, they are still fighting their legal damage claims, in spite of the obvious and well-documented physical impairments they suffered.

Thus it is indeed economically logical that illness and death should occur in places where the foregone earnings will be the least. (Note that the same arguments can be applied to countries internally: it is well known that in the United States toxic hazards are concentrated in poor, usually minority communities where people are seen as less able to protest.)

Summers also thoughtfully provides some good news for the

economically insignificant: in his second argument, he explains that 'the initial increments of pollution' are very low cost. In other words, when you're just beginning to concentrate toxics, you get relatively little illness and death, especially when people aren't very concentrated either. This is why, in the same memo, he confesses to his colleagues that: 'I've always thought that underpopulated countries in Africa are vastly *under*polluted, their air quality is probably vastly inefficiently low compared to Los Angeles or Mexico City' (his emphasis).

We can only salute in passing Summers's brilliant invention of the concept of 'inefficiently low air quality', which means pure. Alas, it is not always possible to make this air quality efficiently high (foul) in low-wage countries because many polluting industries like transport and electric power simply can't be picked up in Los Angeles and set down in Timbuktu. Furthermore, the shipping costs of moving solid wastes from rich countries to poor ones may be prohibitively high. These factors conspire to 'prevent world welfare-enhancing trade in air pollution and waste'. It is a pity but it is a fact of life that, as Summers puts it, 'the consumption of pretty air is a non-tradeable'.

Summers's third reason for facing up to the impeccable logic of waste dumping is basically that beggars can't be choosers. 'The demand for a clean environment for aesthetic and health reasons is likely to have a very high income elasticity,' he writes. In plain English, this means that the more money you have, the more discriminating about pollution you can afford to be. Men in the developed countries may worry about contracting prostate cancer. But poor men living in poor countries have fewer worries on this score because the chances are they will not live long enough to contract it. 'The concern [over toxic agents] is obviously going to be much higher in a country where people survive to get prostrate (*sic*) cancer than in a country where the under-5 mortality is 200 per thousand'. So the demand for pure, 'pretty', inefficient air and for zero toxic waste dumps just isn't there, and even if it were, people couldn't back it up with cash, which, as we have by now understood, is the measure of all things.

Summers's leaked memo predictably outraged environmentalists and many others. Several organizations, including Greenpeace, called for his resignation.* In a letter to Summers, José Lutzenberger, then Secretary for the Environment in Brazil, expressed his views with particular vehemence:

> Your reasoning is perfectly logical but totally insane. [It is] a concrete example of the unbelievable alienation, reductionist thinking, social ruthlessness and arrogant ignorance of many conventional 'economists' concerning the nature of the world we live in . . . [I]t is an insult to thinking people . . . If the World Bank keeps you as Vice President, it will lose all credibility.

Summers's new boss, President Lewis Preston, did not fully agree with Lutzenberger. He was on his first visit to Africa when the Toxic Memo story broke. He, too, denounced it as 'outrageous', but declined to fire its author.[6] In the general brouhaha of unwelcome publicity, the Bank simply issued a standard disclaimer to the effect that the views in the memo did 'not represent the position of the World Bank'.†

Summers himself apologized profusely, saying he had only meant his remarks 'ironically' and as a 'sardonic counterpoint' which would 'provoke debate'. Since then, he has missed few opportunities to say that he made a mistake. He told *Business Week* that his text took 'an aggressively sarcastic tone to try to put some rigor into a very muddled discussion of environmental and trade issues'. Actually, the memo's more controversial passages do not differ significantly in tone from the rest of the seven page text – they merely

---

* Personally, we did not join in the demands for Summers's resignation. Not only do we value free speech but furthermore, as Susan George was quoted in the quarterly *BankCheck*, 'Mr Summers is a perfect example of what the Bank thinks and is, except that the PR staff usually manages to hide the reality. It's been a long time since we've had such an unreconstructed and frank free-marketeer and I say, keep him talking'.

† In a letter to the *Economist* published a week after it had leaked the Toxic Memo, Summers affirmed that 'it is not my view, or the World Bank's view, or that of any sane person that pollution should be encouraged anywhere, or that the dumping of untreated toxic wastes near the homes of poor people is morally or economically defensible . . . I regret that the *Economist* . . . did not consult the Bank before running the story and, therefore, failed to run our statement which put the contents of the memo in perspective'. To which the *Economist* tartly added an Editor's Note: 'The Bank would not have issued a statement had we not published the memo'.

touch on a more sensitive subject. Summers also told the *Washington Post* that the questions he was asking – for example, whether environmental standards should be the same worldwide – are legitimate ones, but fall outside the bounds of 'political correctness' and thus induced a sharp backlash.[7]

Whatever else one can say, Summers got his wish: he provoked debate with a vengeance. In our view, the real debate should centre not on Summers the man, but on the hypothesis that his views, even the extreme ones, *do* in fact represent the position and the basic assumptions of the Bank. One cannot merely discount Summers's job as Chief Economist and Vice-President for Development Economics which made him, for a time, the top 'doctrinal' officer of the Bank; opinions expressed while in that position cannot be judged simply as those of a former Harvard professor or a private individual.

Like any institution, the Bank has its own self-reinforcing culture and its codes which set the limits on what can be reasonably believed and discussed if one hopes to be taken seriously and remain a member of the group. One often hears stories about the arrogance of this or that Bank official. It is not especially pleasant to be on the receiving end of this arrogance, but it is easily explained.

Put in the same place several hundred people who have been trained in the same schools to think in the same way, recruit them precisely because they have excelled in this training, provide them further with high salaries and many benefits, give them power to impose their doctrines on hundreds of thousands of (by definition) ignorant people and you are unlikely to produce a climate of humility and tolerance. (We elaborate on these aspects in Chapter VI.)

The far more probable cultural outcome will be – at least among the economists – monolithic and fundamentalist. Fundamentalism is not confined to matters spiritual. The Bank's parameters of thought and action may appear 'totally insane' to outsiders like Lutzenberger, ethically dubious to humanitarians and ecologically disastrous to environmentalists, but for those inside they are as valid as were the premises of, say, medieval schoolmen for whom issues like the numbers of angels that could dance on the head of a pin, or the sex of the said angels, were serious matters.

Perhaps the Bank's world-view has become about as relevant to today's context and to late twentieth-century problems as that of the schoolmen or of the Flat Earth Society; but this does not mean it will disappear just because it is outmoded or wrong. We may recall that the Catholic Church only got around to rehabilitating Galileo in 1992 although it first condemned his views in 1633.* Twentieth-century economists cling to their beliefs with every bit the tenacity once displayed by medieval theologians and when they are concentrated in a place dispensing power, profit and prestige like the Bank, they have an even greater personal stake in defending the faith against heresy. As the noted economist Albert Hirschman drily remarked, in economics 'a model is never defeated by facts, no matter how damaging, but only by another model'. (We explore some elements of an alternative model in Chapter IX.)

Meanwhile, Summers is as clever a schoolman as one is likely to meet within the confines of his own paradigm and for this reason his world-view is both meaningful and influential.

So who is Larry Summers and how did he become what he is? The short answer is that it runs in the family – both his parents are economists and two of his uncles, Paul Samuelson and Kenneth

---

* See 'Discours de S. Ém. le Cardinal Paul Poupard au terme des travaux de la Commission Pontificale d'Étude de la controverse ptoléméo-copernicienne au XVIe et XVIIe siècles', 31 October 1992 and the speech of Pope John-Paul II on the same occasion. This story is more complicated than popular myth would have it. Irrefutable optical and mechanical proof of Galileo's hypotheses was only supplied some 150 years after his condemnation yet Pope Benedict XIV gave Galileo's *Complete Works* the *imprimatur* (Papal permission to print) in 1741. Books teaching Copernican astronomy were all removed from the *Index* (of prohibited books) by 1846. Even so, many conservative theologians disapproved of these decisions and continued to insist on, and to teach, a geocentric cosmos. At the 1992 meeting, Pope John-Paul II reminded the Pontifical Academy that in Galileo's time, it was inconceivable to think of the world without a fixed physical reference point – whereas today both the earth *and* the sun have lost their central importance in the cosmos. Galileo's arguments were correct as far as they went, but should remind us, according to John-Paul, that beyond two partial and conflicting visions, 'there exists a broader vision which encompasses and goes beyond both'. The Pope also repeated that science has nothing to fear from the Church, since – in the words of his predecessor Leon XIII – 'Truth cannot contradict truth'. Amen.

Arrow, are Nobel laureates in economics.* Summers got his Ph.D.
at Harvard in 1982 at the age of twenty-seven. A year later he
became a full, tenured professor – a record probably unmatched at
Harvard since the seventeenth century. The US National Science
Foundation has given him the largest no-strings-attached grant
($500,000) ever awarded an economist.

He acted as economics advisor to the hugely unsuccessful Democratic presidential candidate Michael Dukakis in 1988. People close
to that campaign say Summers spent his time combating those
who were trying to push Dukakis towards a more progressive
stance. In any case, Summers's nominal status as a Democrat had
not prevented him from serving earlier as a senior staff economist
on Ronald Reagan's Council of Economic Advisors; the Bush administration encouraged his appointment as Chief Economist at the
Bank, itself then headed by Barber Conable, a former Republican
Congressman.

Summers's economic views differ imperceptibly if at all from the
standard neo-liberal 1980s' agenda: free-market, monetarist economics, free (that is, deregulated) trade, privatization, reduction of
the role of the state and downsizing of the public sector, plus cost/
benefit analysis applied to every conceivable object including human
life, as indicated above. Summers has written widely on a variety of
economic topics, including taxes and unemployment, but until his
Bank stint, development economics *per se* had never visibly claimed
his attention.

Since it is unfair to judge the man on the strength of a single
memo, let alone one he has disavowed, let us look at some of his
other views which will also help to explain the culture of the Bank
itself. One of Summers's other public statements concerns the
Soviet Union (as it still then was) and was made during a breakfast
meeting talk to Bretton Woods officials, private bankers and government ministers at the Bank–IMF annual general meeting in Bangkok in October 1991.[8]

Summers is upbeat about the Russians' future and accentuates

---

* Strictly speaking, there are no 'Nobel laureates in economics' because there is no
Nobel Prize in economics. There is a prize awarded to an economist 'in memory of
Alfred Nobel', instituted by the Royal Bank of Sweden in 1969.

the positive, listing several elements in the country's favour: huge oil reserves and plenty of educated people, including a third of all the doctorates produced in the world in science and engineering. Best of all, he says, 'the Soviet Union after seventy years of Communism still does have a work-ethic'. This observation may surprise those who remember the old Soviet joke – 'We pretend to work and they pretend to pay us'. None the less, 'speaking both for myself and on behalf of the World Bank', Summers invites his audience to

> look to the obvious entrepreneurial energy of the black market, look to the large numbers of Soviet workers who are finding jobs in Poland and who are regarded by Polish employers as the best workers they can find, and look to the wage rates for those workers – it's hard to find any plausible exchange rate that gets you to 75 cents an hour. That means that the system can be made to work.

Workers – highly educated ones at that – earning a maximum of 75 cents an hour are indeed a windfall for any employer of any nationality. As for the 'obvious entrepreneurial energy of the black market', it certainly exists, but has been diversely judged. Anecdotal evidence of the nature and the consequences of that energy already existed at the time Summers spoke and was amplified by the *New York Times* Moscow correspondent less than a year after his talk. She reported that Russians were sadly unprepared for the 'breakdown in the trust and discipline that bound their society together'.

> It is not just a matter of crime, corruption, prostitution, smuggling, and drug and alcohol abuse . . . There is also a widespread view that now . . . people are out for themselves and anything goes.[9]

But isn't that precisely the point? Complete freedom for the invisible hand, with or without a gun in it, to work its magic? In late 1991 when Summers was speaking so fulsomely to his colleagues about Russia, the serious crime rate had already risen by an estimated eighteen per cent compared to the previous year, whereas in 1992 the police reported 'a rise [in serious crimes] of 30 to 35 per cent'. 'The situation is substantially aggravated by the illegal sales of arms,' according to the minister of the interior, less enthusiastic than Larry Summers about the trends taking root in his country.[10]*

In his speaking and writing, Summers seems oblivious to social consequences of economic policies and thus asks his listeners in Bangkok:

> What can the West do to drive this process of reform [in Russia] forward? Number one: it can spread the truth. The laws of economics, it's often forgotten, are like the laws of engineering. There's only one set of laws and they work everywhere. One of the things I've learned in my short time at the World Bank is that whenever anybody says, 'But economics works differently here', they're about to say something dumb.[11]

Well before this speech at the Bank's annual meeting or the leaked Toxic Memo, Summers had publicly declared his universalist position. When questioned by the *Los Angeles Times* shortly after taking up his position at the Bank, he declared, 'The rules that apply in Latin America or Eastern Europe apply in India as well . . . [third world governments] need to understand that there is no longer such a thing as a separate and distinct Indian economics – there is just economics'.

All third world countries, he asserted, should imitate the 'aggressive, market-oriented' East Asian dragons, because 'they have to realize that governments can't be omniscient enough to get things right in every market'. The journalist questioning Summers remarked that he had 'become a virtual tent-preacher, touting free-market economics to developing countries'.[12]

Recent history has strengthened Larry Summers's position just as it has that of the Bank. The former socialist countries of Eastern Europe tried to run their command economies with a system of dictated, managed prices – highly subsidized energy or staple food-

---

* Summers would doubtless be intrigued by the cover story concerning the 'obvious entrepreneurial energy of the black market' in Russia which appeared, two years after his talk, in the business journal *Global Finance* (September 1993). Entitled 'Gangster Economics', it provides seven closely spaced pages of appalling news about all-pervading, organized criminal control of the new entrepreneurial Russia. Random samples: 'Corruption is not the exception, it's the norm . . . If you're not a part of it, you're not going to be doing business . . . Stories of threats, beatings and killings are an everyday event'.

stuffs, free education and health care, controlled wage differentials and the like – and they utterly collapsed. From atop these towering ruins, it's easy to assert that 'the laws of economics are like the laws of engineering'.

From there it's only a short step to condemning as useless and stillborn any present or future attempts, under any political system, to make society the master of the economy, rather than the other way around. The fall of the Wall immeasurably reinforced the Bank's doctrine – and not just at the Bank. The bottom line of this doctrine, to put it bluntly, is that everything (and everyone) can be assigned a price determined by the market, that everywhere people are, and indeed ought to be, motivated by greed and self-interest. They will invariably act upon this self-interest because they are 'out for themselves, and anything goes'.

For the Bank or for an exponent of its doctrine like Summers, propositions like these are just common sense, or in more philosophical terms, natural law. And it's quite true that much of economics *is* just common sense – for example, make energy more expensive and people will use less. If Russia uses five times more energy per dollar of GNP than the United States, put an end to cheap oil. That's just what Summers told his Bangkok audience: make oil much more expensive and you can make people stop flying Aeroflot from city to city to sell their vegetables. Such measures would be desirable anywhere, not only from an efficiency but also from an ecological point of view.

The Summers–Bank model, however, places every aspect of human existence under the sign of the marketplace and rarely stops to ask the social or political questions that cannot be separated from economics, except in some notional world where the economic model represents the whole of reality – its 'truth and evidence', to use Summers's phrase.

There is enormous confusion at present about what markets can and cannot accomplish. They can allocate scarce resources, including land and capital, according to the willingness and ability of people to pay for them: this they will do with what we now call efficiency. But it is not their job to provide jobs, which are only a by-product of their functioning. Nor will they provide food, clothing and shelter for all, much less health, education and culture.

In other words, markets cannot be expected to determine social priorities and to get them right – only democratic debate and rough-and-tumble politics (or authoritarian fiat) can do that. Although every society *has* an economy it does not follow that society *is* an economy.

Wherever markets are allowed, unrestrained by law or custom, to make most of the decisions, they will define the social and the political priorities of a community as well. The overlap of economy and society will become more and more nearly perfect until, in the perfect market economy (which is impossible), the two would become indistinguishable.

To apply the market solution to every problem is to take the line of least resistance and the lazy way out, allowing forces other than human reason to determine what constitutes the desirable society. If history is any guide, it is also likely to heighten social tension and exacerbate political conflict. A society which refuses vigorous debate of its priorities will get what it deserves: the market, and those who have the most market value, will make its social and political choices.[13]

Just as we cannot reasonably ask the market to design a blueprint for the desirable society, so we cannot expect it to spare any thought for the future. Markets provide snapshots of reality, they deal with the here and now. Ideas like 'inter-generational solidarity', 'caring for those who cannot yet care for themselves' or 'stewardship of the earth' are political and moral concepts, not economic ones. They can only emerge from a constant, collective effort to define values.

A Bank whose doctrine celebrates the market, whose practice assumes that the market *can* provide for the community and the future, whose energies are devoted to imposing economic laws as universal and immutable as 'the laws of engineering', cannot simultaneously claim that it pursues sustainable development or that the 'sustainable reduction of poverty is [its] overarching goal'. Until the Bank resolves the theoretical and practical contradictions of the market *versus* sustainable development, this claim is a slogan, or a mantra.

Larry Summers, for example, although he has declared that sound ecology is a good investment, tolerates no bars to growth. The following excerpt from the Summerian canon shows that 'stewardship of the earth' is clearly not on his agenda.

> There are no ... limits to the carrying capacity of the earth that are
> likely to bind any time in the foreseeable future. There isn't a risk of
> an apocalypse due to global warming or anything else. The idea that
> the world is headed over an abyss is profoundly wrong. The idea that
> we should put limits on growth, because of some natural limit, is a
> profound error and one that, were it ever to prove influential, would
> have staggering social costs.[14]

Financial Times journalist Michael Prowse summed it up: 'For Mr
Summers, the environment seems to be just a pile of raw material,
something you use up in creating GNP'.[15] Nature gets the same
cost–benefit analysis as people. Larry Summers may be an economic
prodigy but he does not seem to have read much outside his own
field, particularly scientific work over several decades demonstrating
that natural phenomena are not linear and reversible but are,
rather, subject to (positive or negative) feedback loops, poorly
understood amplifying mechanisms and random events leading to
chaotic, unpredictable and irreversible effects.

At the January 1992 annual meeting of the American Economics
Association, Summers is said to have listened in exasperation to
papers by colleagues arguing that global warming could have
grave economic consequences. At that meeting, William Cline,
Senior Fellow at the Washington-based Institute for International
Economics, stressed its cumulative and irreversible effects and
warned that US policy makers have seriously underestimated the
economic costs of global warming.

Summers, for his part, sees no reason to change anything in
present behaviour or institute government abatement programmes.
He says that even assuming the most pessimistic scenario, 'global
warming reduces growth over the next two centuries by less than
0.1 per cent a year ... Raising the spectre of our impoverished
grandchildren if we fail to address global environmental problems is
demagoguery'.[16]

Just as Summers tends to cast the economy as the whole
of society – or at least as its principal social and political arbiter – so he sees the biosphere as subservient to our present
economic preferences or whims. Nature will submit passively,
docilely, never striking back, world without end. This is why
he can affirm, 'the argument that a moral obligation to future

generations demands special treatment of environmental investments is fatuous'.

His key criterion for any investment, environmental or otherwise,
is its capacity to produce the highest possible monetary return. He
argues that this paramount principle will best serve not just present
but future generations as well, by making them richer. This he can
prove arithmetically: 'A dollar invested at 10 per cent will be worth
six times as much a century from now as a dollar invested at 8 per
cent,' Summers writes.[17]

Contemplation of the finite is not his long suit either. Summers
wrote a review article of *Beyond the Limits*, sequel to the Club of
Rome's bestseller, *The Limits to Growth*. The title of his piece asks, 'Is
the World Beyond Its Limits?' and he predictably answers, 'No'.[18]

He also develops in this review the Bank's key concept of the
links between growth, poverty and the environment. Here is his
conclusion, which typifies the Bank's approach:

> The environment is a critical global problem. Environmental prob-
> lems are serious everywhere, but it is only in poor countries that
> they kill and disable millions of people each year, which occurs on
> top of the other crushing effects of poverty. Any strategy for address-
> ing environmental concerns that slows the growth of poor countries
> either by regulating them directly or by limiting their markets is
> grossly immoral. I trust that the world's policy-makers will find
> *Beyond the Limits* beyond belief.[19]

This excerpt illustrates another aspect of Summers's, and the
Bank's, culture. Its claims are not simply for immutable economic
laws, but appeal to a moral – even a religious – vision. The market
and the doctrine of growth are seen as profoundly ethical; they are
genuinely believed to provide the greatest good for the poor, right
now. Our moral responsibility is to serve those living today; this is
the best insurance for tomorrow, which, in a context of strong and
steady growth, will then take care of itself. Summers, for example,
declares in another article, 'I, for one, feel the tug of the billion
people who subsist on less than $1 a day in 1992 more acutely
than the tug of future generations'.[20]

Anyone arguing with the Bank's world-view must remember
that the Bank, too, is committed to those billion people. That city

block in Washington does not by any stretch of the imagination house a collection of moral monsters. Nor can those who oppose the Summers–Bank doctrine expect to win through argument alone – whatever winning might mean. The Bank's doctrine is passionately held, like that of any other orthodoxy drawing large numbers of followers. And all fundamentalists tend to define themselves in opposition to (and only too often in hatred of) others.

Bank fundamentalists believe that unlimited growth through a largely unregulated market is the answer to the world's woes; growth must therefore be encouraged by all possible means on pain of incurring what Summers calls 'staggering social costs' and of demonstrating 'gross immorality'. The Bank's true believers, like other fundamentalists, are not in the final analysis arrogant but righteous.

Belief is not undermined by argument, churches are not shaken because a sanctuary is destroyed here or there. The Bank's doctrinal fencers have long since learned to parry every challenge and thrust from the outside; the institution's foundations will not crumble because one or another of its projects is thwarted.

Intelligent institutions whose stock-in-trade is doctrine know how to revitalize it – in the Catholic Church, this evolution is accomplished through papal encyclicals or conciliar reinterpretations, in the Bank through new operational directives or project guidelines or *World Development Reports*. The Bank will not be converted. Like the concept of development itself, it will only change when it becomes subject to the same political rules as any other worldly, man-made institution, when the sacred and the secular are well and truly split.

Finally, in the spring of 1994, the Clinton administration named a new US executive director, Ms Jan Piercy, to replace the Bush appointee who left in July 1993. It had, however, long before named Larry Summers Under-Secretary of the US Treasury, thus making him the man who will give the instructions to Ms Piercy. He will also define American policy with regard to the Bank, which is to say largely with regard to the South and, to a considerable degree, with regard to the nations of the former Soviet Union and the countries of Eastern Europe.

Chapter VI

L'Esprit de Corps

The World Bank's development model has been criticized in many quarters, but most people, inside and outside, still see it as the world's foremost, most prestigious official development institution. Young graduates with the right credentials and the desire to make a career of development without the financial sacrifices required if one works for a grassroots non-governmental organization, first try for a slot at the Bank before accepting a position anywhere else. By comparison, a regional development bank, or a national development cooperation agency like USAID, would be well down the list. The Bank is in this regard like heaven: many clamour at its gates; few pass through them.

How can such an eminent institution, attracting people of undeniably high calibre, have none the less failed in its fifty-year life span to solve the most basic problems of development? Considering its initial advantages and the odds in its favour, why has it fallen so far short of the historic mission it took upon itself? Here we explore some possible explanations for this paradox, seen through the prism of the Bank's culture and the values around which it has built its institutional *esprit de corps*.

The Bank draws upon a worldwide pool of top talent; it tries to pick its people young and shapes them to what it believes to be its needs. One entry point, if you are lucky, is to join the Bank's summer training programme as an intern while still a Ph.D. graduate student. You stick with it for two summers, as an apprentice, working closely with one or two people, doing their dogsbody research work and learning how the place works. This will give you points later on with the Bank's regular Recruitment Division.

Another way to capture a permanent Bank position is through repeated jobs as a consultant. Ten or twelve years of precarious employment on short-term contracts may be required before one is finally admitted to the inner sanctum. Consultants, we were told by one of them, 'really take a pounding'; their work loads are huge and their professional lives literally depend upon unquestioning respect for the premises of the` institution – a habit of thought which becomes quickly ingrained.

Third world nationals can earn more in a week consulting for the Bank than in months of local employment. Their professional reputations are enhanced by such contracts, which put them on the fast track to high positions in their own countries. They are thus easily and cheaply co-opted – a statement which applies as well to much of the scholarly establishment, North or South.

The royal road into the Bank is the Young Professionals (YP) Program, an immensely competitive, post-graduate fast track to a high-flying Bank position for the under-thirty set. Four to five thousand people apply every year. Thirty to thirty-five are accepted after a rigorous, staged selection process and a series of gruelling interviews.

Applicants represent dozens of nationalities; the YPs chosen during the thirty-year existence of the programme come from ninety-three different countries. Such figures tend, however, to exaggerate the real cultural diversity of YPs. At least in the first fifteen years of the programme, sixty per cent of the recruits came from Part I (rich, donor) countries and ninety-five per cent of the remainder, recruited from Part II (poor, borrowing) countries had received all or part of their education in the North, half of those from top American or British institutions like Harvard, MIT, Oxford and the London School of Economics. These educational attainments provide a clue to the social status of the Southern YPs, who generally come from families at the top of the pyramid in their own countries.[1]

Minimum requirements for becoming a YP are a 'masters degree in economics, finance or a related field' and fluency in English; in practice most applicants have outstanding credentials at the doctoral level, plus significant work experience. In October 1992 eligibility criteria were extended beyond economics and finance to include candidates with a masters degree or equivalent in a technical field, in particular 'agronomy, civil engineering, environment (i.e. solid waste management, industrial pollution, water sanitation) and public health', doubtless reflecting a recognition that the Bank is slipping behind in its traditional fields of strength and needs some new professional blood.

Once accepted, the trials of the YPs have only begun. They (like all Bank staff) 'are on probation for at least one year'; they must successfully complete two six-month assignments, each normally involving a field mission, in different Bank departments. Not all of them make it.

Still, of a thousand and some Young Professionals tapped by the Bank since 1963, more than two-thirds still work there. You wouldn't leave either, with an attractive tax-free salary, a minimum of twenty-six working days of vacation, paid home leaves, health and life insurance, all kinds of free professional or language training courses, subsidized restaurants, gyms and a host of other perks.

Bank staff can certainly count their blessings, but we think critics who pick on them for their high salaries and benefits are on the wrong track – people like the YPs are *la crème de la crème* and would be making top salaries wherever they landed, in some countries (e.g. Japan) handsomer ones than the Bank's. They want to be at the Bank and not on Wall Street because the work is not routine and because they are highly motivated. As one of the YPs who joined the programme in 1990 says,

> I've wanted to work in development since I was 12, so this is my dream job . . . each project takes you beyond your mental, cultural and professional borders. The Bank provides the possibility . . . to do something for world development. The work here is a lot more rewarding than saving some corporation a few basis points on a London borrowing.[2]

One Young Professional who left after nearly two decades at the Bank – a rare case – explained that when he joined, only American salaries were competitive with the Bank's, so financially speaking it was a dream job for practically everyone, Europeans included. Today, citizens of Part i countries could usually earn as much at home in employment at a similar level, but for Part ii country nationals, a job at the Bank remains the biggest plum in the world. They tend to hang on tooth and claw and would be crazy to rock the boat.

Overwhelmingly trained in economics and finance, the YPs belong to an exclusive kind of disciplinary as well as professional club (we hear they tend to eat together in the Bank cafeteria too). They go through a bruising approval programme during the selection process; they are then expected to 'make significant contributions to the work programs of their departments' in each of their two six-month stints. They generally have one or more mentors who make sure they have a workload so heavy that, as one who did not stay on says, 'it cuts off all opportunities for personal reflection'.

People with the YP profile have some extremely attractive qualities, but a bent for dissidence or heresy is not among them: they have neither the time nor the inclination to challenge the Bank's assumptions or to pursue independent lines of thought. Outsiders frequently complain of the arrogance of Bank managers, but there is no reason for people like the YPs to be especially humble. They have, after all, been certified 'Best in Show' in one of the world's toughest competitions.

Furthermore, as the Bank's official historians have pointed out, 'Knowledge on the part of the staff members that they are employed by a respected agency that is empowered to make or withhold ardently desired loans, coupled with the belief that they themselves are more cosmopolitan and experienced than are the representatives of low-income countries with whom they deal, is not conducive to humility'.[3]

Not only have they common training and common experience, which tend to be mutually reinforcing, but also in the countries where they go on mission, they *are* the best, at least according to the Bank's standards. It's not just that they're smart and articulate, which they are, but also that nobody in the South knows as well as they how to manipulate the theoretical, neoclassical economic models the way the Bank wants them manipulated. Only the Bank's people know how to construct and, if necessary, nudge or fudge a project's rate of return to make it conform to the Bank's criteria.

If the borrowing country authorities bring up a problem that doesn't fit the theory or the model, their concerns are easily dismissed. Bank staff also assume that with only minor alterations, structural adjustment packages can be applied as a blueprint to all countries, regardless of their particularities. Detailed, local knowledge is not exactly prized. As one high Tanzanian official wrote,

> Nor can the World Bank claim freedom from ... overweening arrogance ... Its 'experts' have always 'known better'. ... One observed, rather grandly, to some of my colleagues: 'I know what we should do in Tanzania. Of course I haven't been there yet but I'll be out soon and stay long enough to learn all the facts I need to know, probably two weeks'.[4]

Although the Young Professionals Program can be seen as a kind of seminary preparing for the priesthood, or at least as a proving ground, there is no 'ideological training' *per se* at the Bank, nothing so crude as a drilling school for Party cadres or a rote catechism. Passing on and reinforcing the ideology is none the less the job of the whole institution.

Even the Young Professionals who leave after several years of experience may not represent a genuine loss to the Bank or to the YP programme. According to one ex-Bank staffer, 'they often become quite useful at home through their ability to formulate funding proposals in such a way as to make them look "attractive" to international lenders ... YPs may be highly sought after because of the contacts they established within the Bank, their familiarity with Bank thinking and its procedures'.[5]

Surprisingly, very few Bank managers have any training in management *per se* – apparently specific management skills are supposed to be included in one's DNA or absorbed by osmosis. At every level, people are judged not on their ability to manage, to motivate, or to improve the substance of their work for the borrowers, but on their capacity to contribute to projects that will successfully sail past the board.

To be successful, any large organization has to 'socialize' its members and create a group identity. This socializing, integrative task is especially difficult for an international institution like the Bank because the members of the group come from dozens of different national, ethnic, and religious backgrounds (even though their education is often similar). At one level, the Bank seems to have coped with this problem effectively. At another, its coping style has not been without significant costs.

Nearly everyone who joins the Bank stays. Certain cultural problems may thus surface. One is a tendency for the Bank to accumulate burnt-out people who will be hanging around for another ten or twenty years, going through the motions. This is hardly conducive to creativity, innovation or forward movement. Compared to businesses or service organizations, the Bank's personnel turnover rate is extraordinarily low – about three per cent a year (except during the 1987 Reorganization, about which more in a moment). The former US executive director told us that this rate was one half of one per cent for higher-level staff, which may be only a slight exaggeration.

Many Bank people simply do not have time to keep up with recent advances in their areas. The new rhetorical emphasis on sustainable development provides a case in point: the language of sustainability may be adopted, but the techniques and technologies to promote it are not known, and thus not used, by most staff.

Nor can people who join the Bank late necessarily contribute their specific skills to improving its practice. One current staff person, commenting on a draft of this chapter, wrote to us:

> I think your point about the Bank not using the talent it hires is especially relevant to the 'mid-career entry' people and I'm not *just* thinking of myself! There's a tendency for the Bank not to trust people who haven't done 20 years service inside the Bank and so not to give them management positions.

Perhaps because of its Anglo-Saxon origins, the Bank avoided at least one pitfall. Unlike the UN, it never even considered messing about with several working languages.* No time is lost in translation or interpreting and while some may find the linguistic imperialism of English politically incorrect, this choice was both sociologically and financially wise. Although there may be some French- or Spanish-speaking department enclaves at the Bank, people must all, literally, speak the same language, a powerful cultural

---

* Although staff may speak a variety of languages in the field when dealing with borrowers, and the Bank's Economic Development Institute gives some courses for government officials in French and Spanish, reports to the board and internal documents are always in English.

homogenizer. This rule has, however, tended to favour Americans and British (still numbers one and two in terms of staff at the Bank), Commonwealth country citizens, and northern Europeans, with Filipinos in support staff positions.

At least until quite recently, the institution solved its socializing problems through authoritarian or paternalistic methods. For the first twenty-five years of the Bank's existence, the staff had no formal way to express their point of view or their interests. Then the McNamara whirlwind roared in, adding over a thousand new people to staff in its first three years alone. A relatively small multilateral development institution 'where everyone knew everyone else by sight if not by name' was suddenly transformed into a large, impersonal and aloof bureaucracy.

The McNamarian management also went out of its way to classify all Bank employees as either professional or non-professional, with only those at the top end of the salary scale in the first category. Predictably, 'staff who had previously assumed that they were an integral and highly valued part of the Bank work force began to wonder what the implications of such distinctions might be'.[6]

Until the early 1970s, anyone 'unhappy with the work environment, career development opportunities, compensation or benefits' was supposed to appeal through 'normal administrative channels', which sounds perfectly reasonable, except that nobody knew what those channels were – no process had ever been spelled out. According to Bank staff veterans, 'Any formal complaint was viewed as risky . . . personnel officers were often regarded with suspicion. Nearly everyone had stories about personnel officers who passed on confidential matters to division chiefs.'[7]

Since 1972 the Bank has had a lively staff association which now has a democratically elected delegates' assembly, full-time, Bank-financed administrative personnel and about thirty committees. The association is an important tool for integrating people into the institution and it can take initiatives no individual or ad hoc body could take, but it cannot substitute for good management policies nor create a climate of trust and high morale *ex nihilo*. The association does, however, help to identify and to reflect the state of existing morale and for a number of years, many signs indicate that this morale has been shaky at best.

The Bank's socializing system has engendered a good many unnecessary and avoidable losses. By 1978 the staff association was seeking to 'foster [staff] participation in the Bank' because 'an increasing number of staff feel that we will serve our borrowers more effectively if we can reduce the level of competition, distrust and insecurity found among some staff'. The association also wanted a forum where staff could 'express themselves on more global aspects of the Bank's work'.

The staff association believed that

> ground rules can be worked out to encourage a maximum of participation without harming the Bank's image and also defending the individual staff member against any repercussions that making his views known would have.[8]

It also believed that such participation should not present insuperable problems since 'Mr McNamara has recently called internal communication his most difficult problem at the Bank'. Therefore he, and other top managers, ought normally to have welcomed measures to improve it.

This turned out not to be the case. Judging by the conclusions of a survey carried out by a Berkeley Ph.D. candidate in 1980, the association's recommendations were neither welcomed nor acted upon. Using both questionnaires and over 150 in-depth interviews, she examined the attitudes of Bank staff from varied cultural backgrounds towards communication and decision-making in the institution. The 'vast majority' of her respondents felt that

> work pressures and a sense of competition ... inhibit communications across divisional lines. Communication is perceived as a monologue from higher management levels in which staff members are allowed to communicate upwards only in response to management's questions ... Directives are given by senior management without adequate explanation or rationale.[9]

These conclusions reflect the essence of the authoritarian, don't-ask-questions McNamara management style and will surprise no one familiar with the man or his methods. More detrimental to the Bank's stated goals – and thus to people in its borrowing countries

– is the decision-making process itself. In the strictly disciplined, hierarchical atmosphere of the Bank, people felt that they were being

> rewarded on merits such as . . . *quantity of output and cooperation with authority which are not central to one's qualifications or proficiency.* There are no . . . methods to change the structure of decision-making which would encourage their own more active participation in the process. Taking this situation as a 'given', they face confusion in times of change, *inconsistency in managerial decisions,* and *reprisals in response to unpredictable error* (emphasis added).[10]

In spite of such widespread complaints, the Berkeley researcher found Bank people highly motivated. Their commitment to development was a central, shared value and they had a high regard for one another's professional skills. Their motivation was, however, weakened by increasingly burdensome paperwork, 'the emphasis of quantity over quality' and the 'fear [of] reprisals from senior management if they disagree'.

The researcher also discovered that the 'delicate balance' between the staff's respect for the Bank's goals and their frustration with its practices was 'shifting to more antagonistic and less constructive relations among colleagues'. To her surprise, she could detect almost no 'cultural' (i.e. ethnic or national) differences in staff responses – in other words, Chileans, Japanese, Indians, Americans all felt basically the same way about their professional lives.

So the Bank socialized its members, yes, but not around values like participation in decision-making, encouragement for innovative, critical thinking or creativity in designing good development projects. Their institution instead insisted they go by the book – without necessarily specifying what the 'book' was. After putting its staff through an extraordinarily rigorous selection process, the Bank proved unwilling and unable to use fully the potential of extremely talented, highly motivated people. More harmful still, the professional constraints placed on the staff were all too often antithetical to the real needs of borrowers.

In fact, the 'book' staff must go by is loan volume. In a climate demanding quantity over quality and cooperation with authority, it is natural that people who do not wish to lose their jobs should acquiesce and concentrate on volume of output. If authority requires that they push money out the door, they can only respond by designing more, larger and costlier projects. The consequences of those projects – financial, human or ecological – cannot become their professional concern whatever their ethical instincts.

One Bank 'old-timer' quoted by Deborah Shapley in her biography of McNamara put it this way: 'In the old Bank, we were rewarded for finding reasons not to lend. Under McNamara, we were rewarded for finding reasons to go ahead'.[11] And so the prevailing culture has remained.

What is the easiest, most efficient way to push money? Duplication of a previous project, in another place but with the same co-financiers, garners high marks. That is why one is likely to find strings of similar projects (whether dams or ports, agricultural or structural adjustment) causing serial disasters.

In any event, by the time the results of a given project become manifest, managers can expect to be working on something else, somewhere else. Assimilation of the Bank's theoretical and practical culture is assumed to equip staff for dealing with development in general. For example, one of the people most responsible for pushing the notorious Narmada dam project in India, whose funding the Bank finally withdrew in 1992 after a firestorm of criticism (see Chapter VIII), was promoted immediately thereafter to a high position in the Russia country department. Before dealing with India, he had been involved in another of the Bank's most decried environmentally devastating enterprises, the Polonoreste project in Brazil.[12]

Furthermore, individual promotions, at least until 1993, were entirely based on loan volumes. A manager in charge of a $400 million loan for a string of polluting coal plants guaranteed to spew forth millions of tons of greenhouse gases has much more power and prestige than the one who designs a $10 million loan promoting energy efficiency. (These were actual loans in the India country pipeline in 1993; the low relative dollar value accorded environmentally beneficial choices is also clear.)

Some claim that top Bank management sees the world strictly in terms of 'resource mobilization' — i.e. how much additional funding the Bank can obtain from its Part I members for this or that new programme. Empire-building and enhanced power are the point —

whether they come through Women in Development, the Special Program of Assistance for Africa or the Global Environment Facility (GEF) which emerged from the 1992 United Nations Conference on Environment and Development in Rio. In due course, as other issues become 'sexy', the Bank can be expected to add staff and to create new vice-presidencies to deal with them — or at least be perceived to be dealing with them.

The Bank, for example, has become lead manager of the Global Environment Facility and now frequently attaches small, environmentally friendly GEF projects to its own pre-designed larger loans, a practice Susan George has called elsewhere 'tacking environmental tails on some quite nasty dogs'. As of late 1993, for example, about three-quarters of the environmentally friendly loans aimed at reducing emissions of carbon dioxide were attached to standard Bank credits. In other words, so long as new programmes bring fresh capital, they are grist to the Bank's mill, whatever intrinsic interest it may or may not take in women, Africa, the environment, and so on.

People taking the opposite view argue that the Bank is not looking for extra work or increased resource mobilization at all, but rather has tasks like running the Global Environment Facility thrust upon it. The Americans and the Europeans certainly didn't want to create a new bureaucracy to design and implement environmental loans after the 1992 conference in Rio. Furthermore, because 'nobody trusts the UN specialized agencies', donors see no alternative to the Bank. Who else can competently administer their contributions to this or that special fund for developing countries?*

* The donors have a point. Corruption in the UN is considered widespread and many of its agencies are, if anything, less open to scrutiny and amendment than the Bank itself. Some are run as personal baronies, like the Food and Agricultural Organization in Rome where Edouard Saouma held sway until late 1993, under purely nominal board control, for nearly eighteen years. The UN Environment Programme (UNEP) in Nairobi is well-meaning but wholly incapable of managing a billion-dollar budget like the GEF's. Even the more competent UN agencies are inadequately funded and so cannot much improve their performance. The Bank, trusted by the rich countries, also raises money directly on the market and can pay for institutional capacity beyond the reach of the UN bodies. Its hegemony – like their failings – thus becomes self-perpetuating.

Some say, too, that the few extra billions the Global Environment Facility may in time attract will be split into so many small projects it really isn't worth Bank staff time to bother with them. Running the GEF and other co-financing groups is a burden for the Bank, they claim, not an advantage. If staff started spending serious time on the $10 million rather than the $400 million projects, the Bank itself would become less cost-effective and ultimately less solvent, a point not lost on an institution whose staff includes several thousand economists.

Large, traditional project loans may be the Bank's heart and soul as well as its bread and butter but the growing importance of policy-based lending since the mid-1980s has had a profound impact on the Bank, its staff and its culture as well. The focus on structural adjustment has enormously strengthened the dominance of the neo-classical economic world-view. This focus also led directly to the most traumatic event in recent Bank history: the 1987 Reorganization.

This milestone is almost always given a capital R in contemporary or subsequent Bank literature (like the Reformation) and is still commonly referred to by staff as the 'earthquake' or the 'avalanche'. Certainly it was the severest test to date of institutional resilience; some maintain the Bank is still convalescing from the shock treatment applied in 1987.[13]

Like the Reformation, a full-scale Reorganization (or in the case of the Party, a purge) reflects not merely the state of an institution's internal functioning, but also society-wide conditions to which the institution must adapt. The Church has never really recovered from the Reformation – the proof is that the Christian community is still split into two apparently irreconcilable camps (three, counting Eastern Orthodoxy). Nor could purges and prisons save the Party from its own deep failings and internal contradictions. For many reasons, the Bank did not split into rival denominations, each organized around its own Truth; and fortunately its senior management showed no signs of consigning anyone to the gulag.* It still

---

* Although our judgement may be a trifle hasty: the Bank's equivalent of the gulag is the field offices. An ex-staffer wrote to us, 'When someone was posted to a field office, away from the main action and from the opportunity for advancement, one wondered what he or she had done wrong'.

needed to adapt to new conditions in a different world order and that adaptation left a good deal of bureaucratic blood on the floor.

To stretch the metaphor only slightly, the 'project' culture at the Bank represents the 'old-time religion'. As the popular American revivalist hymn goes, 'Give me that old-time religion ... It was good enough for – [Moses, Jesus, et cetera, *ad libitum*] and it's good enough for me'. But projects alone, even as hugely augmented by McNamara (for example, in integrated rural development multi-project programmes), were no longer good enough for the Bank's major shareholders, particularly the United States. They had a new and different agenda in mind for the Bank and they intended to force it through.

When former US Republican Congressman Barber Conable took over the Bank's presidency on 1 July 1986, he inherited a crisis. Reagan's people saw the Bank as both financially spendthrift and politically craven. As far as these neo-conservatives were concerned, the Bank was providing subsidies for government bureaucracies worldwide, including many guilty of that ultimate heresy, protectionism. The Americans wanted their free-market, free-trade, privatization policies pushed energetically and, according to *Business Week*, they especially 'resented the deference Bank officials were forced to grant the policy views of what the Reaganites considered "weaker" nations'.[14]

Not only was the Bank actually listening upon occasion to the 'policy views' of these upstart clients, but it was also spending a lot of money on weaklings who should, according to social-Darwinist, free-market laws, be ignored if not annihilated. Nor had the Reagan administration got the tightly-run ship it had expected from Conable's predecessor, private banker Tom Clausen. So it had sent him back to California and now wanted the Bank shaped up from stem to stern. In a sharp signal of disapproval, just as Conable was about to take over, the US executive director had voted against the Bank's 1987 budget, with two other board members also voting nay and two more abstaining – in the Bank's culture the equivalent of a slap in the face.

Barber Conable may seem an unlikely Martin Luther, but he

knew he had to deliver.* The catch, and catch-all, phrase was 'we have to turn fat into muscle'; the political agenda was, in fact, to push structural adjustment and the US programme throughout the world and to make the Bank an effective instrument of that mission, which was nothing less than to convert the planet to Reaganomics. The new creed of policy-based lending was superseding the old-time religion: though projects might remain in numerical terms the centrepiece, ideologically they would have to confirm the new Truth and conform to the framework it dictated. This conversion required a top-to-bottom overhaul of the Bank.

If the political rationale for the Reorganization was fairly straightforward, its mechanics were much less so. Conable began by choosing a seven-member steering committee to guide the Reorganization, chaired by American Young Professional Edward V.K. (Kim) Jaycox, in 1993 the Bank's Vice-President for Africa.† Besides the seven in-house people, the steering committee included three external members: a former Colombian finance minister, the chairman of the board of the Bank of Tokyo and none other than Robert Strange McNamara.

Part of this steering committee's mandate was to name three task forces to deal with: 1) policy, planning and research; 2) operations; and 3) support units. This accomplished, Conable retired from the fray and told his most senior managers to do likewise, on the grounds that they had vested interests. Perhaps he thought he was being democratic. In fact, as the *Financial Times* reported, 'by giving enormous power to a hand-picked steering committee of young middle-rank high-fliers, Mr Conable succeeded only in exacerbating the personal tensions and jealousies'.[15] Not surprisingly, virtually all these high-fliers were former Young Professionals.

At the end of its labours, the steering committee reported to President Conable, identifying two major 'strategic challenges' facing the Bank:

---

* Mr Conable's arrival at the Bank roughly coincided with the nuclear meltdown in the Ukraine: he was duly nicknamed Barber Chernobyl.

† As Vice-President for Africa, Jaycox is judged by one African economist and development expert we greatly respect as 'one of those few people who have made the Bank less awful than it would have been otherwise'.

> First, *effective macroeconomic management and a sound policy environ-*
> *ment have come to be, and will remain, at the heart of the development*
> *challenge* ... Second, *successful economic development increasingly de-*
> *pends on being able to deal with the interdependence of problems and on*
> *the effective integration of macroeconomic and sectoral issues* (emphasis
> in the original).[16]

On the off-chance that this passage has not put you to sleep, we
should explain what it means when translated from Bankspeak.
First, projects alone are never going to meet the 'development
challenge'. The Bank will consequently move from funding discrete
projects – a dam here, an agricultural complex there – to reorganizing entire economies. Structural adjustment (which will provide the
'sound policy environment') is taking over and will become the
organizing principle for everything else.

Second, to achieve its ends (labelled 'successful economic development') the Bank wields two sorts of tools: structural and sectoral
adjustment loans (SALs and SECALs, the latter for agriculture or
industry or whatever sector needs restructuring according to free-
market, free-trade, privatization laws). The same policy must preside
over all aspects of the economy, everything is to be subservient to,
and integrated with, adjustment.

Consequently, because it intends to reorganize entire countries,
the Bank must also reorganize itself – around SALs and SECALs –
abandoning or downgrading its traditional, across-the-board
departments (e.g. water, education, energy) in favour of a much
sharper country focus. The country manager's job will be to make
sure that no project falls outside the macroeconomic framework
centrally determined by the Bank.* S/he will, in particular, oversee
the 'integration of the domestic economy with the international
trading and financial system', as the steering committee makes
clear. This outward, international market orientation for
everyone is one of the primary targets of structural adjustment.

---

* The importance of such coordination is illustrated by the case of Malawi, where
Bank people negotiating a SAL were pushing the government to remove a fertilizer
subsidy. Another Bank project meant to increase maize production relied for its
success on the same subsidy being maintained. See Paul Mosley, et al., *Aid and Power*
(London, Routledge, 1991), vol. 2, p. 2.

As the steering committee further explains,

> Within the Bank itself, adjustment lending programs, especially in the heavily indebted countries, have posed *major intellectual challenges*, requiring new lending approaches, policies, staff skills and procedures ... The changes in the Bank's mission and role that have taken place in recent years towards broader policy advice, expanded support for economic adjustment and more extensive involvement in aid coordination and co-financing with the private sector thus seem likely to remain at the center of what the Bank does (emphasis added).[17]

There, as stated by the steerers, are the grounds for the Reorganization and the basis for its design. The Bank must extend its reach, it must be in a position to enforce its own policies through a combination of 'advice', 'support for adjustment' and 'coordination' of other donors' aid as well as of private investment. By reorganizing itself, the Bank will respond to the 'major intellectual challenges' this new hegemonic role poses. Again and again in their report to the president, the steering committee insists on the need to reclaim and to maintain 'intellectual leadership', which the Bank must demonstrate if it is to justify its structural adjustment policies.

By 1987, as the steering committee busied itself with the Reorganization, criticism of these policies had already surfaced. The toll adjustment was taking in the Bank's borrowing countries, particularly on the poorest and most vulnerable people least able to pay, was becoming clear. Doubtless shaken more by UNICEF's unflattering appraisal of adjustment than by the critiques and complaints of countless non-governmental organizations, the Bank none the less understood that it had not satisfactorily met those 'major intellectual challenges', i.e. convinced its critics of the beneficence of its policies.[18]

In this context, the challenges for the steerers themselves are clear and they rise to the occasion. As befits an institution seeking to reflect the economic orthodoxy and the corporate ethos of the 1980s, the steering committee urges President Conable to see 'intellectual leadership in the development field ... as a top management concern in the same way that new product development is for high technology companies'. The Bank must first define policy – its high-tech product – for the borrower, then apply this policy to 'specific operational output in the form of loans and economic work in the field'.

Not only must 'the financial aspects of development and of the Bank's role ... be given greater prominence in organization and staffing' but the Bank itself must also become visibly lean and mean: 'The Bank's credibility suffers if it is seen to be "soft" in its own internal management'. That ought to please the Reagan administration.

The steerers thus provide President Conable with a blueprint for reinforcing the already dominant neo-liberal, macroeconomic and financial-policy culture and they make no bones about it. Among the 'major problems' they identify is the Bank's

> failure to deal effectively with a mix of staff skills and capacities that is no longer appropriate to the Bank's evolving mission, producing critical shortages of some skills, e.g. in sector economics, adjustment lending and finance.

In other words, they claim that the circumstances of the Bank's 'evolving mission' demand *even more* structural adjustment-oriented types on staff.

All the committee's recommendations for change flow from the need they perceive to integrate operations, the traditional heart of the Bank, with policy, which is now, universally, to be adjustment. One major change is that every Bank-borrowing, client country will from now on have

> a single senior counterpart/interlocutor ... who can speak authoritatively for the Bank and will be seen as the key decision-maker as far as the country is concerned ... the Country Director and his management team will be clearly accountable for results within a particular country or group of countries.[19]

The Bank's doctrine should thus become much clearer because it will be articulated by a single senior official speaking – how else? – authoritatively to the state. The government of the adjusting country will need the blessing of this key decision-maker for all its economic and financial undertakings.

The committee's remaining task, internally, was to shift the Bank's machinery into full structural adjustment gear. People would have to be diverted from the classic project, or sectoral, focus to a policy, country focus. The Reorganization was to be put in place a.s.a.p. and the steerers decided that this should *proceed in a top-down fashion*.[20]

And so it did. As it did, the actual business of the Bank ground to a halt for several months. Top-down, also known as the cascade system, meant that except for the *very* top, everyone would be suspended from his or her position. After this forced mass resignation, the senior vice-presidents would choose their subordinates, who would choose their subalterns, who would choose their underlings, who . . . and so on, all the way down to support-level staff.

A system, in short, not unlike that of the Catholic Church, or in an analogy preferred by many Bank staff people, a feudal system of suzerain–vassal relationships; or again, in more contemporary terms, a complex hierarchy of patron–client arrangements, as in any well-run Mafia. As the staff association remarked in its own assessment after the Reorganization was completed, 'The criteria by which staff would be chosen were not known'.

It was a wonderful time for rewarding the docile and for settling old scores. We spoke at length with one former division chief, a 'Level 26' man – in the Bank pay scale, 26 and above is about the top three per cent of the Bank – who learned he had not been chosen when a friend came up to him in the street and said, 'Gee, I'm sorry'. He had in the past dared to argue with his superior (who *was* reinstated) about setting up agricultural processing plants in several countries which he knew would be unprofitable under all foreseeable market conditions for the commodity in question. His behaviour had naturally been regarded not as an exercise of responsibility towards the Bank's borrowers, but as a barrier to getting the money out the door. He could have moved to another department but decided enough was enough.

He is now glad he left and his many remaining friends in the Bank say he made the right decision, one many of them wish they had found the guts or the freedom to make. At the time, however, he was particularly disgusted not just because the cascade process legitimized personal patronage networks but also because about a quarter of all the division chiefs who *were* selected – some thirty to forty people out of about 130 division chiefs in all – were not Level 26-ers at the time or were not even eligible for promotion to that level. They were selected instead on the basis of loyalty to their superiors.

Even the personnel department reacted to this situation. It sent a memo to President Conable naming names and pointing out that all the previously established rules for promotions were being broken, but it made no difference and no action was taken.

The staff association did what it could but it couldn't do much since all the work of the steering committee and its task forces took place behind closed doors. Although the association did have some meetings with the steering committee, the circulars coming down from management about the implementation of the cascade system did not 'reflect the understandings that had been reached between the association and the steering committee'.

Suddenly, in the midst of this process and without forewarning, on a Friday afternoon at 5.00 p.m., the staff association was handed a completely new draft of the Staff Rule – a complex, sixteen-page, twelve-section document governing most of the aspects of the staff's working life. It was expected to comment by '3.00 p.m. the following Monday, so that the Bank could issue the Rule immediately'.

From then on, as the 'Reorganization juggernaut gathered momentum', it was all downhill. One of the staff association's newsletters of June 1987 captures the mood:

> Never before has the morale of the Bank staff sunk so low . . . The credibility gap between the management's statements . . . and the views of the staff is as wide as it could ever be. Our soundings indicate that very few staff have confidence that job selections have been or will be made fairly or that the mechanisms for review and correction of unfair decisions will work adequately . . . [21]

The numerical result of this trauma was 576 staff 'terminated by the Bank' – about ten per cent of the total. The human and institutional price, for the Bank and for its borrowers, cannot be estimated. The ex-division chief we interviewed says, the Reorganization killed any sense of fairness or equity. On paper, when you see the organizational chart, it may look rational, but in the final analysis it's based on personal affinities. People know that loyalty is the thing.

A year later, little if any improvement was discernible. In July 1988, thirteen months after the Reorganization ended, the staff association issued a 'Staff Survey Report' it had commissioned. The survey was conducted by an outside consultant, an industrial psychologist who had already 'assisted the Bank in the past with staff surveys'; that is, he had previously been retained by management, not staff, and knew the place well. He wrote the report, over which the staff association 'exercised no editorial control'.[22]

Responses came from about sixty per cent of the people who could have completed the long questionnaire in time; remarkably high for an in-house survey conducted on short notice during a very busy time of the year, according to the consultant. The conclusions were not encouraging (in the following quotes emphasis is in the original throughout):

> Overall satisfaction with the Bank as an Institution, and reported morale, are low ... A further finding ... is that only 12% reported favorable answers when asked how much mutual trust and confidence exist in the relationship between senior management and staff ... Such data would be considered compellingly disturbing in most organizations known to me.[23]

As for the Bank's *raison d'être*, its borrowers, its lending policies and its institutional goals, he found that:

> Lack of consensus is the outstanding feature of the relevant data. Only 36% of the professional staff indicated that institutional goals and directions for borrowers are clear. In addition, only 48% of all responding staff expressed a belief that borrowers' most important needs are being met by the Bank's lending policies. And 30% indicated that the Bank's move toward structural adjustment or policy based lending has *decreased* their feeling of commitment to the Bank; only 12% said their commitment had increased because of this direction.[24]

In conclusion, the consultant's results

> confirm that the Institution is in deep internal difficulty ... *the data clearly show that reconciliation and renewed trust between senior management and staff are sorely needed.* They also show that the Institution's changing goals and lending policies remain unclear to large numbers of staff, at *all* levels, and controversial to many.[25]

Morale seems to have improved since 1988. Two further staff attitude surveys have been conducted, commissioned, however, by senior management rather than by the staff association, in 1990 and in 1993. Comparisons between the 1988 and 1993 surveys are tricky: the methodologies differ, the questions aren't put in the same way and fewer than a quarter of the same substantive categories are covered. In the 1993 survey there is no narrative, interpretative material at all — and although there are forty pages of bar graphs it's not clear how the 1988 results were transformed into bars and reproduced in the 1993 survey.

Insofar as comparisons are possible and keeping these caveats in mind, on a scale of 1 to 6 the 'mutual trust and confidence in the relationship between senior management and staff' was 2.1 in 1988, 2.9 in 1993. 'To what extent do you perceive the institution as a well coordinated, internally cooperative organization?' gets 2.3 in 1988, 2.9 in 1993. The capacity of information and views from staff to influence the decisions of senior management rises from 2 to 2.6; having a sense of personal accomplishment from one's work improves from 3.7 in 1988 to 4.3 in 1993. The summary, 'overall satisfaction' index is up from 2.8 to 3.6.[26]

Interesting questions about the Reorganization remain. Why did it so utterly demoralize the staff? Not just because their jobs were threatened (ninety per cent of them stayed on); nor even, we think, because of the crassness and palpable bias of the process. We believe, rather, that the staff's commitment to their 'central value' of development was stretched to the limit, perhaps even damaged beyond repair. One result of the staff study noted above – that commitment to the Bank because of its structural adjustment or policy-based lending had increased for only twelve per cent of respondents and had decreased for thirty per cent – is surely significant. (NB: No questions concerning values figure in the 1993 survey.)

We were told that a further 600 to 800 new orthodox macro-economists were hired in the two or three years following the Reorganization, a figure we have no way of verifying. If correct, the culture will naturally have been skewed even further in favour of structural adjustment and the liberal, free-market, free-trade agenda. Those with different ideas will be overwhelmed by the sheer neo-classical mass, drowned in the doctrinal sea.

It took the Church several hundred years to convert only a part of humanity to Christianity – large areas of the globe have always remained beyond its reach. It took the Bank little more than a decade to impose structural adjustment worldwide, or very nearly. In the single year 1987 it was able to reorganize itself from top to bottom the better to serve this recent but all-pervading doctrine. By any standards, this is a stunning performance. The Bank is without contest the premier policy institution deciding how the South and the East are to be organized. Nobody else even comes close.

The price the Bank has paid for this ideological triumph is not, however, without consequences. It has reinforced those aspects of the institution through which the dominant culture forces bright and talented people, who ought to be creative and have minds of their own, to behave like fundamentalists. There is no salvation outside the free market. Those who hope to succeed and to remain within the fold must either espouse the doctrine as true believers or be consigned to outer darkness (or at least to other employment or perhaps a field office . . .)

> [G]iven the periodic reshufflings, it is important for employees to build mechanisms for self-protection. Becoming an accepted member of one of the many pyramidal clans that exist at the Bank and that usually have a senior manager at their apex is therefore a good idea.[27]

The Bank's management style is at once capricious (much depends on personal patronage, 'rules' may be made up or effaced as one goes along) and wasteful, since its authoritarian manner of functioning guarantees that much talent is stifled and encouraged to confine itself to loyalty and obedience.

To put the matter rather differently, we find it hard to escape an unattractively scatological analogy: professionals who really are *la crème de la crème* are swallowed and absorbed by the Bank, digested and, in the end, are destined to produce what any other digestive system produces. It is not enough to recruit top talent and hope that its quantitative juxtaposition will automatically produce quality results.

The Bank can, with this system, maintain orthodoxy; it cannot alleviate poverty or contribute to anything reasonable people would term development. The fact remains that under specific political circumstances, the Bank *did* carry out a vast and thorough Reorganization oriented towards the single goal of universal adjustment. Presumably, then, under different political circumstances, with different goals and the desire to create a different *esprit de corps*, it could do so again.

The Namland Coup

Jonathan O'Donnell was a man of methodical habits who enjoyed a few creature comforts. Every weekday morning at half past seven he stopped at the same metal box on the corner of 17th and Pennsylvania, put $1.25 in the slot and retrieved his *Financial Times*. Then, his fresh pink paper under his arm, he proceeded a bit further along Pennsylvania Avenue to Au Bon Pain. Here he served himself a large Colombian coffee, chose a croissant from the basket of baked goods and took one of the tables next to the window where the light was best.

He liked this place – it was clean, the employees knew him and were pleasant but left him alone, and the classical music in the background was unobtrusive yet blocked out the noise of downtown Washington coming to life. You could sort of ease into the day. Jonathan always turned first to the stock market quotations to see how his portfolio was doing, then read the news for half an hour or so. He would be in his office across the street on the sixth floor of 'J' building by a quarter past eight.

This routine was one of the small luxuries O'Donnell allowed himself since being promoted to division chief at the World Bank. He could have all the *Financial Times* he wanted delivered to his office; his secretary was a Filipina and not even adverse to fetching him coffee, but he liked this moment of quiet self-indulgence before the ever-growing pile of reading matter and meetings meetings meetings took over his life for the rest of the long day.

This was a perfect Washington spring morning – 1996 seemed to be confirming the warnings about global warming but for the moment O'Donnell was enjoying it. He took his first sip of coffee and was about to turn as usual to the market quotations when he suddenly blanched and nearly knocked over his cup: there on page one of the *FT* was a story headlined, 'Coup Against the World Bank in Namland'.

'Sweet Jaysus', O'Donnell whispered, his oath for major occasions that took him back to his Irish roots. Namland was one of the Bank's model countries – the only one, in fact, in sub-Saharan Africa. The Bank held it up to its more recalcitrant pupils as a sterling example of a Properly Adjusting Country, pointing to its positive balance of payments, increased exports, healthy growth rate, controlled inflation and the lowest ratio of government employees to total population in Africa. And to make sure it remained such a shining macroeconomic beacon, the Bank corralled other donors to contribute and piled loan after loan on Namland, granting it the softest possible terms and inventing extra programmes with barbarous acronymic names like PAMPER: the Program of Action to Maximize People's Economic Returns. It was hard to tell whether these transfusions were rewards or insurance money.

'Get a grip on yourself, man,' said O'Donnell to himself. The worst of the shock was that he knew the prime minister of Namland, in fact very well. You could even say they were comrades in arms – the Bank had chosen both of them as Young Professionals in 1975, Nyamba straight out of the LSE and O'Donnell fresh from his Ph.D. at Harvard. They had climbed the same ladders, swapped stories in the cafeteria and even worked out in the Bank's gym together. Nyamba had been lumbered with some God-awful missionary name like Nicephorus or Nicodemus but everyone called him Nick, he was a great guy, a bloody good economist – in a word he was One of Us.

To no one's very great surprise, least of all the Bank's, Nick had been called home to run his country's fortunes in the mid-1980s, his former employer having argued the case persuasively not to say unanswerably with the previous Namland authorities. One does legitimately prefer to deal with a person who speaks one's own language, doesn't one?

Nick not only spoke the language, he knew the music and all the dance steps as well. You almost didn't need to send a mission – it was a pure formality – because Nick could write a structural adjustment programme for Namland, just as he had done for various other countries, practically blindfolded. The Bank had just set up a new African regional mission in his capital city too – one of the tallest and handsomest buildings they had. And what in God's name was a '*coup* against the World Bank' anyway? The Bank wasn't the government; Nick was. Why hadn't they overthrown him? Better settle down and read the damn piece.

The *FT* had done its usual thorough job in next to no time – you had to ask yourself how these guys managed. First, the journalist – a certain Julian Cray – described what had happened. Late the previous afternoon, Namland time – which is why O'Donnell hadn't caught it on the evening news – a huge mob of people – men, women and children – had gone 'dancing and singing' ('dancing and singing'?) down the broad avenue that led to the new Bank headquarters, swept up the stairs and swarmed into the offices. Employees were given a few moments to collect their personal belongings 'but were not permitted to take computers or diskettes with them'.

They were then hustled down the stairs to where a small fleet of Toyota vans ('some apparently commandeered from UNICEF') was waiting to take them to the airport. The crowd seemed to be having a wonderful time and there was no violence of any kind. At the airport the Bank's people were given a choice of three destinations and politely told that their spouses and children would be given safe conduct and their household goods would be packed and sent to any forwarding address they might care to leave, all 'at the government's expense'.

'That last bit,' thought O'Donnell, 'can only mean one thing – Nick is mixed up in this somehow. Whoever Julian Cray is, he's clearly enjoying himself and the paper is giving him all the space he wants – they're playing this story as a world first.'

O'Donnell read on. Cray rattled off all the right figures, the successes, the reasons why Namland was teacher's pet as far as the Bank was concerned. Some of Cray's other numbers O'Donnell found less welcome – the increases in urban unemployment and the amount by which Namland's foreign debt had increased (more than two-fold) since the country had entered its period of 'successful' adjustment. The International Labour Organization claimed that fifty-nine per cent of the population of Namland was now living below the poverty line, compared to thirty-seven per cent in 1990.

Even worse, this Cray dwelt on 'social indicators'. Fair enough, they were probably accurate, they came from UNICEF, but they showed that the percentage of people who had access to health services or safe drinking water had significantly declined since the early or mid-1980s when the Bank had taken Namland under its wing. The country had made great strides in commodity exports, although like everybody else it had had to accept lower prices, while food production was stagnant.

There was also clear evidence, said Cray, still quoting UNICEF, that child mortality rates were rising. In 1985 deaths of children under five had been 153 per thousand; by 1990 they had been reduced to 140, but in 1992 had shot up to 170. Statistically speaking, a Namland child had a better shot at survival fifteen years previously than today. Namland had always been poor, yes, but it used to rank forty-second on UNICEF's score sheets, which meant that at least it had a lower child mortality rate than forty-one even more awful countries to raise kids in. Now it was number twenty-seven.

O'Donnell's whole professional life revolved around numbers but at the Bank one rarely dealt with this sort – these were for the soft social-science types, and of course outfits like UNICEF loved them, they positively revelled in sniping away at the Bank. But Cray wasn't finished. Somehow he had also found time to interview Nick. This piece ran separately, on page six, where the page one story continued.

Well, you could see why the *FT* was squeezing this story for all it was worth: Nick had clearly lost his marbles. 'Poor bastard,' thought O'Donnell, 'he's gone completely round the bend.' The tale Cray had got out of him was totally weird.

Nick had apparently had a call, relayed by drums if you please, from his ancestral village. His father's cousin ('who, as you know, in our culture is as close a relative as one's own biological father') had summoned him home. Cray called this cousin the shaman of the village, but in plain English, he was a witch-doctor, right? So Nick drops everything, orders an Air Force helicopter and takes off for the village ('I could not refuse the summons of one of my fathers').

As soon as he arrives, this witch-doctor gives poor Nick the most incredible song-and-dance you ever heard. He tells him the ancestors are waking him every night, that they're furious because the people are unhappy, the children are dying and some very heavy things are going to happen – things like locust plagues, famines, tidal waves, you name it – if Nick doesn't shape up Namland pretty damn quick.

So then Nick and this old guy – he's about eighty-five – talk all night long and at dawn Nick gets back into his helicopter and goes home to put on his native costume covered with embroidery (the *FT* carries a picture of Nick in his fancy dress as well) and then he goes straight to the NRTC – the Namland Radio and Television Corporation – just when most people are getting ready to go to work and are listening to the radio or are having a coffee in a café with the TV turned on.

O'Donnell can't believe the speech. Can *this* be the Young Professional, the honours graduate of the London School of Economics, the man who spent eight or nine years doing the Bank's business abroad before returning to do it at home?

'My dear fellow Namlanders, my dear brothers and sisters,' Nick is saying, 'I, your Prime Minister, Nicodemus Nyamba speak to you this morning but it is not only I who am speaking. I have asked for and received this night the counsel of the ancestors and they have promised also to speak through me. As the radio and the television are vessels for my voice and image, so I feel myself a vessel for the voices of our fathers and mothers.

'They are sad voices. They watch over our country and they see a few Namlanders growing exceedingly rich but the people perishing. Our forests where the spirits dwell are felled and sold so that we can pay our debts. We no longer grow our own maize and beans. The ancestors have heard foreigners saying that our country is the healthiest of the whole African continent and they do not know whether to laugh or to cry. They can see this is not true, that we have forgotten how to live and, above all, we have forgotten them.

'Our friends from the World Bank have taught us a great deal that is valuable. I myself have learned much from them. But I have come this morning to tell you, my sister and brother Namlanders that: when the power of an institution is greater than its knowledge;

when an institution demands that proud men and women submit
to its laws; when it makes this submission a measure of human
value and disobedience to its doctrine a cause for punishment;
when the authority it has taken upon itself comes to seem natural
and good to those over whom that authority is exercised; when it
makes us so dependent on its money and its wisdom that we come
to cherish our own dependency; when it chooses in our place how
well we may treat our sick people, our parents and our children by
telling us that we shall devote such or such a part of our wealth to
them; when it draws its legitimacy not from the law of the ancestors
or from the people but from within itself; when it continues to
govern indefinitely without the consent of the ancestors or of the
people; when it considers the whole Earth its natural home and all
Earth's people as its subjects; when it is never satisfied with its
present domains but sees always new fields to conquer; when an
institution makes power, not truth, the basis of its ethics and the
proof of its doctrine; when it claims it will build the future by
destroying the past; when an institution believes itself to be an
instrument of Providence in the cause of universal salvation; when
we ourselves say, "There is No Alternative"; then, my brothers and
sisters, we should get down on bended knee and bow our heads, for
we are in the presence of a new faith and we have embraced it.

'The ancestors have called upon me to tell you they refuse this
new faith.

'My own position is of no importance. I will remain as your
Prime Minister or not, as you will. No one has been more faithful to
the Bank than I, no one has carried its doctrine further. Now I have
heard a different voice and I am returning to my village. You are
the people and the children, you must do as you must.

'Goodbye.'

O'Donnell was stunned. He paid for his coffee in a kind of daze
and somehow reached his office across the street. The phones were
ringing off the hook. He hung up on a journalist from the *Washington Post*, the ultimate idiocy. He felt ill and shaken, he needed to
talk to Nick, because clearly one of them was crazy.

Thank God he had a little time to settle down. The meeting
wouldn't start until half past ten when O'Donnell was scheduled to
present to the board of executive directors the new structural

adjustment programme for Vambiso, the country as it happened adjacent to Namland's south-eastern border. But O'Donnell knew he would impress the EDs. He had all the figures down pat – growth rates, balance of payments, inflation, debt service, commodity export volumes – everything could be notably improved in Vambiso through the good offices of the Bank. No question about it.

It goes without saying that any resemblance between Namland and an existing African country, for which figures could have been derived from UNICEF reports on *The State of the World's Children* for 1987, 1992 and 1994, is purely coincidental.

Between 1980 and 1989 some thirty-three African countries received 241 structural adjustment loans. During that same period, average GDP per capita in those countries fell 1.1 per cent a year, while per-capita food production also experienced steady decline. The real value of the minimum wage dropped by over twenty-five per cent, government expenditure on education fell from $11 billion to $7 billion and primary school enrolments dropped from eighty per cent in 1980 to sixty-nine per cent in 1990. The number of poor people in these countries rose from 184 million in 1985 to 216 million in 1990, an increase of seventeen per cent.

(With grateful acknowledgement to the fact sheet 'The World Bank and Hunger: Facing the Facts' prepared by the Development Group for Alternative Policies (D-GAP) of Washington for the Bank-sponsored Conference on Overcoming Global Hunger, Washington, DC, 30 November–1 December 1993.)

Chapter VII

Governance: The Last Refuge?

The Bank's double bind – the promise to change the lot of the poor while remaining a profitable institution – lies, we believe, at the heart of its recent and increasing preoccupation with governance. In the Cold War days, the Soviet Union was accused of fomenting unruliness, subversion and chaos throughout the South. In the 1980s, ill-effects of structural adjustment were ascribed to governmental incompetence or stubbornness. If sustainable poverty reduction turns out to be just another mirage, institutional responsibility for failure must not be seen to be the fault of the Bank itself. The only other possible culprits will be the Bank's partners who, today as yesterday, are the governments of those countries within whose borders large numbers of the poor are to be found.

Governance provides a new tool-kit, an instrument of control, an additional conditionality for the time when the traditional blame-the-victim defence again becomes necessary. It further offers the opportunity both to instil Western political values in borrowing countries and to fault them if things go wrong. In the new era dawning the stakes are higher and the Bank's strategies of self-justification must become more sophisticated. Victim-blaming must either be given a whole new dimension or abandoned – in which case the Bank's version of development is a dead duck. Already, the onus of failure is coming uncomfortably close to being laid on the Bank's own doorstep.

When we examined the case of McNamara faced with the insoluble contradictions of channellling development to the poor and weak through the rich and powerful, we considered three hypotheses: 1) he was naïve to believe developing country social and political élites were motivated by moral concerns; 2) he was beset with delusions of grandeur, believing that he, McNamara, could give them orders and thus obtain the desired results; or 3) he was concerned to increase his personal power, using the pretext of the absolute poor to expand the Bank.

Whichever is true, McNamara convinced himself and many others that he was behaving not just efficiently and rationally but ethically as well; that he was doing good, in Vietnam for his country, at the Bank for the poor. Whatever his motives, he was among the first to see that the self-interest and ultimately the security of the United States and the West depended on raising the living standards of the poor in the third world. He trusted the Bank's version of development to fulfil that mission and hugely extended the institution's capacity to intervene. Yet poverty continued to flourish no matter how much money was thrown at it.

In the 1990s, the Bank's perennial problem, growing more acute with every passing year, is still the one McNamara faced in the 1960s and 1970s: what on earth are 'we' to do with the poor? They are outstripping all efforts of the Bank, and everyone else, to improve their lot and to reduce their numbers. More and more, they are perceived as threatening political stability. The Bank also blames them for undermining the planet's ecology.

McNamara feared perhaps more than anything the population explosion – typically applying warlike metaphors to the phenomenon. It was the theme of his maiden speech to the Bank's board of governors in 1968, in which he compared the proliferating poor to an atomic bomb: 'Casting its shadow over all . . . is the mushrooming cloud of the population explosion', an explosion which was 'blowing apart the rich and poor and widening the already dangerous gap between them'.

The following year he had the guts to make another speech entirely on the population issue in that bastion of Roman Catholicism, the University of Notre Dame in South Bend, Indiana. Here he pointed to the spectre of a minimum twenty-first century world population figure of 15 billion, possibly attaining . . . 60 billion!

In nineteenth-century France, the bourgeoisie referred to the poor as the dangerous classes. In the 1960s, RSM remained firmly within that tradition, viewing the poor's potential to blow things apart and their burgeoning numbers as a threat to global security ultimately more dangerous than the enemy to the east. In this,

McNamara was not just a throwback to a bygone era but curiously ahead of his time. His fears and fantasies are, in the 1990s, coming to be more and more widely articulated. *Les classes dangereuses* are alive and, so to speak, well.

With the demise of the Cold War and the West's concentration on integrating the former Eastern bloc, largely at the expense of the third world, the new mythology of the dangerous classes is becoming clearly identified with the South (as well as with Southern immigrants in the North, a theme we cannot deal with here). Today's uneasy bourgeoisie, inside and especially outside the South, would prefer to ignore them but realizes implicitly or explicitly that, somehow, these masses will have to be held in check and managed.

In a book published in France titled *The Empire and the New Barbarians*, Jean-Christophe Rufin takes a hard look at Western democracies suddenly deprived of their historic Cold War enemy. He sees them staring across a widening gulf at what they see as a chaotic, radically different and frightening South. He thinks Western countries will react by erecting a latter-day *limes*, the frontier that separated the Roman empire from the barbarians beyond the walls.

For Rufin, in the New World Order now under construction, the empire perceives itself as unified (around Judeo-Christian-Hellenic-democratic values), finite, orderly, and stable. The barbarians, on the other hand, are constantly shattering into an infinity of tribalisms; they are innumerable, unruly and nomadic. The empire believes in Science, Reason, and Law; the barbarians are arbitrary, fanatic and violent. The empire is prosperous and frugal; the barbarians miserable and profligate.

In a word, Rufin's book is about the forging of a new ideology in a new world configuration. As with any unfolding myth, the 'facts' are immaterial – any or all of the above statements may be demonstrably false. What matters is that a new belief system is supplanting an old one:

> The mythology of development was universalist: behind the East–West opposition, there was general agreement on the idea of one world, and on the need for those who were backward and 'behind' to catch up. The ideology which now opposes the North and the new barbarians, on the contrary, accepts and intensifies their division. It

identifies not one world but two, it transforms priorities and opens a new phase of history, that of the confrontation of these two worlds.[1]

On the other side of the Atlantic, foreign-policy scholars like Samuel Huntington of Harvard pursue similar lines of argument – although Huntington is less sanguine than Rufin concerning the cultural cohesiveness of the empire. For him, we are finally emerging from the historical period of 'Western civil wars', fought first among princes, then among nation states and, in this century, among ideologies. The dawning era will be one of conflict of the 'West versus the Rest'; one in which the

> great divisions among humankind and the dominating sources of conflict will be cultural . . . the fault lines between civilizations will be the battle lines of the future [and these] fault lines are replacing the political and ideological boundaries of the Cold War as the flash points for crisis and bloodshed. The core of global politics will be the interaction between the West and non-Western cultures . . . the next world war, if there is one, will be a war between civilizations.[2]

Huntington's views and his tone (far more than Rufin's) contribute, we think, to the very split and mutual mistrust and enmity they profess to describe; but if these authors are correct, as many newspapers suggest many days, then the Bank will be required to deal with this new world disorder. We see the Bank visibly positioning itself as a major political actor in the next phase of world history. What better breakthrough for a middle-aged institution peddling a worn-out development formula than to become the arbiter of the great new North–South, empire–barbarian divide? As it gropes for a new role, and as so often happens with the Bank, it is plunging ahead in an ad hoc and contradictory way.

On one hand, much of the Bank remains a bastion of the *ancien régime*, still proclaiming the one-world, universalist ideology of development and the doctrine that the poor can somehow catch up with the rich. For those who believe that the era of one-worldism is done for, that 150 countries cannot become Asian dragons (if only because the planet would collapse), that gap-closing is illusory, the Bank is necessarily fighting a rearguard action, doggedly defending its traditional practices and the conventional wisdom.

On the other hand, because of its financial power, its capacity to dictate policy and its ability to mobilize the resources of other institutions, the Bank is in the vanguard; it really is in a position to alter fundamentally the course of future events. It can influence the direction and the depth of Huntington's civilizational fault lines; it could even help to prevent them, just as it played a significant political role during the Cold War by shoring up Western client governments.

One way or the other, the issue is still to 'manage' the barbarians. Paradoxically, the poor are at once the Bank's *raison d'être* and its enduring, institutionally life-threatening problem.

The Bank needs the poor far more than the poor need the Bank. The mere physical presence of more than a billion absolute poor justifies the Bank's existence and its recurring if so-far ineffective commitments to poverty reduction. After decades of failed development, which has itself generated vast numbers of marginalized people, what other excuse is there for the maintenance of this ageing bureaucracy, if not massive and increasing poverty? The Bank is no longer needed as a Cold War player on the side of the West but it can bet its chips on the latest security threat: the new dangerous classes.

The argument from poverty is morally satisfying too: plenty of people, inside and outside the Bank, still want to believe that the North–South gap can somehow be diminished if not entirely closed, that justice among the nations will eventually prevail, that the poor will *not* always be with us. Few other institutions still put up a brave front on such matters. Mass poverty furnishes the institution with the perfect justification for its protean role of bank and Bank; provider of commercial loans at market rates and humanitarian.

Committing the institution, as President Preston has done, to sustainable poverty reduction is none the less a risky business. If the Bank's strategy misfires one more time, if the poor cannot be helped by outside intervention, however benevolently intended, if the empire really does become fed up with – or terminally frightened of – the barbarians, it could be the Bank's swan-song. Failure will not be excused for ever and, at the very least, must be justified.

The obvious way for the Bank to justify its institutional existence is actually to do something lasting and constructive about mass poverty. It is duly issuing new operational directives and devoting much more staff time to the subject than in the past. It is not, however, visibly altering its basic market-based development model which is specifically designed not to include everyone, nor its traditional methods, particularly those of adjustment which augment social polarization. The Bank has never been able to reach the absolute poor and it is not clear why this deficiency should suddenly disappear.[3]

As we have already tried to show, an exclusively market-oriented philosophy and a 'poverty focus' with a hope of success are mutually exclusive. The Bank has convinced people the contradiction can be resolved by giving adjustment 'time to work', that is, by pushing the problem into an eternal future. It has also managed to pin the blame for its shortcomings on others.

The Bank has explained in any number of publications that adjustment policies are certifiably correct: the problem lies, rather, with the 'adjustees' who haven't applied the proper remedies hard enough or long enough; their hearts simply aren't in it. Similarly, the development model itself is never seen to be at fault; failure is attributed rather to the degree of perseverance and competence with which the Bank's borrowers apply it. This line of argument was, for a time, reassuring: in the 1990s it is wearing thin.

For decades, the Bank has had a free hand to carry out its policies, especially during the 1980s following the onset of the debt crisis. Surveying the results, some critics make the mistake of proclaiming that development has failed. It hasn't. Development as historically conceived and officially practised has been a huge success. It sought to integrate the upper echelons, say ten to forty per cent, of a given third world population into the international, westernized, consuming classes and the global market economy. This it has accomplished brilliantly.

A decade or more of structural adjustment has given marked impetus to the process of global integration. Elites everywhere have managed to make their poorer compatriots pay the costs of adjustment, whereas they, on the whole, have profited from it or at the very least have lost, proportionally, far less. They profit because much of their money is in foreign bank accounts: every time their local currency is devalued, they become richer at home. Luxuries are readily available when import controls are dismantled. Servants (including security guards) and workers are plentiful, docile and cheap. Public services may be disintegrating, but élites can afford private ones.

Years of unimpeded Bank policies have helped to transform McNamara's 'dangerous gap' between the rich and poor worlds into a chasm. According to the United Nations Development Programme (UNDP) this gap has doubled since the early 1960s. Now, however, the breach lies not just between North and South but also between rich and poor, the 'ins' and the 'outs', the consuming classes and the excluded *within* the less developed world. These deep divisions make the new fault lines even more difficult to predict, much less control. (Think of Iran, or of the volatile situation in major countries at the edge of the *limes* like Egypt or Algeria, even Mexico.)

Meanwhile, the poor – the barbarians – are perceived as endangering the globally integrated world – perhaps a third of humanity all told – the Bank has done so much to create. Fears of international class or religious warfare, terrorism and mass migrations which could swamp the industrialized countries are now the stuff of both the reflections of sophisticated strategists and the bugbears of the popular imagination.

Whether fully conscious of the fact or not, the Bank is currently staking its reputation, its influence and perhaps its existence on its capacity to turn the world – and itself – around. When President Lewis Preston proclaims that 'sustainable poverty reduction is the overarching objective of the World Bank', he unwittingly affirms a thorough overhaul of the institution's theory, practice, personnel and machinery.

If the Bank can't transform itself and actually use its billions to keep the North and South, the 'West and the Rest', from irrevocably splitting along Huntington's or Rufin's fault lines, then there is little justification for its continued existence. President Preston admits as much when he declares, 'Sustainable poverty reduction is the benchmark by which our performance as a development institution will be measured'.

Measured by whom? Presumably, the Bank's own flying squads will determine whether or not sustainable poverty reduction has actually occurred, just as the Bank has trusted its own evaluation teams to judge the economic impact of its projects and the effects of its structural adjustment policies. The poor themselves, duly noting that their poverty has or has not been reduced, are unlikely to be given a voice in the matter.

Preston doesn't say either which criteria will measure the Bank's performance. These could conceivably be anything from several thousand more television sets in the *favelas* of Rio de Janeiro to increased proportions of female children in primary school, to higher per capita disposable income, to zero cases of cholera and vitamin-A blindness – with a prodigious variety of quantitative and qualitative measurements in between. The vexed, value-laden question of development indicators is completely glossed over. We aren't told how sustainable poverty reduction will be measured any more than we are told who will measure it.

In addition, no timeline is set. When may we reasonably expect to see other marks lined up against Mr Preston's benchmark? In a decade? A century? Even the word sustainable in Bankspeak should set off an alarm since it could easily provide an excuse to defer judgement indefinitely. So long as the Bank itself sets no temporal limits for achieving sustainable poverty reduction, sustainable means indeterminate and this institution is a past-master at buying time.

Preston, however, has taken the pledge and must expect others to keep him to it even if his own staff does not. He has laid the Bank on the line. Under such circumstances any non-suicidal, self-respecting bureaucracy would be crazy not to cover its institutional backside in case of failure.

In his statement heralding the new operational directive (OD) on poverty reduction, Preston serves notice on governments that 'the Bank's volume of lending *should be linked to the strength of a country's efforts to reduce poverty*' (emphasis added).[4]

This crucial phrase amounts to a declaration of a new condition in addition to those already in force. 'Stronger government commitment to poverty reduction warrants greater support,' says Preston; 'conversely, weaker commitment to poverty reduction warrants less support'.

Governments are thus on notice to get their acts together. To describe this process and this requirement, the Bank has chosen the rather archaic word governance. 'Government' would have been a bit too blatant since the Bank, according to its Articles, is not allowed to intervene in politics at all. To circumvent this difficulty, much fancy legal footwork has been contributed by the Bank's staff, not least by its Vice-President and General Counsel Ibrahim F.I. Shihata, whose reflections on the subject of governance constitute a valiant if not wholly convincing effort to preserve what he calls 'this delicate balance' between respecting the Articles and actually getting something done.[5]

Being against good governance is like being against motherhood and apple-pie. The Bank's official definition, published in 1992, is also one most reasonable people would accept and is spacious enough to accommodate many a legal obstacle. Governance is defined as:

> the manner in which power is exercised in the management of a country's economic and social resources for development. Good governance, for the World Bank, is synonymous with sound development management.[6]

This definition nicely circumvents the issue of politics by focusing on the Bank's own legitimate concerns which, according to its charter, must be solely economic. Political considerations are supposed to be irrelevant, as Shihata explains, 'especially as the Bank's credibility and strength has (*sic*) traditionally depended on its status as a quintessential technocracy exclusively concerned with economic efficiency'.

Politics none the less quickly rears its head. Two other high Bank officials, Pierre Landell-Mills and Ismail Serageldin, respectively Senior Advisor and Vice-President of the new department of Environmentally Sustainable Development provide a comprehensive list of the characteristics of good governance.*[7]

---

* Although these authors specify that their paper does 'not necessarily reflect the views of the World Bank', they presented it at an official Bank conference in 1991 and it does not seem to have provoked strong rebuke, since both authors have subsequently been promoted.

Their inventory goes well beyond the bland, catch-all definition above; it also hews quite close to the norms Shihata himself arrives at after a lengthy argument. Landell-Mills and Serageldin draw their core governance values from the Universal Declaration of Human Rights which implicitly underlies the properties of governance they regard as least controversial, or minimal. Taken together, however, these values begin to sound suspiciously like a political programme – again, one with which virtually everyone (at least in Western nations) would agree. In summary:

The political rulers and government officials are held accountable to the ruled for their actions through clearly formulated and transparent processes ... the legitimacy of the government is regularly established through some well defined, open process of public choice, such as elections, referenda, et cetera.

The safety and security of citizens is assured and the rule of law prevails, such that contracts can be fairly enforced both among private operators (individuals or enterprises) and between a private operator and the state. Moreover, citizens should be legally protected from arbitrary or capricious actions by public authorities.

Public agencies are responsive to the need of the public and social and economic development is promoted for the benefit of all citizens in an equitable manner.

Information is readily available, thus permitting accountability to be practised, laws to be correctly applied, markets to function and people to be creative and innovative.

Freedom of association and expression of opinions is guaranteed.

Who wouldn't want to live under a government respecting these principles? Although we doubt that any known earthly power conforms perfectly to these norms, although we do not wish to fire cheap shots at an easy target, we are still bound to point out that the Bank shows scant interest in adopting such high-minded principles for its own use. What it deems imperative in the outside world, at the national level, is readily dispensed with by the Bank itself, operating internationally. Even though the Bank's decisions influence far more lives than the most corrupt and despicable third world régime, it does not hold itself to any of the standards it now seeks to enforce with regard to its clients.

Thus the Bank is not held accountable for its actions, except to a board of executive directors whose members are in turn appointed, in many cases by undemocratic régimes, and whose sociological characteristics often preclude meaningful opposition to whatever the Bank's own hierarchy has decided. (See Chapter x.)

The Bank is not transparent. It justifies its opacity by the need to protect the confidentiality of its relationship with borrowing members who are themselves then enjoined by the Bank to be, precisely, transparent. Since many governments are unwilling to allow their own people, much less outsiders, to learn what Bank projects may have in store for them, the Bank's refusal to divulge such information places it at the same level of poor governance as those governments it criticizes for their lack of transparency. Its confidentiality defence is not just hypocritical but absurd.

If the legitimacy of a government should be 'regularly established through some well defined process', and if the same standard were applied to the Bank, one would have to conclude that it has avoided any further external legitimation process since its establishment at Bretton Woods fifty years ago. Even its General Capital Increases have rarely been a matter of public debate. Environmentalists and others have had to express their opposition to Bank projects on an ad hoc, case-by-case basis. Occasionally they may even win – but the legitimacy of the institution itself, much less of the development model it practises, is not called into question.

While the Bank quite properly demands that governments afford legal protection for citizens 'from arbitrary or capricious actions', hundreds of thousands of 'oustees', the displaced persons forcibly removed from their homes by Bank dam or transmigration or enclosure projects, must feel its actions have been not only arbitrary and capricious but cruel as well.

As for development promoted 'for the benefit of all citizens in an equitable manner', this is sadly and demonstrably not the case with the Bank's own projects and programmes from which élites have generally drawn far greater advantages than their poorer compatriots.

Given the ambiguous, indeed contradictory status of governance with regard to the Bank's own Articles of Agreement; given the controversial and unwelcome nature of such a programme in a great many of its client countries; given, finally, the Bank's own flagrant nonconformity to the principles it exhorts others to follow, why has the Bank chosen to venture into this minefield? And why now?

Partly, perhaps, because the United States Congress is showing signs of revolt. The internal Wapenhans Report (see Chapter XI) showed that over a third of recent Bank projects have failed, even when measured in narrow economic terms. The Sardar Sarovar fiasco (see Chapter VIII) was another warning. The Bank's problem is that sooner or later people are going to notice, including people who buy Bank bonds and those who subscribe to its General Capital Increases.

Then, too, the Cold War is over. Time was when the Mobutus of this world needed only to knock at the Bank's door. In Biblical fashion, they asked, and loans were given unto them. Now, lots of places that used to be strategically important no longer are. Dictators can't count on aid just because they're there, even if they are still prepared to serve certain Western interests. Those interests have shifted and the West, like the Bank, can now afford a moral stance. In the old days, nobody wanted to talk 'politics' and strict observance of its Articles suited the Bank's reigning ideology perfectly.

Today, Communist subversion cannot be blamed for the crisis of development which is hurting morale even inside the Bank. Landell-Mills and Serageldin themselves detect a 'sense of failure and self-doubt' afflicting development professionals. After much soul-searching and debate, they announce that 'there is a growing recognition [among such professionals] that the relatively neglected issues of governance lie at the heart of the problem'. In other words, if development is such a patent failure, it's because the developers have hitherto left certain vital factors out of the equation.

What, then, went wrong? The authors propose several a priori explanations which are in fact hypotheses presented as established and universal facts: market economies are successful whereas government planning is not; authoritarian régimes are abusive; public enterprises and public agencies are inefficient and therefore the role of the state must be re-examined; corruption is widespread and, finally, ethnicity is everywhere resurgent.

From Landell-Mills and Serageldin's list, one would never know that the Bank had ever made loans to abusive, authoritarian and/or corrupt régimes or that the practices of development donors might have contributed in any way to the present crisis. Their paper implicitly dismisses the possibility that some of the third world's present problems could be remotely related to debt, trade barriers, disastrous commodity prices, structural adjustment measures or other policies and practices emanating from the North in general or the Bank in particular.

Worst of all, the Bank's institutional credibility is at stake and the proliferating poor can bring it down. Its development narrative is running out of steam, the story could come to an abrupt end. In the next phase of its existence, the Bank will have to prove that it *can*, finally, help to make the barbarians less chaotic, unruly and nomadic.

Samuel Huntington claims it is in the West's interest 'to strengthen international institutions that reflect and legitimate Western interests and values'. The Bank will have to show its major funders that it is indeed first and most deserving among those international institutions; thus it must devise ways of protecting those interests and advancing those values. At the same time, it must be ready to defend itself in case the poor fail to cooperate with its plans to alleviate their poverty and to reduce their numbers.

The preoccupation with governance was triggered inside the Bank by the mess in sub-Saharan Africa; the term entered official Bankspeak with the major study *Sub-Saharan Africa: From Crisis to Sustainable Growth*, published in 1989. Landell-Mills was one of its principal authors.[8]

This study identified governance as a basic issue for the economic development of the region and announced point-blank that 'Africa needs not just less government but better government'.[9] Structural adjustment hasn't worked in Africa and the promised private investment hasn't turned up.* Wealthy Africans aren't bringing their flight capital home and many local firms have gone under because they must now face much tougher competition. Nascent industries aren't competitive on world markets and aren't even allowed time enough to get on their feet.

So, by 1989, the Bank was compelled to ask itself why investment had failed to materialize and it answered, 'poor governance'. General Counsel Shihata also speaks on the issue straightforwardly:

> [T]he Bank's increasing concern with issues of governance in its borrowing members seems to have come as a logical last step in its gradually expanding involvement in policy reform through adjustment lending, which has been extended to social sectors.[10]

Political conditionality is nothing new. The difference is that during the Cold War, a country's foreign policy alignment determined how it was treated, whereas domestic policies were considered its own affair. The Bank has moved from purely economic support – often of human-rights violators but Cold War allies – to intervening in social sectors and finally to politics because, in the final analysis, everything is connected to everything else. Whatever goes on in a country can be linked to the Bank's legitimate, legally sanctioned mission of economic development. Hence the new-style political conditionality, which authorizes the Bank to determine how much help a given government can expect from the World Bank as reward or punishment for adopting the right domestic policies.

Long before the governance debate got under way and despite its apparently restrictive Articles, the Bank had already acquired broad experience in changing institutions – political as well as social ones. Shihata notes that to ensure the efficacy of its adjustment lending – no small sum, since a third of all IBRD loans and twelve per cent of the IDA's were devoted to SALs and SECALs during the 1980s – the Bank has had to deal with 'the overall organization of civil

---

* OECD figures confirm this failure: between 1984 and 1990, private charitable agency (NGO) grants to Africa exceeded direct (foreign) investment by 25 per cent. In two of those years significant disinvestment occurred.

service, the size of public administration and the size and structure of the public sector' as well as introduce many other measures requiring

> extensive legislative changes, particularly in the areas of labor regulation, investment, taxation and generally in what has become known as the 'enabling business environment'.

Major Bank shareholders provide support for political conditionality. The United States has already enacted legislation instructing its executive director at the Bank to oppose loans to any country exhibiting 'a pattern of gross violations of internationally recognized human rights'.[11]

The British also served notice in mid-1991 that 'our aid policy towards individual countries and its level will be influenced by human rights and democratic records as well as broader good government criteria'. Foreign Secretary Douglas Hurd said candidly that 'concern to improve human rights performance, democratic government and sound economic policies, means that donors use carrots and sticks.' And Lynda Chalker, Minister for Overseas Development, added,

> To those who argue that we have an obligation to provide aid whatever the circumstances, I would say . . . aid cannot be given in a policy vacuum . . . Our resources are finite and neither we nor recipients of our aid can afford to see them wasted. Some might call this conditionality. I call it common sense.[12]

In 1990 the Bank's then President, Barber Conable, told his African governors:

> Allow me to be blunt: the political uncertainty and arbitrariness evident in so many parts of sub-Saharan Africa are major constraints on the region's development . . . I am not taking a political stance here, but I am advocating increased transparency and accountability in government, respect for human rights and adherence to the rule of law. Governance is linked to economic development, and donors are showing signs that they will no longer support systems that are inefficient and unresponsive to people's basic needs.[13]

Shihata's careful legal arguments, formulated in 1990–91, have been overtaken. He was worried about having to amend the Bank's Articles, or worse, violating them. Such legal niceties no longer hinder or bind. And if the Landell-Mills–Serageldin list of minimum conditions is to be demanded, it's anyone's guess how many governments in Africa or elsewhere can possibly measure up. Few developed country governments could be absolutely sure of a place at this exclusive table. Shihata is by now defending a lost cause when he stresses that

> the following activities are legally prohibited by the Bank's Articles and thus *may not be carried out under the guise of promoting 'good governance'* . . . The Bank should not be influenced by the 'political character of the member . . . It should be immaterial to the Bank if the country is a kingdom or a republic, follows a Western-style or another form of government . . . political choices, *along with their underlying values* . . . are for each country to make; the Bank's concern is for the economic effects and the resultant degree of efficiency in the allocation of resources . . . Regardless of how simplistic (*sic* – does he mean simple?) it may be to attempt to introduce political transformation through the conditionality of external lending, *such conditionality would not in my view be consistent with the explicit provisions of the Bank's Articles of Agreement* (emphasis added).[14]

The general counsel's view has, it would seem, been superseded by President Preston's.* Governance is no longer in the domain of internal Bank debate; the matter has been settled. Everything, particularly the prized goal of private investment which alone can validate the pain of adjustment, is related to how the government

---

* For example, in his foreword to the Bank's April 1992 publication *Governance and Development*, Preston asserts that virtually everything falls within the Bank's mandate: 'Poverty and the environment are two critical areas of country strategy which present particular challenges of governance'. So do 'public sector management', 'reforming the civil service', 'promoting deregulation', 'improving the working of markets' and 'parastatal reforms'. '[The Bank] has often encouraged borrowers to introduce new laws and regulations . . . without always examining whether the legal system as a whole is operational and whether laws will be implemented effectively. *This situation has changed rapidly in recent years*' (emphasis added).

behaves. This behaviour thus becomes the legitimate concern of the Bank. Shihata should have another look at his law books and stretch his arguments to fit the Bank's Procrustean bed.

The official Bank document on *Governance and Development* provides a further, clinching argument in favour of an activist policy: whether one calls it intervention, conditionality or common sense. The Bank cannot hope to alleviate poverty or preserve the environment if it lacks a free hand with governments. 'Even in societies that are highly market oriented' (presumably the best kind) 'only governments can provide two sorts of public goods: rules to make markets work efficiently and corrective interventions where there are market failures'. But poverty alleviation and environmental protection programmes can be

> totally undermined by a lack of public accountability, corruption and the 'capture' of public services by elites. Funds intended for the poor may be directed to the benefit of special interest groups and the poor may have inadequate access to legal remedies. Similarly, the enforcement of environmental standards, which benefit the population as a whole but which may be costly to powerful industrial and commercial groups, can be emasculated by poor governance.[15]

Like the Landell-Mills–Serageldin list of democratic, human rights principles, the demand for legal standards that protect the poor can only be positive for third world peoples. Transparency necessarily requires a free press, publishing genuine information, and freedom of public debate. Accountability means that citizens have the capacity to 'throw the rascals out' at regular intervals. The rule of law supposes an independent judiciary. Such things are desirable in any society.[16]

If, however, the Bank starts to insist on multiparty democracy, or even a Western electoral system in general, the whole governance thing, as George Bush might have called it, could blow up in its face. At last count, in 1992, there were over two hundred political parties in Zaïre . . . All too often, in Africa in particular, multiparty is code for multiethnic; its imposition could shatter fragile national consensus where it has been established.

Still, the Bank has a startling opportunity to do great good. Were it actually to cause a shift in favour of transparency, accountability and human rights – all of which remains to be seen – it would also be immediately denounced, sometimes by its major clients. At the UN Human Rights Conference in Vienna in 1993, for example, several delegates argued that the West, by insisting on universal standards, was practising 'human rights imperialism'.

'Imperialism' may still work as a buzzword in some quarters, but no persuasive case can today be made against good governance on grounds of national sovereignty. In small, weak countries under structural adjustment – and in many larger, stronger ones as well – sovereignty has become a fiction anyway.

Therein lies another contradiction for the Bank. It has spent more than a decade eroding the capacity of the state to act independently. Monetary policy is decided for them: if told to devalue, they devalue. Macroeconomic policies also emanate from the Bretton Woods sisters, which, after a period of rivalry, now apply 'cross-conditionality'. This means that a government must obey the one or receive no help from the other. The effect – and the intention – of structural adjustment has been to weaken the state and to make sure that many of its traditional functions are taken over by outsiders, acting on behalf of the global market. Hans Singer puts it well:

> Governments are depicted as centres of corruption, policy failures, rent-seeking, ignorance and so on while the Bank has acquired a self-confident position of being in possession of the Holy Grail of good policies and an ability to sort out the 'good boys' from the 'bad boys'.[17]

The next logical step is the substitution of supranational for national authority, under the banner of governance.* Military spending is already beginning to receive attention. It was one of the centrepieces of the Bank–Fund meeting in Bangkok in 1991 where Landell-Mills, on behalf of the Bank, told participants that over the past ten years, the Bank had 'expressed concern at the level of

---

* The governance strategy will not work in the East Asian nations which are not subject to Bank–Fund conditionality. Their insistence on behaving as they choose could well contribute to the latent conflict Huntington masks as 'civilizational' but which will be, as usual, economic and political.

military expenditure in at least twenty cases'. Although he 'viewed with particular alarm' the rising number of local conflicts since the end of the Cold War, Landell-Mills stated that even in the face of increased civil unrest, the World Bank should not 'ignore the challenge posed by excessive military expenditure' and he argued that the 'problem should be viewed as an aspect of governance'.[18]

The ultimate attribute of the state – the capacity to defend itself – thus becomes the province of outsiders. The governments in question may richly deserve surveillance and punishment and their citizens may well be better off, but spades should be called spades.

The Bank can influence a country's bilateral donors as well. If these donors are already unhappy with the way a country is governed, the Bank can orchestrate concerted pressure to obtain significant political changes. Countries whose currencies are non-convertible cannot do without the Bank's approval if they hope to borrow from other public or private sources, receive export credits, obtain debt relief and the like.

Nor is the Bank's clout limited to its leverage over monetary, economic or military policies. Through its projects and programmes, it exercises more influence over education than UNESCO, over health than WHO, over the conditions of workers than ILO, over agriculture than FAO, over the environment than UNEP, and so on.

To sum up, we argue that the Bank's new insistence on governance is tied to:

Continuing and refurbishing the 'blame the victim' defence, the enterprise begun with structural adjustment. The locals will be at fault when and if the unwanted and unruly poor continue to multiply.

Gaining time for the institution. Governance is at the centre of an excellent and well-conceived advertising campaign whose human rights pillars no one can fault. Like any advertising campaign, the point is not to inform (or only marginally) but to manufacture believers and consent.

Positioning the Bank itself for the twenty-first century. With the engineered decline of national sovereignty in the former second world and the third, unelected technocrats will play a growing international political role, however much their rhetoric may try to disguise it. In this world-order scenario, leadership remains in the hands of the G-7 countries. GATT or its successor World Trade Organization is in line to become the International Ministry of Trade. The International Monetary Fund will press its claim to be the International Ministry of Finance. The way history is moving, the way the institution is playing its cards, the Bank is the prime candidate for the Ministry of Everything Else.

Chapter VIII

The Environmental Battlefield

[The environmentalists' challenge is] going to turn the Bank into a real swamp. It's a major threat to what the Bank has been, because it involves a new kind of people, religious people, who have no particular respect for traditional forms of quantification and who insist on looking at the long run.

Richard Webb, co-author of the official fiftieth anniversary history of the World Bank, 1992[1]

Mr Webb has good cause to be alarmed. Environmental organizations, particularly in the United States, have challenged the Bank's development model forcefully enough to win his accolade as a 'major threat'. It's true that their ultimate goal is nothing less than to provoke a wrenching internal cultural shift, which the institution may or may not be able to accommodate. If it meets the test successfully by recognizing the environment as the inescapable partner in all its development endeavours, the Bank has a future. If, instead, it treats the biosphere and the planet as hindrances or enemies, it is destined for fossilhood.

In the second case, however, many environmentalists believe that we are all destined for fossilhood. If the Bank continues to devote billions to worldwide, business-as-usual development – huge dams, predatory fishing and forestry, coal and oil-fired power plants, roads for mass automobile transport and the like – they say that sooner or later we can kiss the earth goodbye. Rightly or wrongly such people see the Bank's development model literally placing human survival at stake. If this makes them 'religious', so be it. Environmentalists are making the point that although the planet may survive as it has done for some four billion years, it may perfectly well do so without us.

As more and more people recognize that unlimited growth is a physical impossibility and the dominant development model nothing short of suicidal, a major doctrinal battle seems unavoidable. When Mr Webb describes the environmentalist threat as stemming from 'religious people, who have no particular respect for traditional forms of quantification and who insist on looking at the long run', he clearly fails to grasp that the Bank's side is also composed of 'religious people' who worship traditional forms of quantification and insist on looking at the short run.

Webb adds that the environmentalists are 'prepared to place much greater weight on uncertainties than has been the case. So [in the Bank] there will be lots of noise, lots of delays'.[2] Right again, Mr Webb. The environmental movement sees these 'uncertainties' as early warning signals; it abides by the Precautionary Principle, which states that when a given action risks harming the earth and its inhabitants, those who propose the action must prove that it is safe; it is not up to opponents to prove that it is dangerous. The Bank, in contrast, maintains that every dollar spent is somehow doing good for beneficiaries. The best thing we can do for the future is to promote more growth today.

Since 1989 the Bank has begun to take environmental issues more seriously but its dominant culture is extremely slow to change. The majority still espouses the Larry Summers view: nature is basically a reservoir of raw materials to be used up in creating growth, to which there are no physical limits. The planet can also serve indefinitely as a universal dustbin for the by-products of growth – anything from CO_2 to toxic wastes.

When the green challenge first surfaced, the Bank saw it as an 'image problem'. As late as the end of 1986, the vice-president for external relations told the Bank's in-house magazine that

> environmental issues are the most important image problem the Bank has to deal with in view of the growing public criticism of the Bank's policies and operations (most frequent targets: the Botswana livestock project, the Brazil Polonoreste development program, the Indonesia transmigration projects and the India Narmada dam project).[3]

These projects, like many others one could cite, were and are not just image problems but authentic, vast and costly environmental disasters richly deserving of every ounce of criticism that has been levelled at them. From an institutional point of view, however, the Bank, in carrying them out, performed rationally and according to the logic dictated by its own internal requirements. Management demands huge, expensive, ecologically destructive projects from staff partly because the Bank's administrative and overhead costs are colossal – in the 1994 budget, they amounted to nearly $1,400,000,000.[4]

Gigantism feeds on and reinforces itself. If the institution had a portfolio of small, environment-enhancing loans and grants, it is hard to see how it could remain financially viable – at least at present staffing levels. The green camp insists that *not* spending (no loans for megadams, deforestation, coal-fired power plants and the like) plus smaller, more precisely targeted loans with the participation of local organizations, would provide greater benefits on the ground for the poor and for the environment than the Bank's present portfolio can possibly promise. Unfortunately, the Bank's own comparative advantage is in megaprojects.

If the Bank listened to the greens, it would have to reduce turnover substantially and downsize like some banal transnational corporation laying off staff. Demands on staff time for the preparation and execution of more complex, environmentally beneficial loans would necessarily increase. As presently organized, the Bank is simply not geared to such activity; it has little choice but to keep spinning money.

A confidential mission report by a European Community representative describes the Bank's predicament succinctly. When he visited the Bank in May 1993, he learned that:

> In general, the Bank staff are extremely nervous about environment issues. It has a major credibility and public image problem which, despite massive investment in staffing and assessment procedures since 1989, has not resolved the issue. I was told that the average time it takes from project identification to approval is five years and costs an average $500,000 in staff time alone. Since the environmental procedures were introduced in 1989, *no project which has been subject to these procedures has actually been right through the appraisal process*. Even so, the Environmental Review report, submitted to the Board in April [1993] was remarkably frank about the difficulties in

implementing the procedures. It has not yet been officially released because the Bank is understandably reluctant to 'wash its dirty linen in public' . . .

This nervousness was heightened by the US Congressional hearings on IDA X [he refers to the Tenth Replenishment of the International Development Association soft loan funds] which were taking place in Washington while I was there. There is an open split on the Board of the Bank on the extent to which the Environmental Assessments should be made public [publication is at present mandatory] with many of the Bank's major beneficiaries [India, China, Pakistan, et cetera] pressing for confidentiality of these documents (emphasis added).[5]

Staff nervousness is doubtless heightened because environmentalists, taking advantage of the Bank's own environmental impact assessments, routinely make its life miserable. Because these assessments are at least theoretically public documents and its operational directives for project execution are also obtainable, the Bank can, for the first time, be taken to task if it fails to follow its own specified guidelines.

President Barber Conable instituted the Bank's first serious environment programme in late 1989. Only then did projects become subject to screening for their probable environmental impact. Between 1989 and mid-1993, about 300 projects were screened.*

Since the late 1980s the Bank has unquestionably improved its performance, at least in terms of resources devoted to environmental issues. When asked 'How much?', it can't quantify exactly staff effort devoted to the environment 'because environmental concerns

---

* This screening process classes projects A, B or C, depending on their expected degree of environmental impact. While an education project can without debate be classed C (no environmental assessment required), debate focuses on the degree of scrutiny to which other projects should be subjected. The task manager, not the environment department, determines the category into which his or her project falls and has no incentive to ask for rigorous screening. Critics find that even in category A, the supposedly toughest criteria are insufficiently strict. Structural adjustment loans – about a quarter of all Bank lending – are not assessed at all. Their numerous, if indirect, environmental consequences therefore go officially unrecognized by the Bank. For the environmental impacts of debt and subsequent adjustment measures, see Susan George, *A Fate Worse than Debt* (Harmondsworth, Penguin, 1988) and *The Debt Boomerang* (London, Pluto Press, 1992).

are now integral to a wide range of Bank activities'. In 1992 'there were 140 higher-level and long-term consultants in the Environment Department and four regional Environment Divisions (up from 54 in 1990) ... Overall, some 279 staff years ... were devoted to environmental issues in 1992'.[6]

By 1993 it had 200 specialists and expected to add another sixty-five environmental positions before the end of 1996. Five hundred Bank staff participated in environment training programmes in 1993. A vice-presidency for environmentally sustainable development was also instituted in 1993 with authority over the departments of environment, agriculture, urban development and transport. The environment department itself got a new subdivision for social policy and resettlement to deal with the thorny questions of people forcibly displaced by Bank-funded projects. Considering that the institution boasted all of five environmental specialists in 1985, this is progress indeed.[7]

But not enough. Some department members note privately that numbers do not tell the whole story; more environmentalists hired does not necessarily mean that the Bank is now suffused with an emerald glow. Many, they say, behave like anti-environmentalists put in place to prevent a real cultural shift, more the Summers hue than truly green. The Bank's new environmental staff – ecologists, foresters, anthropologists, sociologists, land-use planners and the like – are attempting to make up for lost time and count themselves satisfied when and if they can prevent some of the more predictable ecological disasters from occurring.

The Bank's official environmental assessments of proposed project loans frequently have gaping holes in them. Crucially, they do not estimate a project's potential for creating greenhouse gas emissions. The ex-head of the Bank's industry and energy department stated publicly that for the Bank, 'global warming is not a concern'.* As the environmental movement pushes harder on the issue of climate change, the question of CO_2 and other greenhouse gas emissions is

* Mr C— is the 'ex'-head of the industry and environment department because environmental NGOs successfully undermined his position there, but at this writing he is ensconced as senior advisor in private sector development; not necessarily a safer spot from the planet's point of view.

likely to become another terrain in the conflict between the greens and the Bank.

The Bank's overwhelming need to spin money and its refusal to entertain the notion that increased CO_2 emissions might be dangerous are illustrated by its 1993 decision to support a massive, long-term expansion of power plants in India. The tale of the National Thermal Power Corporation loan is exemplary.

Energy is the Bank's second largest lending sector and by 1993 it had already loaned $9.1 billion to India, its biggest customer, for fifty-six energy projects, heavily biased towards the state-subsidized coal industry. Suddenly, however, after forty-three years of such loans, the Bank woke up. In the words of its own staff, India was plagued by 'a capital and energy-intensive pattern of development' characterized by 'inefficient production and use of energy'. Government policies not only provided no incentives for energy conservation but positively encouraged its profligate use through the pricing system.[8]

Meanwhile, the Bank had taken over near-total control of the Global Environment Facility, a $1.3 billion fund pledged at the 1992 United Nations Conference on Environment and Development in Rio de Janeiro. This fund is intended to contribute to preventing global warming (forty-one per cent of its projects as of 1993) and to have a 'catalytic effect' on the Bank's much larger loans, that is, steer them towards reducing CO_2 and other greenhouse gas emissions. So while global warming may not yet be, officially, a concern for the Bank, it is still obliged to pay it some attention via the Global Environment Facility. India duly got one of the Facility's loans, to help make wind, solar and small hydropower schemes commercially viable.

Furthermore, many technically sophisticated and credible studies by institutions with impeccable credentials have shown that India *does not need* more thermal power capacity because it is sitting on top of an 'energy-efficiency goldmine', as USAID put it. In addition to these findings, in 1993, the Bank's own operations evaluation department called spending for more power capacity in India 'a losing game' and recommended that the Bank and the Indian government concentrate on demand management and energy efficiency instead.[9]

Given all this, one might think, wrongly, that the Bank would heed its own best advice and make energy efficiency a priority in India. On the last day but one of its 1993 fiscal year, however, the Bank's board approved a $400 million loan to the Indian National Thermal Power Corporation to finance two new power plants and the expansion of coal mining in the Singrauli region, where conditions created by previous Bank-financed power plant and coal mining activities, as described in yet another Bank report, are characterized by:

> unemployment, particularly of the original local population, inadequate resettlement and rehabilitation compensation, inadequate housing and the growth of slum settlements, inadequate sanitation and pollution of drinking water sources and degradation of forest resources.[10]

At the same meeting, the board announced that two further loans to NTPC of $400 million each were under consideration for disbursement before 1997. No loans for energy efficiency or conservation seemed to be contemplated.

These new loans to India will compound social and environmental problems locally. Their global impact will also be significant. According to the US Environmental Defense Fund, the extra CO_2 pumped into the atmosphere by this huge project will 'in all probability be the single biggest new source of greenhouse gas emissions on earth'.

The Indian power loan may be one of the more spectacular disasters-in-the-making but it is far from unique. David Batker of the Greenpeace Multilateral Development Banks unit has examined the shortcomings of several of the Bank's other environmental assessments. One, for a coal-fired thermal power project in Java, does not refer to greenhouse gases – this is standard – but does not consider problems posed by coal-mining, increased acid rain, mercury and heavy metals emissions, fresh- and sea-water pollution, or solid and liquid waste disposal either. Similar criticisms apply to projects from Bolivia to Malawi to Malaysia.[11]

The Bank's current guidelines require that local people be consulted with regard to projects affecting them. Batker has shown for several projects that local people have never been approached.

In the case of the Mae Moh mine and power development project in Thailand, the Bank foresees resettlement of 'near-by villages to reasonably distant locations', but the number of people concerned is not specified and there is no indication that they have even been notified, much less consulted. Both the Java and Thai projects – a tiny sampling – were approved without opposition by the Bank's board in December 1991.[12]

The environment is a battlefield between non-governmental organizations and the Bank but it is also, inside the Bank, turning into a major geo-political conflict between North and South. The split between donors and recipients, Part I and Part II countries, is increasingly acute, as the EC visitor's report, cited above, attests.

Although it would be difficult to consign the Bank's environmental assessments to the vaults now that the principle of their public availability has been established, many governments of large and populous third world countries like India, China or Pakistan would like nothing better than to conceal them because they want to keep the money flowing, even if proposed loans risk becoming environmental nightmares.

Borrower governments read environmental protection clauses in loan agreements as code for 'this project is going to cost us a lot more and will include completely superfluous but mandatory components we'll have to pay for'. These governments argue that the additional financial burden they will bear for unnecessary ecological frills may even price their goods out of the world market.

Many of the Bank's customers view environmentalism with deep suspicion, either as a new kind of conditionality, as an underhanded reintroduction of trade barriers or as a way of holding them back from developing. They say, with ample justification, that the West built dirty smokestack industries, produced abundant toxic waste, chopped down its forests, constructed dams for electricity or irrigation and roads for private automobile transport and got rich. Having done so, it now seeks to deprive poorer countries of the same privileges. If the West has only discovered the greenhouse and other environmental dangers in time to prevent developing countries from contributing to them, that is, in a word, tough.

India *wants* its next $1.2 billion for the National Thermal Power Corporation. China *wants* its $310 million loan for development of coal-fired power plants, $150 million for oil and gas development and more than $1 billion for fossil fuel-based transport systems. And the Bank intends to finance them. Alongside this megamillion dollar Chinese portfolio for traditional, massive greenhouse gas-emitting projects, the Global Environment Facility has allocated a paltry $2 million for assessing lending opportunities which might at some unspecified future time *reduce* CO_2 emissions in China. Because this project is too small to merit any Bank staff time, it has been handed over to a consultant with no connection to the Bank's real work. And, once more, the relative size of these loans provides a reliable guide to the Bank's – and its clients' – priorities.*

A good part of the Bank's staff, including much of its middle and upper management, would cheerfully do without any environmental considerations at all. Their standard line is: 'Development and growth first, which will bring riches, which will then allow a country to take care of the environment'. Or as Larry Summers put it succinctly when he presented the 1992 *World Development Report*, centred on the environment: 'Promoting development is the best way to protect the environment'.[13]

The Bank continually refers to something called sustainable development but its daily practice takes into account neither the long-term environmental impacts nor the uncertainties to which Mr Webb, cited at the beginning, so strenuously objects. Reorienting the institution in this direction would require resolving the money-spinning dilemma and designing an unending stream of small projects which would respect the Bank's own guidelines from A to Z. Each would cost a minimum of $500,000 in staff time, while little money would actually be moved. Ask any busy Bank task

* According to press reports, China is seeking a total of $25 billion for its electric power industry and is proposing lucrative incentives to foreign investors. Ontario Hydro, one of the two largest utilities in North America, announced from Beijing in October 1993 that it was founding (with two partners) the Asia Power Group Inc. to invest in power projects in China and other Asian nations. The Chairman of Ontario Hydro is none other than Canadian multimillionaire Maurice Strong, who previously served as General Secretary of the United Nations Conference on Environment and Development (UNCED), the greenfest held in Rio de Janeiro in 1992 (Reuters and AP dispatches, 'A Power Hungry China', *International Herald Tribune*, 7 October 1993).

manager: s/he would much prefer to handle large projects based on long-established procedures. For the moment, David Batker affirms that '*All* World Bank projects I have seen violate the environmental assessment requirements. Most Bank task managers do not even know what those requirements are'.

Officially, however, the Bank thinks its assessments are fine: its first Environmental Assessment Review (covering fiscal year 1992) concluded that 'environmental assessments are proving to be a valuable tool for identifying project problems and the means to solve them, even in countries with little or no previous experience in this area'.[14] Perhaps in some cases they are.

Against this checkered background, the recently-named head of the Bank's environment department, Mohamed el-Ashry, announced in late July 1993 a new and startling policy. As part of an 'action plan', the Bank is supposed to carry out an annual review of its *entire* portfolio, including the environmental aspects. Projects begun years ago will – it is claimed – be reviewed and some could be cancelled. Staff promotions are no longer to be pegged to 'how many dollars they are able to lend'. From now on, performance reviews 'will also take into account how loans within a particular country are helping to meet the World Bank goals, which include alleviation of poverty and environmental protection'. All of which, according to el-Ashry, spells 'a change in culture, a change in attitude' at the Bank.[15]

If put into practice, it certainly does. Whatever else happens, the public announcement of such a plan shows that the times they are a-changing and the contradictions they are a-sharpening at the Bank. One hopes that the plan is backed to the hilt by management, right up to the President, because even he may not understand the extent of the cultural revolution being proposed.

We have here no less than an attempt to take an army of neo-classical economists, most of whom share the Larry Summers world-view and have spent their lives preaching and practising the Gospel of Growth, and convert them to environmentalism. Not only would they have to abandon the faith of their fathers; they would also have to change not just their standard cost-benefit analysis but also accept the purely institutional costs, including reduced loan volume.

Many of their more highly-paid skills, the ones for which they were recruited, would become obsolete. Their macroeconomic training would be maladapted. What would they do all day? In other words, the degree of cultural resistance is likely to be high to insurmountable, unless the incentive structure can indeed be drastically overhauled and the Bank's own massive overheads substantially curtailed.

In the technical sense as well, such a plan stands in stark contrast to established Bank policy in its many technical departments. As the Indian thermal power example shows, Bank energy lending would have to be shifted from the huge greenhouse gas-spewing loans to energy efficiency and renewable energy sources. The Bank's own energy division, however, after estimating its loans for 'classic' energy projects at close to $16 billion for 1992–95, has already stated categorically that 'Energy conservation loans will represent over the fiscal year 92–95 period only 1% of Bank lending'.[16]

To convey more graphically the obstacles to a cultural shift and the nature of the philosophical clash between 'long-run' green 'religious' people and 'short-run' economic dogmatists, here is an anecdotal illustration. In the past, the degree of alienation sometimes attained by Bank staff, to the point of unconscious public displays of contempt for the supposed beneficiaries of the Bank's projects, could be astonishing, even painful to observe. We have already presented Robert McNamara and Larry Summers as emblematic of certain of these aspects of the Bank's culture.

If they are high priests, then the Canadian agricultural development specialist David Hopper, the Bank's senior vice-president for policy, planning and research until 1990, is a worthy acolyte. Hopper the man is not targeted: he has simply made more public statements than most high Bank officials past or present; we quote him *in extenso* to illustrate the dominant Bank culture. In the following excerpts, Hopper shows considerable bravery as he unveils before a knowledgeable audience the complete inanity, indeed wilful destructiveness, of the Bank's quantitative approach to development. His remarks were made to British members of the World Wildlife Fund (now the Worldwide Fund for Nature) in 1988:[17]

Towards the end of February 1978, I recommended to the Board of Executive Directors of the World Bank the financing of an irrigation project in a South Asian nation. I had been in the Bank a little over a month and this project severely tested my principles. As a researcher and agriculturalist with more than ten years of living and working on agricultural development issues in India, I had seen too many acres become useless from water-logging and salinity.

Irrigation projects ignored the necessary investments in drainage, water-hungry and inexperienced farmers overirrigated their lands, and the hot summer sun and the short rainy seasons parched the soil, wringing out the surface and sub-surface moisture, depositing the earth's salts in the root zones to sicken and kill future seeds. I promised then, that if ever I had the chance, I would see that no irrigation investment would be unaccompanied by appropriate drainage, and that no irrigation project would be without its component of farmer demonstration and education.

The project I sent forth in February was without drainage, without demonstration, without farmer education. Yet I sent it forward. I protested to my staff in the South Asia Projects Department and they, rather wearily, explained to their newly appointed Vice-President that the project in question barely met the test of a ten per cent economic rate of return, and that if drainage or demonstration or education were added, the extra cost would make the project uneconomic and, thereby, eliminate it from the lending programme ... It was obvious they were right. Proper drainage would have tripled the cost of the investment ...

A few months later, I sent to the Board another project to add drainage to irrigated land now water-logged and saline from decades of farming ... This time the investment met the economic rate of return because unproductive acres were to be returned to productive use. But the costs were high, much higher than if the investment had been made concomitantly with the initial irrigation project; and investment that would have insured the long term, sustained, productive use of the land.

The peculiar anomaly of this story is the fact that there was an accepted economic justification for proceeding with the investment that was certain to lead to a degrading of the resource base, and there was no acceptable justification for protecting those resources from destruction.

This 'accepted economic justification' is based on the premise that natural capital, as opposed to financial capital, costs nothing.

Even the neo-classical economic principle that the cost of a resource should rise as it is depleted or destroyed is ignored. For the farmer, however, productive, living soil is capital: if it is ruined, he will be ruined too. If a development institution deliberately finances projects which it knows will waterlog soils and render them saline and sterile, it has in fact wilfully cheated the farmer, the country and its people of a part of their capital stake and their inheritance.

An accepted economic justification can be found for such wanton behaviour only because those who design such projects arbitrarily assign the environment a value of zero. It then follows, equally arbitrarily, that environmental destruction has no cost either. The justification for degrading the resource base ensues from the initial premise.

The pertinent question concerning the accepted economic justification is, 'Accepted by whom?' As the Bank's official historian, Mr Webb, quoted at the beginning of this chapter, quite rightly observes, environmentalists 'have no particular respect for traditional forms of quantification'. Why should they? Why should belief in these traditional forms of quantification or accepted economic justifications supersede the perfectly obvious and rational observation that natural capital has a value greater than zero, that its destruction entails serious costs? By what right do those who knowingly undermine natural capital and the people who depend upon it (ultimately all of us) impose their demented orthodoxy on everybody else?

Hopper goes on to make the point that development ought to conserve or improve the natural resource base and should ensure that the environment within which development takes place can 'continue to sustain over time the new activities that intrude upon it'. He also regretfully recognizes that 'this simple but central concept has not been easy to convey to development professionals'. None the less, Hopper guarantees his audience that the 'business of the World Bank is sustainable development' and he praises its environmental record over the previous *twenty* years during which he affirms the Bank 'has had an active environment programme'.

This is stretching the truth more than a little. McNamara may have created a position called 'environmental advisor' in 1971, but the office had no discernible influence over Bank practice. The proof is that most of the 'image problems' (a.k.a. environmental disasters) it would later contend with were conceived in the 1970s. Certainly the 'natural capital is worth zero' bases of cost–benefit analysis, by Hopper's own admission, were left unchanged during the McNamara years.

Hopper also informs his listeners that the Bank is introducing environmental considerations in all aspects of its projects and that its borrowing country members may object to these new constraints. What happens if they do? Hopper claims that:

> Many potential Bank loans or credits are dropped because the negotiators were not able to reach a mutual acceptance of project details. The Bank staff are negotiating with sovereign nations and may not dictate terms. The Bank can only refuse to lend if the project is unacceptable.

In the case of Bank projects requiring large-scale human resettlement and rehabilitation, according to Hopper,

> The Bank has provided assurances that it will give full attention to the special problems of resettling minority and indigenous peoples who may be deprived of their traditional homelands through Bank-assisted projects. Unless suitable resettlement arrangements are made, the Bank will not finance the project.

The available evidence suggests, rather, that the Bank hangs on tooth and nail even in the face of the most damning environmental or human rights evidence. This was precisely the case in the Narmada Valley in India, particularly the Sardar Sarovar dam project, with which Hopper was closely involved from the moment of its inception in 1985.[18]

The ostensible purpose of the Narmada Valley project, covering a vast area in three Indian states, was to provide drinking water, irrigation and electric power to 40 million people. If carried out as planned, the project would comprise 30 megadams (including the super-mega Sardar Sarovar), 135 medium-size and 3,000 small dams, plus canals and irrigation works. As conceived, it would become the largest irrigation scheme on earth; just the sort of project to quicken the hearts of the Bank's – and the Indian government's – techno-cultists.

Critics, on the other hand, pointed to the easily foreseeable, detrimental environmental impact and to the huge number of people who would be displaced, variously estimated from 250,000 to well over a million (if all the dams were completed). The Sardar Sarovar dam alone, 455 feet (140 metres) tall, would submerge all the lands and people of 245 villages.[19]

Countering Bank claims of benefits to be showered upon all and sundry, the Indian *Narmada Bachao Andolan* (Save Narmada Movement) published a highly documented paper showing that proposed irrigation would enrich only already rich landowners, that the promised drinking water or electricity benefits were a 'mirage'; that the proposed 'resettlement' would instead be a 'human tragedy'.[20] Many Narmada opponents undertook non-violent protest actions to support their claims.

The Bank contributed an initial $450 million to this complex project in 1985; in 1992, two other loans totalling a further $440 million were pending. But even as David Hopper spoke, in late 1988, the project had become a *cause célèbre*, outside and inside India, where hunger strikes, mass commitments to self-immolation by drowning, police violence and arrests of dam opponents, had turned the project area into a virtual war zone.

The furore reached such a pitch that Bank President Conable decided to commission an unprecedented independent review, chaired by his old friend and colleague, Bradford Morse. Morse, a venerable member of the American establishment, was, like Conable himself, a former Republican congressman. As former Under-Secretary-General of the United Nations and Administrator of the United Nations Development Programme his international credentials were impeccable as well. The independent review was co-chaired by the distinguished Canadian jurist and former British Columbia Supreme Court Judge Thomas Berger.

Never before had an official, independent body examined a Bank project prior to its completion. The review's conclusions, submitted in a 363-page report, were devastating. It accused the Bank of flouting its own guidelines. Morse and Berger wrote to Lewis Preston (who had meanwhile replaced Conable at the head of the Bank) that the 'situation is very serious. We have discovered fundamental failures in the implementation'.

According to the review, the Bank had ignored its stated directives on resettlement; people forcibly uprooted from their homes were clearly not going to receive adequate compensation. Nor were any proper environmental assessments ever made. 'The Projects proceeded on the basis of an extremely limited understanding of both human and environmental impact ... involuntary resettlement resulting from the Sardar Sarovar projects offends recognized norms of human rights ... The history of the environmental aspects is a history of non-compliance [with the Bank's own guidelines]'.[21]

Although both the Bank and the Indian government had complicated its task by purposely withholding relevant information, the review's own assessments pointed to thousands of coastal fishermen who would lose their livelihoods, 'serious problems with waterlogging and salinity' as well as a 'large-scale increase in water-borne diseases'.

The review pointed out that one of the Bank's own consultants, in a separate report, had already described parts of the project as 'death traps', guaranteed to bring malaria 'to the doorsteps of the villagers'. The Bank had disregarded his report. For Morse and Berger, it seemed 'clear that engineering and economic imperatives have driven the Projects to the exclusion of human and environmental concerns'.[22]

What does an institution like the Bank do when confronted with a uniquely negative report, commissioned by its own President? In the present case at least, its management circles the wagons and lobbies the executive directors unrelentingly. The Bank's board subsequently votes, in September 1992, fifty-nine to forty-one per cent to *continue* funding Narmada, prompting the US executive director, Patrick Coady, who voted no, to warn his colleagues that the vote

> will signal that no matter how egregious the situation, no matter how flawed the project, no matter how many policies are violated and no matter how clear the remedies prescribed, the Bank will go forward on its own terms.[23]

All the directors voting against the project represented Part I countries (the US, Germany, Australia, Canada, Japan and the Nordics). All the Part II countries voted with India to keep the cash flowing, confident that India would sooner or later return the favour.

The board's decision immediately triggered blanket condemnation from the world's environmental community. More startling, perhaps, was the scathing, five-page, single-spaced, 'nothing left to lose' letter from Morse and Berger to President Preston and the executive directors denouncing the Bank's response to their independent review. This response, entitled *Next Steps*, was in effect a blueprint for business-as-usual on the Narmada projects.

We quote at length from the Morse–Berger letter because it demonstrates how far the Bank's management was prepared to go to salvage a huge project for its largest all-time borrower. Throughout the lifetime of this project, the government of India was an enthusiastic and deliberate accomplice to the Bank. In short, Morse and Berger accuse the Bank's management of lies, fraud and wilful misrepresentation of their report to its own executive directors (most of whom would not then have had the opportunity to read the original):

> We have an interest in seeing that our report is not misrepresented. [The Bank's response on the Narmada project, *Next Steps*] ignores or misrepresents the main findings of our Review [and is] at variance with what we wrote . . . Unless the Bank recognizes the failure of its . . . strategy, the well-being of tens of thousands of people will continue to be at risk . . . *Next Steps* omits any reference to those parts of our report describing how the project continues to disregard the environmental requirements of both India and the Bank. Most of these have been in place for a decade or more. To continue to ignore these standards places the environment at risk. The risk becomes greater the further along construction proceeds . . . You will note that something as basic as the Environmental Work Plan is still unavailable (legally required by the Bank before the end of 1985) . . . The Executive Directors are given the assurance in *Next Steps* that the hydrology issues raised in our Report have been addressed. This is not true.

(Several paragraphs follow on the slipshod technical work of Bank staff people hastily assigned to salvaging Narmada. They did not trouble to read the independent review report nor avail themselves of data on hydrology and sedimentation issues repeatedly offered, vital to the impact and lifespan of the dam but not even mentioned in *Next Steps*.)

> *Next Steps* ignores the fact that there has never been a proper environmental assessment of the Sardar Sarovar Projects. Because there was no impact assessment we had to do an enormous amount of work that was not originally seen to be part of our terms of reference in order to create a database . . . We are concerned that it has become necessary to write this letter. The Bank may choose to reject our findings . . . It is clear, however, that the Bank's *Next Steps* document has sought to present a version of our report that is at variance with the report itself . . . The Bank may decide that overriding political and economic considerations are so compelling that its Operational Directives are irrelevant when decisions have to be made about the Sardar Sarovar Projects. But it should not seek to reshape our report to support such decisions.[24]

Finally, with a storm of criticism raging within and without, the project was dropped – but not by the Bank itself. According to the Press Trust of India, the government of India requested that the Bank cease funding the project because 'Everybody is holding inquiries into what India considers its domestic problem . . . [this] was not in keeping with the country's self respect'.[25]

India's request appears to have been mostly a face-saving exercise. Observers noted the interestingly timed visit to India by Bank Senior Vice-President Ernest Stern prior to the Indian government's declaration.* They noted also the $2.7 billion worth of loans to India approved in fiscal 1993, up by a comfortable $487 million

---

* Stern is frequently cited as 'the power behind the throne', the '*éminence grise*' or simply 'the guy who really runs the Bank'. He served, for example, as Acting President in 1993 while Lewis Preston was recovering from major surgery. Stern is reported (by *Die Zeit*, 1 October 1993) to have put pressure on the board to rush through the $400-million Indian National Thermal Power Corporation loan at the tail-end of fiscal 1993 in order to compensate the Indians for the loss of Narmada. Ernest Stern may not be overly sensitive to environmental issues but one has to admire his *chutzpah*: he declared at a press conference on 12 July 1993, only three and a half months after the government of India had 'asked' the Bank to cease funding Narmada, that the Bank's own portfolio performance reviews had led to the cancellation of 'projects worth $1.3 billion in India', just as if the Bank had taken the initiative, just as if $400 million for unneccesary power plant expansion had not been approved a fortnight earlier.

(twenty-two per cent) over the previous year, handsome compensation for the loss of the undisbursed portion of Sardar Sarovar ($170 million). They noted, finally, that the Bank, chairing the Aid India Consortium meeting only three months after the Narmada débâcle, urged donor countries of the Consortium to pledge $7.2 billion, including $1.8 billion in 'fast disbursing funds not tied to specific projects but geared to policy changes that would further economic reform'.[26]*

Now let us cut for the last time, in flashback, to David Hopper, this time on-screen in Nicholas Claxton's 1987 film *The Price of Progress*.[27] As Senior Vice-President of the Bank and a man intimately involved with the project, Hopper is being questioned about Narmada.

CLAXTON: How serious are the social and environmental implications of this project?

HOPPER: They're quite serious and it would be wrong to say they're not ... but you can't have development without someone getting hurt before the benefits that are going to accrue. I wish you could. We try to carefully weigh benefits against costs. Among the costs obviously are the costs of relocation, the costs of dislocation for people. Among the benefits are the irrigated land ... and obviously the power benefits. As we go about this, we try to put various kinds of numbers on these costs and these benefits to ensure that there is a favourable weight to the benefits.

On screen: Hundreds of women in brilliantly coloured saris are marching in a seemingly endless line across the top of the rising dam. They balance baskets of concrete on their heads; they are being paid meagre wages to participate in the destruction of their own villages. The dam, when completed, will obliterate their homes.

CLAXTON: What will be the impact on the people who are forced to resettle?

HOPPER: They will move out of areas which traditionally they've occupied, their technologies in gaining a livelihood ... will be made redundant, they

---

* One of the Bank's lesser-known functions is to chair over two dozen aid consortia for individual countries through which it can exert significant power over other public donors.

will not find it as easy to gain a livelihood elsewhere . . . There are always people who are dissatisfied, there are always people who want more, more compensation, more of this, more of that, but there are techniques in India, it's a democratic country and there are techniques for expressing yourself both through the ballot box and through the courts to try to get the best deal you can make.

NARRATOR: The villagers have been fighting their case for five years and have taken it to the Supreme Court of India to fight for a better deal, but the dams are going on regardless.

[*Claxton then interviews anthropologist Thayer Scudder about resettlement in general. Scudder explains that you can predict the increase of death and illness rates among relocated people. They suffer acute personal anguish ('What's going to happen to me?') and more generally they are victims of economic and socio-cultural stress.*]

SCUDDER: The food economy of these people is tied to a given habitat, their knowledge is tied to a particular place . . . At the same time, the credibility of the leadership is undermined . . . [If the leaders support the displacement they're seen as traitors; if they can't prevent it, they're seen as impotent.] I would say it's about the worst thing you can do to people, to force them to move, next to killing them.

HOPPER: [*quotes* SCUDDER] 'Force them to move. Next to killing them.' [*continues*] Over the course of time we hope we'll gain more experience, that the Bank will gain more experience in how you handle this kind of a situation. Initially we're going to be subject to criticism, because we just don't have that experience, we're going in as rather new carpenters and we're likely to botch the first job, but we'll learn and so will the government of India, and that's where there's a give and take . . . The tribals themselves will learn, the oustees will learn. ['Oustee' is the term used to describe people ousted from their land.]

Hopper illustrates better than we could hope to do the familiar dialectics of error and learning, repentance and forgiveness. We don't actually know what we're doing, we're likely to botch the first job as 'new carpenters', but we'll learn, at someone else's expense.

Despite the termination of Bank funding, the Indian government has vowed to go it alone in completing the Narmada projects. In a sense, *even a financial failure can become an ideological and cultural success for the Bank.* The Indian élite, like so many others, has perfectly assimilated the Bank's own orthodoxy; its development model is so deeply internalized by borrowing governments that they can be counted on to perpetuate it, if need be, by themselves.

At the same time, by *not* continuing to finance Sardar Sarovar, the Bank has displayed openness and disarmed some of its fiercest critics, at least until another egregious case like the thermal power plants comes along. Indians say that at best, if environmentalists have won a victory, it applies to the next dams – which may not get built – not to Sardar Sarovar.*

What is to be learned from the Bank's environmental record? First, that it has been extremely successful in having its cake and eating it (the more graphic Italian image is to have the wine-barrel full and the wife drunk; the Bank manages both). While reinforcing its environmental staff, capacity, et cetera with one hand, it continues to lend to expensive impending environmental disasters with the other. Bank people whose views parallel the Hopper–Summers model are promoted; an outstanding environmental economist like Herman Daly returns to academic life (January 1994) after languishing for several years in the Bank without advancement.

Second, its major borrowers have themselves taken up the torch of the Bank's original 'natural capital equals zero' development model, placing the Bank in a good position to say now, 'We only do what the customer wants'.

Finally, the Bank will continue to seek more ways to combine a limited degree of environmental protection with profitability, proper rates of return and, above all, growth. In late 1993, the Bank issued a discussion paper entitled 'Towards an Environmental Strategy for Asia', citing exponential growth of pollution, energy

---

* One should not assume that the withdrawal of the Bank from its flawed projects will improve matters for people in the project area. Consider the following from the Indian organization *Development Alternatives*, whose magazine editorialized in August 1993: 'Ever since the World Bank withdrew funding support for the Sardar Sarovar Project, there has been no check on the government which has paid scant regard to the rights of the tribals affected by the dam. [An Indian human rights organization has sent several teams to the Narmada Valley to report on the situation and has found that some people would accept resettlement.] However, "the tragedy is that there is no land available for people who want to be resettled".'

use and number of vehicles in the region far beyond the capacity of the environment to sustain. The director of the Bank's Asia technical department says, 'The environment in Asia is one of the greatest development challenges in the world today'. The report still promises that most measures to curtail these threats 'involve little or no cost' and affirms that there is 'no trade-off between environmental protection and economic growth'. 'The solutions don't lie in stopping growth, but in making that growth more sustainable'.[28]

The cake has been eaten and is still on the table; the barrel is brim-full and the inebriated wife is staggering. The Bank is incorporating the language and occasionally even the practice of its opponents. The environmental movement has won some project-by-project skirmishes but it has been strategically and ideologically outflanked. Through a combination of reassuring rhetoric and some genuine improvements, the Bank has distanced itself from outright hostilities with the opposite camp.

Like other religious institutions the Bank uses solemn words and magic formulas to transform reality. Growth, when pronounced sustainable, is no longer threatening. Inherently destructive processes no longer destroy because sustainability confers on them the promise of a never-ending future. The environmental movement which fears for that future is stripped of its conceptual weapons and meanwhile, the borrowers have made the Bank's aims their own.

If the religious war over the planet's future does take place, as Richard Webb feared, it will be because environmentalists manage to challenge the Bank's magical manipulations of language, remain a major threat to its credibility and prevent the battlefield itself from slipping into the realm of illusion.

The Clans

Once upon a time, before time was, the Great Ancestor reigned over all creation. His throne stood on a mountain at the exact centre of his domain, which extended to the whole world. He ruled over the land, the air and the limitless ocean and all they contained. Mortals cannot say the name of the Great Ancestor, but his abode was called by the Greeks 'Oikos', and ever since he too has been called that way – in our own language, his name has come down to us as Eco.

After many ages had passed, Eco came to regret ruling alone, so he brought to his bed first the Lady of the North Wind, then the Lady of the South Wind, then the one, then the other, in a ceaseless dance. Eco would not and could not choose between them. The Ladies themselves understandably loathed each other but despite their pleas and their weeping, Eco remained torn between them throughout his days, never accepting to renounce one or the other. From these two unions were born two irreconcilable clans: one called the Nomos, the other called the Logos, the descendants of Eco.

Each clan claimed to be more worthy of their great common ancestor than the other. Each one said its members alone respected the teachings of Eco while accusing the other of abandoning them. The Eco–Nomos and the Eco–Logos could not sit down at the same table for even a few moments without throwing the crockery at each other. Both clans sought to rule at the other's expense and there was constant bickering and rivalry between them. They simply could not see anything in the same light.

As time went on and as each clan schemed and plotted in order to lord it over the other, one member of the Eco–Nomos grew to remarkable manhood. Day after day, he was proving himself a true hero of the old school, accomplishing one brilliant exploit after another. His people affectionately called him Dev, though his whole name was longer, and he seemed destined to reign over a great part of the world, as it then was.

Meanwhile, a lovely girl had been born into the clan of the Eco–Logos, so beautiful that her people grieved. Yes, they grieved because theirs was a patrilineal, patrilocal society in which a girl is necessarily destined to leave her own clan to join her husband's. She was called Ecosphere and she combined to perfection the four great attributes of her clan: air, water, earth and life (or, as they were sometimes called, atmosphere, hydrosphere, lithosphere and biosphere).

No two beings could have been more different than Dev and Ecosphere. Ecosphere was moved by love, all her endeavours were bent towards preserving harmony between the elements of her nature, air, earth, water and life, to nurturing and sustaining them. Dev, on the other hand, was a man of large appetites and ambitions, always wanting to make everything bigger and better than it was, to harness the water and force the earth to do his will; he insisted that all the elements – and men and women as well – be 'efficiently managed', as he always called it.

These two beings were, in sum, almost caricatures of the feminine and masculine principles and they personified the sharpest contrasts of their clans as well. Dev and the Nomos thought of themselves as active, dynamic, energetic, optimistic – and excellent investors and administrators. Naturally, they saw Ecosphere and the Logos as the opposite of all these qualities – passive, lazy, fearful, pessimistic sticks-in-the-mud, incapable of running anything.

Ecosphere and the Logos saw themselves, rather, as tender, prudent, careful and frugal, as poets and healers with a knowledge of what really made life worth living. As far as they were concerned, Dev and the Nomos were brash, foolish, profligate and downright dangerous.

The least one can say is that Dev and Ecosphere did not seem made for each other. And yet, in both clans, the elders were becoming worried. Among the Nomos, there had recently been some serious setbacks. People were actually daring to revolt against the leadership of the Nomos elders, saying that they didn't have the answer to everything and that they should leave them alone. And some of their favourite undertakings, for example their huge hydro-management projects, were turning out to be nightmares. For the first time, the Nomos and even Dev were not feeling entirely self-confident.

But things weren't altogether well among the Logos either. 'Poetry and beauty are all very well,' many of them were muttering, 'but for one thing life isn't as beautiful and poetic as it used to be; and for another we live in a serious, workaday world and we have to start taking some responsibility for it.'

At last the elders of both the Nomos and the Logos decided there was nothing left to do but to get together. They met, they signed a truce and, as is always the case among rival clans, they determined that their precarious *entente cordiale* should be sealed with a marriage. Dev and Ecosphere would have to wed.

Easier said than done! Both Dev and Ecosphere had minds of their own. All the same, he admitted she was quite, well, attractive and she recognized that he had a certain strength of character, even if he was insufferably macho. The elders could tell matters were progressing and decided it was time to celebrate the engagement. Afterwards, people said they had picked the wrong place, that it was no wonder the wedding didn't come off. At the time, however, Stockholm had seemed an excellent choice, especially fine in the summer. Hundreds of people from all over the world had come to the event and eloquent declarations of intent had been made.

The elders, however, had not taken the fundamentalists into account. On both sides, but especially among the culturally more pugnacious Nomos, some forces refused to yield an inch. They were being sold out, they said, their heritage was being sold down the river, their birthright was being sold for a mess of pottage – they had a whole string of mercantile metaphors to recount their rage. They stirred up the rest of the clan so that finally all agreed that there could and should be no compromises with those weakling, wishy-washy Logos.

Little by little, the carefully designed project lost ground and the marriage of Dev and Ecosphere seemed more remote than ever. Finally, the Nomos and the Logos elders, in desperation, walked in a procession together far into the Northland to visit the High Priestess, who alone might still save the day. Her name was Gro, and she was very wise. She told the elders to return home and wait. She would call a Council and by the deliberations of that Council, the marriage of Dev and Ecosphere might still be salvaged. The elders departed, once again full of hope.

The High Priestess Gro was as good as her word. She brought the priests and priestesses of every clan in 'the world to her Council table and set them to settling the interminable quarrel between the Nomos and the Logos. Everyone there had a preference for one clan or the other, but little by little they drew up a compromise agreement which, this time, seemed ironclad and sure to be accepted by both the Eco–Nomos and the Eco–Logos. And, as generally happens when something which had looked well-nigh impossible suddenly seems to be coming true, hundreds, indeed thousands of well-wishers turned up to say, 'I knew it all the time', 'I told you so', and, 'Of course, you realize they never could have done it without *me*'. Dozens of similar mini-Councils were held throughout the world.

Now everyone was in on the affair. Everyone, too, had an opinion on the subject of the Dev–Ecosphere wedding and was trying to make it heard above the others. People were making a terrific din and jostling each other, usually siding with one clan or the other in the final negotiation, which was to be concluded by the signature of the marriage contract.

Then, unexpectedly, a pall fell: the negotiations were said to be breaking down. The bridegroom was insisting that his bride-to-be change her name. Not just her clan name, but her given name as well. He insisted that Ecosphere was a name straight out of the ivory tower, just the sort those dreamy Logos would choose: he wanted something more down-to-earth and practical, like Environment. Development (which was his full name) and Environment, or even Environment and Development – he was willing to make a concession and let her go first – sounded right together, whereas Development and Ecosphere sounded completely idiotic.

Now Ecosphere wasn't getting any younger – it had already been nearly twenty years since the first attempt to get her to the altar with Dev had been sabotaged after Stockholm – and her clan encouraged her to give in. 'You might as well,' they said. 'What have you got to lose?' They pressed her to make up her mind and to remove this final obstacle to the much-desired match, especially since all kinds of people were lining up, begging to be allowed to contribute something to her dowry. Finally Ecosphere said yes, because secretly she really wanted to get married and was afraid if she refused to change her name, Dev would find someone else and she would be left out in the cold, an old maid.

At last the triumphant elders were able to name the date and the place for the wedding. This time they were careful to choose a venue where the weather was sure to be glorious and the ambience festive – Rio de Janeiro. The invitations went out *urbi et orbi* for June 1992.

Absolutely everyone came. It was an enormous happening and it lasted ten days. Those who could not be there in person were able to watch the festivities on their screens every evening. The Nomos clan somehow got the best seats. They were ecstatic – all their most important members were present, including the chief executive officers of fifty mighty global corporations and the presidents of many nations as well.

The Logos complained that they had been excluded from the main events and forced to settle for second-best, in far-away fora; but the Nomos said 'Nonsense' and told them not to worry – nobody was a Nomos or a Logos any longer: everyone was *both* and the radiant couple, Environment and Development, was there to prove it. But the Logos weren't at all sure – they kept trying to attract attention to their own concerns but all the television people were otherwise engaged. So the Logos thought they might as well try to throw themselves into the spirit of the wedding and they danced the samba night after night, at some distance from the rest of the guests.

Stories used to end 'And they lived happily ever after'. But this is a post-modern story and it doesn't. In fact, no one knows for sure now exactly which way it will go, or what new turns it might take. The sad fact is that almost immediately after the wedding decorations had been taken down in Rio, Dev and Env began quarrelling. They have had a child too, christened Sustainable – not a pretty name and another of Dev's ideas – but the child has not cemented the marriage – quite the contrary. Environment has grown more and more melancholy. She feels she was wrong to give up her lovely name Ecosphere because somehow the ideals of harmony, beauty and balance seem to have flown away with it. Her husband has reverted to type and instead of valuing and cherishing her for herself, wants only to manage her and make her conform to his way of doing everything.

Still, he is her husband and she is constantly torn between her love for him and nostalgia for her childhood and for the values of her clan, for the way the Logos used to be. She fears that Dev's clan, the Nomos, never really changed at all and were only using her, so they could have one more domain to run, to direct, to manipulate.

She sees them taking over her child as well and feels helpless to prevent it. The last we heard, she had been taken to hospital, suffering from acute depression. The poor thing is clearly not herself just now but perhaps if she finds the right therapy and the right therapist, a cure is possible and she still has a chance to live with Dev, happily ever after.

Chapter IX

Intellectual Leadership and the H Street Heretics

I once asked [the Administrator of the Research Advisory Staff] about what he thought the burning issues facing the Bank in 10 years' time would be. 'That's an easy question,' he answered. 'We're consistently about 10 years behind the times. Therefore just look at the issues that are "hot" in the US and Western Europe now – those are the ones that will be "hot" in the Bank in 5 or 10 years' time.'

Internal Bank memo from the Chief of the Water and Sanitation Division to the Deputy Director of the Environment Department, 4 March 1993

The blueprint for the Bank's 1987 Reorganization (see Chapter VI) refers repeatedly to the intellectual challenge the Bank faces, to the Bank as a 'knowledge-based institution' and to its duty to provide 'intellectual leadership'. The authors call on the Bank's senior management to make 'intellectual leadership in the development field' their top priority – the equivalent of new product development for a high-tech company. Identifying major questions confronting the Bank, they ask, 'Is the Bank providing the intellectual and moral leadership in development issues that is expected of it?'[1]

The Bank's close attention to its intellectual role, stature and reputation is understandable, considering its claims to have the answers to the practical problems of development in the field. It follows that the theoretical underpinnings of its practice should be solid and its intellectual work of high calibre. We will argue here that despite its pretensions to excellence, the Bank is not only sadly behind the times, as its research administrator humorously (or perhaps cynically?) admits in the above remark, but is also wary of – even hostile to – ideas that contradict its own preconceptions. It cannot therefore create a climate conducive to intellectual leadership.

At the end of the chapter, we outline briefly the contributions of the 'H Street Heretics', who, from obscure offices in the Bank's environment department, have quietly laid the foundations for a much-needed theoretical renewal, of which their employer has, so far, taken absolutely no notice.

If money could buy intellectual leadership, then the Bank should be the front-runner. The sheer weight of its research presence, especially in economics, broadly defined, is daunting. Its designated research budget in 1991 was three and a half per cent of the administrative budget (about $22 million) but when the money spent on economic analysis, policy and sector work by the central research department and the geographic or technical departments is added, the annual outlay is closer to $150 million.[2]

The Bank's researchers number in the hundreds. Since they are spread throughout the organization and are not all full time, they cannot be quantified precisely. Permanent staff plus consultants in 1991 produced 450 formal Bank publications and 176 journal articles, plus a further 220 informal working papers of which about half eventually appeared as articles, symposia contributions, book chapters, and so on. Included in the informal publications category are twenty-seven different series of sector working papers – in agriculture, environment, energy, trade, et cetera. The Bank also publishes two journals: the *World Bank Economic Review* and the *World Bank Research Observer*.[3]

Quantity aside, the Bank's strength, but ultimately its weakness as well, derives from its homogeneity. Unlike any university, institute or independent think-tank, it can cover the development waterfront so massively that virtually no intellectual space remains for serious inquiry outside the boundaries it sets. The Bank necessarily tends to dominate the literature and the debate in several areas. In so doing, however, it risks sterility, avoiding the kind of critical thought, exposure to harsh light and confrontation with unfamiliar or unfashionable ideas which could help it to advance. To make the point differently, in a human community, if intermarriage is the rule and no fertilization from outside gene pools takes place, the result is physical and mental degeneracy. The same holds true for intellectually homogeneous institutions.

Furthermore, the Bank's practice constrains its theory as much as the other way around. If a particular set of practical economic measures is preferred, indeed insisted upon, then the Bank cannot, intellectually speaking, take into account, much less integrate, the criticism of people like Colin Stoneman (Chapter III) or Stuart Holland (Chapter IV) showing that its economic approach is static and dated. Like medieval doctors, the Bank's intellectual workers have built up an astonishing *corpus* of theological commentary in economics and related fields but research is not encouraged (i.e. is not paid for) outside the accepted doctrine.

A substantial portion of the Bank's research relates to its project areas (water, energy, agriculture, et cetera). Although we do not believe that so-called technical work is ever undertaken in an ideological and political vacuum, we make no attempt to deal with this part of the Bank's production. More characteristic of its public profile is its vast output on economic and policy subjects. The annual *World Development Report* alone is typically distributed in 120,000 copies and is doubtless the world's most widely-read publication in the field of development.

The Bank's research output influences academics and their students, certainly, but our main reason for discussing it here is its performative nature, in the sense of the grammatical performative mode. When God says, 'Let there be light', there is light. When the king says, 'Off with their heads', the executioner swings into action. When Joe or Jane Bloggs says the same things, nothing happens.

Similarly, the work of independent Joe or Jane Researcher dealing with questions of power, even if demonstrably true, rarely alters the reality of power relations (as the present authors are in a good position to attest). But when the Bank decides to take up a given issue and massively commissions work on it, its publications speak in the performative mode and the Bank is in a particularly advantageous position subsequently to claim that research supports whatever policies it has decided to implement. One scholar calls this capacity the intellectual–financial complex. His own illustration is the Bank's growing hegemony over education policy in developing countries but the institution is also capable of setting the agenda in any number of other fields.[4]

The Bank indubitably holds the reins of this intellectual–financial complex in development research. It not only chooses the topics and the scholars (and pays them generously) but also 'specifies the types of research that it will regard as legitimate and capable of generating valid results'. Critical peer review is absent; 'limited, tentative and partial findings' are all too easily ennobled as fact. As a result:

> Research that would not withstand broad exposure and critical examination entrenches selected approaches and methods, filters explanations and legitimizes particular courses of action. At the same time, research whose approach is at odds with the prevailing style is readily rejected. Orthodoxy masquerades as pluralism.[5]

We saw in Chapter IV that despite its serried ranks of economists the Bank was unable to spot major economic trends and consequently to give its borrowers worthwhile advice. The Bank has lagged behind in several major areas of enquiry and with few exceptions has proved to be an intellectual under-achiever, as an authoritative overview by Professor Nicholas Stern, then of the London School of Economics, now chief economist at the European Bank for Reconstruction and Development, makes clear.[6]*

---

* Nicholas Stern's paper is to appear in the Bank's official fiftieth-anniversary history (publication expected sometime in 1996). In 1968, the Bank called upon the Brookings Institution in Washington to chronicle its first twenty-five years. Edward S. Mason and Robert E. Asher led this project, publishing *The World Bank Since Bretton Woods* in 1973. The Bank again commissioned Brookings for its half-century history, a $2 million project to which the Bank is contributing one-fourth. Richard Webb and John Lewis are writing Volume I, an overview. Volume II is a collection of essays examining the Bank from various angles and geographical perspectives, of which Professor Stern's paper on 'The Bank as "Intellectual Actor"', which he most generously supplied to us in draft, is one. According to a Bank memo, 'The history team works with complete independence ... [with full access to Bank documents] ... Prior to publication the Bank will be given an opportunity to review and comment on the completed manuscript; the Bank will have the right to require revision or deletion of material which would disclose confidential information with seriously adverse effects on the Bank's relationship with member countries or its ability to perform its functions'. As the reader will probably agree having read our ample citations of his chapter, it is much to Stern's credit to have been so frank in a Bank-sponsored project, as it will be much to the Bank's if it publishes his paper as it stands in its official history. (Quotes in this note from World Bank Memo, 'History of the World Bank Group: Recent Developments', SecM93–177, 28 February 1993.)

Stern's study is highly valuable for anyone who wants to know in detail how the Bank's intellectual–financial complex has responded to events in the outside world as well as to its own internal economic and political agenda. Whereas this agenda in the 1950s and 1960s centred on 'growth through industrialization and import substitution, with the government playing a central role in the process', and in the 1970s hewed closer to McNamara's absolute poverty concerns, stressing 'targets and means to achieve the targets', by the 1980s, structural adjustment had become pivotal.[7]

Being a leader doesn't necessarily mean that the cause one is leading is morally just – a fair observation since the authors of the 1987 Reorganization blueprint, cited above, themselves ask if the 'Bank is providing the intellectual and *moral* leadership in development issues that is expected of it'. The Bank's intellectual work in the 1980s certainly furnished what the Reagan and Bush administrations 'expected of it'; its moral leadership is another matter. As Stern says, 'It was during the 1980s and on this topic [structural adjustment] that the Bank was seen to be "leading the charge" of the neo-classical resurgence'.[8]

Certainly the Bank put adjustment and all its associated measures (tying national economies more closely to world markets, 'getting the prices right', et cetera) at the centre of its intellectual concerns – and thus put those same concerns very much on the map elsewhere. In this sense one can say that the Bank exercised leadership. Professor Stern none the less remarks,

> The Bank's record on structural adjustment since 1982 is not, however, one of unrelieved glory. Its attention to equity issues from 1982 to the end of the decade appears to be somewhat token . . . The costs of adjustment for the poor can be very high . . . and McNamara's warnings in his 1980 speech on the need to take account of the poor in the adjustment process do not seem to have been consistently heeded within the Bank.[9]

The Bank is not without intellectual strengths. Stern cites as examples its cross-country analyses of the determinants of growth (it had more in-house expertise and more data than anybody else); poverty alleviation mechanisms (at least during the McNamara years); and more specific topics such as China, urban problems, agriculture, transport and taxation. He also gives high marks to its individual country reports – at least the more confidential, less bowdlerized among them, where the authors are speaking frankly. On the other side of the ledger, however, 'There have been subjects on which the Bank has followed the [development economics] profession only very slowly . . . debt, the environment and cost-benefit analysis'.[10]

Stern underlines (as we did in Chapter IV) how vastly wide of the mark were the Bank's debt forecasts in the 1980s. As for the environment,

> The Bank also has often appeared to respond to environmental issues only reluctantly, seeing them as political irritants that get in the way of making project loans . . . the subject was one of intense interest both academically and politically for a decade or two before the Bank became involved.[11]

So much for leadership on the environment. As for cost–benefit analysis, given that the Bank has always been a project institution, it might have been expected to excel, but once again its culture gets in the way. The primary practical goal is invariably to get the money out the door and as Stern says,

> In these circumstances, careful appraisal is regarded as a distracting interference rather than as a crucial and productive input. Serious cost–benefit analysis takes time and analytical resources of quality and is therefore seen as both managerially irritating and costly.[12]

Everyone in the development field (including us) cites the numbers in the Bank's *World Development Report* tables, but we should be exercising more prudence because these figures turn out to be frequently unreliable. Stern, basing his view on evidence compiled by Professor T.N. Srinivasan, concludes that:

> Many of the numbers come from highly dubious sources or have been constructed in ways which leave one skeptical as to whether they can helpfully be used . . . Given its unusual position, the Bank could have been a much stronger leader here in terms of appropriate caution and discussion of the presentation of the data, in the

development of superior systems and in the cross-country analysis.[13]

Aside from their faulty tables, what about the body of the annual *World Development Reports*, the Bank's best-known and most widely disseminated publication? These, according to Stern, have never sought to be 'innovative intellectual statements in their own right'; their aim has been, rather, to 'bring to the reader an understanding of available contributions to a particular topic' and in this they have 'succeeded rather well'.*

Even so, still according to Stern, their 'documentation has fallen far short of that which would be acceptable in a scholarly publication' and since they must avoid offending politicians in any member country, they display 'a pervasive weakness on matters of political economy'. Even work which has no path-breaking pretensions can still, says Stern, 'show real bite, insight, perspective and judgement'. Alas, 'the *WDRs* have rarely, if ever, risen to this level'.[14]

A striking example of the orthodoxy-masquerading-as-pluralism syndrome and the less-than-scholarly character of the *WDRs* was encountered by David Woodward, who has studied the impact of structural adjustment on health.[15]

Coincidentally, the Bank's 1993 *World Development Report* also centres on health.[16] Only two pages of text (of 171) in this *WDR* are devoted to the impact of the Bank's own structural adjustment policies on health budgets and human welfare. This limited space (including what Woodward calls a 'very misleading graph') is in itself revealing, given that UNICEF and many others have documented how harmful this impact has been.[17] In this brief section of the *WDR*, the Bank concludes that while health spending declined everywhere in the developing world in the early 1980s, it 'recovered much faster in countries with adjustment programs'.[18]

As Woodward observes, the *WDR*'s bibliography for this section (even though it does not include UNICEF) gives the impression

---

* On 'available contributions', particularly if they dissent from the Bank's views, we would be less sanguine than Stern: see the experience of David Woodward described below.

that its conclusions are based on a 'very impressive list' of a dozen or so research publications, comparative country studies, et cetera. On closer examination, however, one finds that:

> All but one of these were produced by or for the Bank or were written by past or present members of the Bank staff or by consultants regularly used by the Bank. The one exception is my book, which is in fact completely ignored by the text and which was included in the list only after I had pointed out that all the references in the earlier draft were directly connected with the Bank.[19]

This is a good example of research capacity – and spending – used to create a false impression of consensus on a given topic (particularly one in which the Bank has a vested interest) and to shore up homogeneity. David Woodward's own research on behalf of Save the Children or the Institute of Child Health in London comes to quite different conclusions from those of the Bank. He and other dissenting scholars like him remain free to publish – but who can believe that their work will have the same audience, or be cited as often, as the Bank's *World Development Report?*

Another peril for intellectual rigour is the Bank's unquestioned status as the pre-eminent employer of consultants in the development field, a state of affairs coinciding with the much greater dependency of academics, university departments and development institutes on income from consultancy work. We can think of at least three past critics of the Bank's adjustment policies whose views became more muted just as their names began appearing on Bank research publications. The direct involvement of so many academics in Bank-funded work is incompatible with a healthy intellectual debate and with pluralism. It would seem that if you can't sell consensus on some issues, you can, arguably, buy it.

Nicholas Stern's final appraisal of the Bank's intellectual leadership is tempered if somewhat weary:

> [A]fter more than 20 years with a research establishment its role as an intellectual creator has been a modest one. Whilst taking due account of its objectives, internal structures and external pressures, one cannot suppress the feeling that rather more might have been achieved.[20]

Why should the Bank with its hundreds of in-house Ph.D.s, access to the excellent minds of a full array of consultants and a multimillion dollar research budget end up such a 'modest' intellectual creator? One is first tempted to answer that all that cash and security are bad for the brain – as Lord Rutherford, in charge of British science policy immediately after the Second World War, told his staff, 'We haven't the money so we'll have to think'. But this doesn't explain much. When it comes to promoting the spirit of free and fearless enquiry – surely the essence of intellectual leadership – the Bank isn't just a nice warm cocoon but a structured and suffocating hothouse where, as Professor Stern again explains:

> Researchers are not free to follow intellectual inspiration. They are under constraints of designated priorities . . . Further, there is quite a strong hierarchy and the atmosphere is much more deferential than one would find in universities. There is an understandable concern with what superiors will think of conclusions.[21]

Take that paragraph out of context and it describes perfectly the conditions under which intellectual enquiry would take place in the Pontifical Academy (where paradoxically there might well be rather *more* freedom) or in one of the numerous Soviet research institutes in the heyday of centralized Party control.

Another explanation for its failure to attain intellectual prominence is the symbiosis between the Bank's academic agenda and the foreign policy concerns of the United States with regard to the South during the 1980s (including the Baker and the Brady Plans for dealing with third world debt, in which the Bank played a practical, financial role). Such unswerving intellectual support for an external agenda is troubling to anyone who believes that the job of the social scientist is not to shore up the powerful but to expose them and the mechanisms of their power. But even without introducing the constraints brought to bear by outside forces, the Bank in-house is not well placed to avoid a sterilizing uniformity.

The research staff it recruits and the consultants it hires are overwhelmingly trained in the same macroeconomics curriculum, in the same American or British institutions, to think in the same ways. Their perspective is then reinforced and rewarded, with money, publication and prestige, by the Bank. They are trapped inside the glass walls of their own world-view and led to believe that theirs is a monopoly on truth. Once you are working within the comfortable confines of those walls, as the invaluable Nicholas Stern again observes, 'opposition can be regarded as misguided, uneducated or malevolent'.[22]

During the 1990s, according to its 1993 *Annual Report*, the Bank intends to apply its research capacity to the priority areas of 'poverty, equity and social-welfare issues, with a growing emphasis on environmental analysis and human resources development', whereas 'attention to the more "mature" topics – structural adjustment, debt and trade – has declined'.[23]

Is the Bank better equipped to exercise leadership on these currently fashionable issues than it was in other decades, on other topics, now considered 'mature'? In the domain of 'poverty, equity and social welfare', we have our doubts and fear that once more the constraints of the Bank's culture will thwart its ambitions to intellectual excellence. It's not just that the pressure to keep spinning money is likely to supersede careful social cost–benefit analysis – more profoundly, the Bank's philosophical view of poverty and equity issues is not conducive to the kind of deep knowledge that could lead to corrective action in the field.

One of McNamara's more pernicious legacies to the Bank was to wed indissolubly the concept of poverty and the numbers approach. First of all, even quantitatively speaking, there are myriad ways to measure the numbers of the poor and each method is grounded in its own (often unexamined) ideological pre-suppositions. For example, two recent estimates of the numbers of the 'absolutely' or 'extremely' poor worldwide differ by a factor of nearly 600 million people. Who is to arbitrate between the Bank's estimate of 630 million and the Worldwatch Institute's 1,225 million?[24]

Perhaps it doesn't matter, since poverty can also be measured not absolutely but relative to any number of criteria – national poverty lines, dollar or parity purchasing power, access to standardized commodity baskets, ownership of land or other assets and a whole gamut of other cash-and-kind yardsticks.

Such questions could and should be the subject for an entire, separate volume: all we can reasonably do here is to point out that poverty is not so much a *condition* – which is how the Bank has perceived it ever since McNamara – as a *relationship*; first and foremost a relationship to those who are *not* poor, but also to the state, to legal and social frameworks of individual and collective rights, to local, family or other solidarity networks, to the world economy, and so on. Poverty is not simply a state of greater or lesser individual deprivation but an expression of one's relative place in a given society and one's access to a range of material and non-material goods and services. This is why a great contemporary economist like Amartya Sen refers in all his work to rights and entitlements and speaks of hunger and famine – which afflict only the poor – as 'failures of entitlement'.[25]

The Bank, dependent as it is on the good will of its richest and most powerful members and unwilling to offend the élites of its borrowing countries, is not in a good position to examine poverty in its relationship to wealth, to the state, to power structures of all kinds. Proper social science research, especially on subjects like poverty, *should* be offensive to some – otherwise the scholar hasn't done work worth doing. Since 1988 the Bank has no longer even published income distribution figures in the tables of the *World Development Report*; not, we suspect, because such figures are impossible to come by, but because they would show that the rich are getting richer, especially in countries long under structural adjustment, whereas the poor are losing the little they had.[26]

Outside of vaguely promoting growth (actually sustainable growth, whatever that is) the Bank has no particular plans for improving the lives of the poor, even assuming it can figure out who they are. It is arithmetically impossible, for example, to provide a livelihood for large and growing numbers of poor people arriving on the labour market every year with standard, Western, growth-dependent job-creation tools, when the creation of a single job costs a minimum of $30, 000. The Bank wants foreign direct investment (from transnational corporations) to reward structural adjustment, but does not seem to have noticed that TNCs destroy far more jobs than they create.

It knows next to nothing about labour-intensive production which its projects have frequently discouraged, nor about the informal sector where the poor create their own jobs. When it talks about the private sector – as it constantly does – the Bank is stuck in the capital-intensive, management paradigm of its Part I countries. The institution is also overwhelmingly peopled by macroeconomists, who are not the finest connoisseurs of what goes on at the microlevel, where the poor, concretely, live and move and have their being.[27]

The Bank is also ill-favoured to reduce poverty, sustainably or otherwise, so long as it remains ideologically and even technically unable to assess honestly the impact of its own projects and policies on the poor. Environmental impact assessments – flawed though they may be – are at least required for many projects. Social impact assessments are not. Since mid-1993 there is some evidence that the Bank intends to develop a set of social indicators to measure the human impact of its projects, but these are apparently not to be applied beyond social sector loans (health, education, and the like) which account for a mere thirteen per cent of Bank lending. The other eighty-seven per cent would apparently be assumed to have no social impact, which is clearly absurd.[28]

Nobody, including the Bank, even knows exactly where the poor are. Intuitively, one imagines they are concentrated in ecologically threatened, fragile or marginal environments, but no overlapping distributional maps exist to prove it.[29]

If the Bank does not develop a credible methodology to monitor the impact of its classic project loans and its structural adjustment policies on the poor, it cannot expect to have its overarching objective of poverty reduction – much less its intellectual leadership – taken seriously. Does it plan to get the necessary information about the poor directly from its people in the field? This task is not necessarily within the capacity of present staff, one of whom confided to a reporter from the *Guardian*,

> It [poverty assessment] is another burden on our shoulders when we lack resources, which will mean a half-hearted effort. We'll take a quick trip to a poor neighbourhood and collect a few statistics to show that something is being done.[30]

Above all, the Bank has to recognize that the rich and powerful – including most of the people who arrange for the Bank's missions to be met at the airport – are not on the whole interested in sacrificing anything for the poor. If the Bank continues to respect (and to hide behind) 'the wishes of its sovereign borrowers' in this regard, it hasn't a prayer of arresting or reducing poverty. The Bank may seek to brush off this fundamental contradiction, which since the McNamara days it has refused to face, by telling us that rising tides of growth will lift all boats. However, as is by now well known, without some protection from storms, smaller and weaker boats get swamped and sink and rising tides in one place imply ebbing tides somewhere else. If the Bank is serious, perhaps its new self-conferred powers of governance can be used here to good effect.

The 1993 *Annual Report* declares that in addition to poverty and equity issues its research agenda will favour 'a growing emphasis on environmental analysis'. This is excellent news; still we wonder what sort of environmental analysis is meant. Max Planck said, 'A new truth does not triumph by convincing its opponents and making them see the light, but rather because its opponents eventually die, and a new generation grows up that is familiar with it'.[31]

This is precisely the situation we face with regard to the Bank's intellectual attitude towards the environment. Without calling openly for anyone's demise – Planck's Law notwithstanding – we introduce here the H Street Heretics who represent a long-shot hope for the Bank's intellectual and practical future.

Some years back, the President of Brazil invited Prince Charles and Bank President Barber Conable to accompany him for a cruise on the Amazon River aboard the presidential yacht. Conable, otherwise engaged, declined. A telegram shot back from the President's office: 'Then please send Herman Daly'. People who know the pecking order of the Bank find this story funny because the hierarchical space between the President and Daly approximated the distance between Earth and Neptune.

Daly, an outstanding environmental economist, stayed at the Bank for six years. With his colleagues, particularly Robert Goodland and Salah el-Serafy, he tried with patience and unfailing good humour to show the Bank why its economic world-view was archaic and inoperative in the late twentieth century.

Environmentalists see the pursuit of economic growth – based as it so often is on the destruction of natural capital – as worse than mindless: suicidal. Gross national product is a fallacious measurement of welfare – you can increase it by having a nice big oil spill, or better still, a war. GNP improves when we treat the skin cancers people get because of the depletion of the ozone layer (destroyed by CFC production which also increased the GNP), and so on. Development as currently practised is, in their view, liquidating our natural assets and orthodox economics is powerless even to describe what is happening, much less halt the damage. Orthodoxy says the market will take care of the earth – environmentalists reject this claim as fraudulent in a short-term, profit-oriented economy. The market does not give a value to a species facing extinction. The cost of runaway global warming could be infinite, but the market is never going to tell us to stop contributing to it, or only when it is too late.[32] The market may be reasonably efficient at setting prices but it can tell us almost nothing about costs, particularly the longer-term ones.

Daly and his colleagues argue that we have passed a turning point in human history and are now living in a 'full' world. Imagine the world's economy as a rectangular box, with sharp corners. The activities it contains necessarily take place in the biosphere whose capacity and finite size cannot be increased by a single cubic centimetre, whatever our technological ingenuity. This economy is dipping liberally into all the resources of the biosphere, processing them in its box and discarding the wastes – heat, pollution, et cetera – into the biosphere as well. A hundred years ago, the size of the box relative to the confines of the sphere was so small that human activity made little difference. Today, however, the size of this activity is growing exponentially and the economic throughput, as Daly calls it, is drawing ever more heavily on both the sources and the sinks the biosphere affords. The sharp corners of the box are inching towards the fragile membrane of the sphere, and like all bubbles, this one can also burst.

The stress humans place on the environment can be described by the simple equation: Impact = Population × Consumption × Technology. Those who blame the poor for degrading the environment generally fail to notice that while Population may be the crucial factor in the South, a rich OECD citizen's Consumption (for example, of energy) is at least twenty times greater than that of a poor person. Impact can be limited by improving Technology (using fewer resources or creating less waste per unit of Consumption) but this is a race environmentalists believe we are losing. In any event, in 1990, world economic throughput had grown more than twenty-fold since the turn of the century – in other words, a $20 trillion global economy produced as much in seventeen days as was produced in the entire year 1900.[33] If development means generalizing the Northern model of consumption to the South, we are all done for because the sphere will shatter.

Daly and his colleagues argue that whereas man-made capital used to be the scarce, or limiting factor, *natural* capital is from now on the scarce resource. Put more graphically, it doesn't matter how many sawmills you have if there are no more trees, nor how many fishing vessels if the fish stocks are depleted. This is why counting natural capital as income (see Chapter VIII) is unforgivably stupid in purely economic terms.

Herman Daly gave a farewell lecture when he left the Bank in January 1994. We draw upon it here, much abridged, for the excellent advice he bequeathed to his colleagues. These 'Daly principles' are still considered heretical in ordinary Bank thought and practice.[34]

Stop counting the consumption of natural capital as income. Income is by definition the maximum amount that a society can consume this year and still be able to consume the same amount next year. Sustainability will ensue if income is properly defined. If not, it won't. Revenues from exports of non-renewable resources should not be counted as income. Applying this principle would drastically change not just national accounts but also the calculation of user costs and balance of payments accounting (many countries that think they are in the black would be seriously in the red if they counted their non-renewable resources properly).

Tax labour and income less and tax throughput more. This recommendation is based on the common-sense principle that we should tax what we want less of (pollution, waste, depletion) and not tax what we want more of, e.g. jobs. But 'the present signal to firms is to shed labour and substitute more capital and resource throughput, to the extent feasible'.[35]

Maximize the productivity of natural capital in the short run and invest in increasing its supply in the long run. This brings us back to the 'limiting factor' argument. The fish catch is limited not by the number of boats but by the number of fish remaining in the sea and their capacity to reproduce faster than they are caught. The capacity of the atmosphere to absorb CO_2 and other greenhouse gases may be much more limiting than anybody knows. We can't create non-renewable natural capital (if we could it wouldn't be natural but man-made capital) but we can invest in renewables, reduce our rates of depletion and improve throughput efficiency. The above-noted taxes would encourage this.

Move away from the ideology of global economic integration by free trade and export-led growth and towards a more nationalist orientation that seeks to develop national production for internal markets as the first option, having recourse to international trade only when clearly much more efficient. This is the ultimate heresy, the completely-at-odds position. Daly is anti-free (that is, deregulated) trade; the Bank was a front-line defender of GATT. Daly believes in production and consumption based on local and national markets first; the Bank wants maximum integration into world markets and export-led growth. These are articles of faith.

Daly, to the contrary, sees global competitiveness, in whose name these doctrines are preached, as a competition to lower wages and standards, including environmental standards, and to export ever-increasing amounts of natural capital at bargain basement prices. The Bank is supposed to exist to serve national communities, that is, nation states. 'It has no charter to serve the cosmopolitan vision of global integration – of converting many relatively independent national economies, loosely dependent on international trade, into one tightly integrated world economic network upon which the weakened nations depend even for basic survival'. In such a cosmopolitan system, there are no mechanisms to defend the common good. We have no world government (nor, probably, do we want one) to regulate global capital in the global interest – all we have are fast-eroding nation states.

Daly is an economist in the eighteenth-century tradition of political economy, when men like Adam Smith or Thomas Malthus considered themselves moral philosophers and recognized that there is no such thing as pure economics without social and political dimensions. Should the Bank one day recognize this as well and welcome heresy as an escape from its present mediocrity, it may yet be able to claim intellectual leadership.

Chapter X

Ruling the Realm

Washington is not a city of skyscrapers. Though the Bank operates at eighteen different addresses, none of its buildings rises more than thirteen floors. Nor do Bank people seem prone to superstition: here, an office on the thirteenth floor is the best of all bureaucratic omens. Though many important Bank people are housed lower down, the commanding heights of the eleventh to thirteenth floors are irreverently referred to by lesser mortals as the 'Nosebleed Zone'. In these altitudes dwell not just the President and his immediate subordinates, the three managing directors (twelfth floor), but most of the executive directors, or EDs as they are usually called.

A board of governors (usually the finance minister or central bank governor of each member country) formally administers the Bank. The governors come together only in the spring and especially at the jamboree Bank–Fund annual general meeting in the autumn. With 176 member countries as of 1993, their numbers would guarantee cumbersome decision-making at best and their role is thus less to decide than to assent.

Most of the governors' powers are delegated to twenty-four executive directors who make up the Bank's board and who are supposed to be in charge of the direction of Bank policy. They work full-time at the Bank out of vast, handsome and commodious office suites to fulfil the Articles of Agreement which prescribe that: 'The Executive Directors shall function in continuous session at the principal office of the Bank and shall meet as often as the business of the Bank may require'.[1] The Bank, not their home governments, pays their salaries.

We say the direction of Bank policy is 'supposed' to be in their hands because there is some doubt they are really in charge. Some matters are statutorily out of bounds – the directors cannot expel a member of the Bank or 'decide to suspend permanently the operations of the Bank and to distribute its assets'.[2] But the formal limits are not the only constraints on the powers of the EDs. The dominant internal view at the Bank on how best to deal with the Board is often summed up as the Mushroom Principle: 'Feed them shit and keep them in the dark'. More on this in a moment.

Because voting strength in the Bank is proportional to subscribed capital shares, the United States has always had the most votes. The five EDs representing the Bank's major shareholders, the US, Japan, Germany, the UK and France, are appointed by their governments. In the old days they could command a majority by themselves, with the US grandly voting nearly a quarter of the capital stock. As the Bank has grown, the power of the Big Five has been diluted; in 1993 they controlled thirty-nine per cent of the votes.[3] In contrast, one of the African EDs represents twenty-one countries casting a mere 2.19 per cent of the votes; the other represents twenty-three countries with an insignificant 1.64 per cent – the smallest share to be voted by anyone on the board.

Aside from the Big Five, the other directors represent groups of countries and are elected (by the governors) as opposed to appointed. The country in the group with the most shares often names one of its nationals as ED or the job may be rotated among the larger members. Saudi Arabia and China both have EDs who are nominally elected, but each represents only itself on the board. A board member is elected or appointed for two years renewable, with no assigned limit to the number of terms. In 1993, the longest serving member had been on the board for nine years.

Country groups usually make geographical or linguistic sense (but usually not both!). Spain surely feels at home with the six Central American countries, plus Mexico and Venezuela. One could stretch a point for the Philippines, the single Asian lumped with the Central Americans – at least it used to be colonized by the same people as the Dominican Republic. One hopes for his sake that the Canadian ED has need for frequent winter consultations in the eleven Commonwealth Caribbean island states he represents (as well as Ireland). It is not clear why Ghana, alone among African nations and not particularly Muslim, should be grouped with

Afghanistan, Iran, Pakistan and three North African countries. Other traces of political horse-trading are visible.

When the Bank opened for business, its Articles specified twelve directors; their numbers gradually grew to twenty-two. By 1993 there were twenty-four: the earthquake in the former Soviet Union added a new chair for Russia and when the Swiss finally decided to become a member of the Bank in a hotly contested referendum in 1991 they got a seat on the board as part of the deal. The Swiss ED also votes for Poland and the central Asian republics of the former USSR. The rest of the Soviet break-up added countries to the portfolios of the Netherlands and the Nordic directors.[4]

Legally, the 'Executive Directors shall select a President' – in fact, the US director informs his board colleagues of his government's choice and that person, 'by tradition', gets the job. The President of the Bank is *ex officio* chair of the board. The IMF across the street is always headed by a European.

The Bank's executive directors are virtually unknown even in their home countries yet shoulder great responsibilities. They approve all the Bank's loans, whether from the IBRD (including structural adjustment loans) or grants from the IDA. They also approve Bank policy; anything that ultimately becomes part of the canon – environmental or poverty directives, for example – must first get past the board and may occasionally originate there.

Since the EDs also determine the Bank's budget, they could theoretically orient the use of staff and resources in new directions if they chose to do so. The operations evaluations department, charged with assessing the performance and impact of Bank projects and programmes, reports directly to them. And like all boards, this one has final responsibility for the accounts.

Is an executive director of the World Bank a person of advanced years, wisdom and *gravitas*, drowsing at the eventide of a distinguished career, rather like the caricature of a director of one of the more venerable British banks? If the title evokes this image, the reality is different: most EDs are impressively competent, patently workaholics and relatively young.

Dynamic and distinguished as its individual members may be, the board is not necessarily the appropriate group to steer an institution which, after a long hiatus, has declared a renewed interest in the poor and the 'overarching objective' of sustainable poverty reduction. If this really is its mission, getting the Bank into the twenty-first century in one piece will require characteristics significantly different from – or at least additional to – those dominant among board members in 1993.*

Sociologically speaking, and despite twenty-four different nationalities, the EDs have a surprising amount in common. Most are about as old as the Bank itself – two-thirds of those serving in 1993 were born in the 1940s – and have thus lived their lives in the shadow of the Cold War, tending collectively to reflect what Henry Luce and *Time* magazine called the American Century.

Although there is only one American board member, half his colleagues received all or part of their education in the United States. They generally have top academic credentials, Ph.D.s or the equivalent. Although there is one diplomat, one agricultural engineer and even one chemist (the UK ED, who seems very quickly to have dropped his test tubes for higher and higher positions in H.M. Treasury), World Bank directors are almost always economists and finance specialists.

With the sole exceptions of the Bush administration's American appointee and the Canadian director, both of whom came from private investment banking and departed the Bank in 1993, EDs are career civil servants and administrators. Before coming to the Bank they had accumulated vast collective experience in matters of trade, foreign exchange, credit, taxation, budgeting, economic planning, debt negotiations, exchange rates and monetary policy. Ten have taught at university level and several boast impressive lists of scholarly publications in economics.

Half the EDs also share prior experience of the Bretton Woods Institutions. Some served as alternate (deputy) directors for the same country group they now serve as EDs; others occupied top

---

* The following analysis is based on the *Biographic Statements* supplied by the EDs to the Bank and to us by the Bank Information Center in Washington. Our sample is the EDs on the board in the spring of 1993. It thus provides a snapshot, not a film, but we doubt that the previous (or for that matter future) sociological composition of the board was or will be notably different. When we ran it by someone who served as an assistant in an ED's office from 1986 to 1988, he found it a fair description for that period.

administrative or policy positions in the Bank itself. In other words, these two dozen people speak the local language and understand, frequently from the inside and from long experience, the local culture. They cannot be bluffed or put down by the Bank's Harvard and Oxbridge squads because they've been there themselves. In an institution notorious for its supercilious attitude towards non-members of the club, this has to be a plus.

In addition to similar academic and professional backgrounds, thirteen of the twenty-four directors come from OECD countries – or fourteen, counting the Russian, from the North. Geographic origin does not prevent anyone from holding strong convictions regarding poverty, the environment, social equity and the like – or if so, the present authors should be disqualified on similar grounds. The fact remains that (at least in 1993) directors who are not native to the Bank's borrowing countries dominate the board where they control roughly seventy per cent of the votes (although some now vote for borrowers as well, a new development since the demise of the USSR and the Eastern bloc).

Perhaps more significant is the background of the ten remaining, nominally Southern, EDs. Eight of them received their higher education abroad, mostly in the United States. Four have Ph.D.s from American universities, all in economics (though one is in development economics). Between them, these third world men have, in addition to their US doctorates, six American masters degrees, again usually in economics. The Indian is an Oxford *and* Cambridge man (though he took his Ph.D. in economics in Bombay). The only Southern ED with hands-on development experience – including experience at the Bank – studied agriculture and development management in France. Only the Frenchman, the Algerian and the Chinese, are, educationally speaking, entirely home-grown products.

The interlocking and interacting similarities of age, *métier*, common academic discipline, heavy US educational bias and previous exposure to the Bretton Woods system ensure basic adherence to the Bank's standard development paradigm and traditional project lending and no one seems to be dissenting from the rationale of structural adjustment either. In principle, board decisions are arrived at by consensus. Still, built-in conflicts exist, if only between Part I and Part II countries, causing one observer to refer to the board's twice-weekly project approval sessions as the 'Tuesday (or Thursday) morning miracle when people who hate each other's guts sit down and decide to give each other money'.

Lack of board cohesion may be partly due to having doubled the number of members since the Bank's origins. The board also has a relatively high turnover. One researcher has calculated that from 1970 to the beginning of 1994 the Bank has had 121 executive directors and they stay three to four years on average. Even three or four years may not be long enough to master the numerous and complex questions the EDs are supposed to decide.[5]

The board's problems are compounded by lack of access to timely and relevant information. According to at least one director, the Mushroom Principle is routinely applied; information is 'scrubbed' as it moves upwards through the Bank to the EDs.[*]

Still, one in-house source gleefully reports that: 'The board is starting to be almost a nuisance to the Bank'. Executive directors have been stung by the evidence of marked decline in project quality as documented in the Wapenhans Report (see Chapter XI) and are trying to make sure it improves. The newly required environmental assessments have also opened a door to more critical input of information on which the EDs can judge projects.

But they still need to be able to get in on the ground floor in order to influence projects and programmes before these are cast in concrete. Internally this is called the 'quality at entry' issue and it is gravely worrisome. So far, for example, no compulsory process comparable to environmental assessment exists to estimate prospective *human* damage before a project is voted through. Policies, too, may come before the board after being worked on for months by Bank management and staff – only to have the EDs reject them. This occurred, for example, with a grossly inadequate forestry policy. Such an obvious waste of everybody's time could be easily avoided if the board were consulted earlier.

---

[*] The mandate of one professional editor of Bank documents, whose name is not cited for obvious reasons, specifically includes replacing all negative words or phrases with appropriate euphemisms. 'Whatever grains of uncomfortable truth might get through this "quality control" process are almost inevitably lost among the chaff of bland Bank-ese and the editing process is intended to maximize the likelihood that they stay lost.'

The directors have prodigious workloads which grow even heavier whenever new policy guidelines are contemplated or old ones are under review. Due to outside lobbying pressures, this is increasingly the case. Towards the end of the financial year, too, according to a former assistant to an ED, 'there is a desperate scramble to get all the loans which were in preparation through the board, so that several billion dollars of loans might be approved in a week, with much less rigorous attention than they would have received earlier in the financial year'.

Directors are expected not only to approve loans and sector policies, but they are also ultimately responsible for individual country policies, particularly since the 1987 Reorganization when the Bank adopted a much sharper country focus. Because they also review the Bank's completed projects, the EDs are in principle the guardians of its historical memory as well and should be the ones to prevent it from making the same mistakes over and over again.

When an ED represents several countries, especially more recent and inexperienced members, s/he has a further, unwritten role in guiding and assisting them in negotiations with the Bank and helping to push loans for the protégés through the pipeline. Sustainable poverty reduction and the environment may receive more attention than they once did; the standard project and structural adjustment agenda is still the meat and potatoes.[6]

How much control is exercised over the Bank by its more powerful members? There are no simple answers. Numerically speaking, as new members have joined, voting strengths have been diluted so that the US now holds 'only' 17.5 per cent of the stock. Does this mean the Bank is less under American influence than it once was?

Many observers from both North and South have long insisted that the Bank is and always has been basically an American instrument. In Chapter IV we quoted, for example, UK economist Stuart Holland who affirms that the US used to set the direction for all the G-7 Directors of the Bank, a situation he felt in 1993 to be significantly changing.

Filipino critic Walden Bello disagrees. For him, from the postwar era straight through to the President Preston period, 'the Bank has consistently maintained its overarching commitment to the interests of the United States'; it has been 'a closely held and controlled arm of United States foreign policy'.[7] The US has been able to prevent loans for its blacklisted countries (e.g. Nicaragua) from reaching the board and the right to name the Bank's President is a trump card.

Then there is the simple fact of the Bank's being in Washington. It might have been a quite different place had it been established in London, Paris or one of its Part II countries. Given that it is legally sited in the country with the most stock, American influence is likely to remain predominant. 'The United States could send Mickey Mouse to the board and he would still have enormous influence,' according to one ED.[8]

A prior question about US influence might also be, '*Which* United States?' Patrick Coady, the US Executive Director from 1989 to 1993, readily acknowledged that he sometimes received incompatible instructions from Congress and the executive branch: 'The State Department wants friends and Congress and the EPA (Environmental Protection Agency) want everyone to apply the same environmental standards as the US'. At least interested Americans can learn how their ED has voted on a given loan: most countries, including a majority of the nominally democratic ones, still do not disclose this information, although the Australian ED is responsible to Parliament and the Swiss ED has announced that his positions will also be made public.

As for the Bank acting as an agent for the G-7, Mr Coady rejected the notion that the Bank might, for example, be acting as a debt-collection agency for the commercial banks of its Part I countries (e.g. by imposing structural adjustment stressing export earnings, which can then be used for debt service). He argued that the private banks had taken real hits and if they were being bailed out by the World Bank, then 'Please don't bail me out like that!' Developing countries pay back of their own free will because 'the benefits of honouring your debts are enormous'. The Bank has had little or nothing to do with the behaviour of borrowing countries with regard to their private creditors.[9]

On the other side of the argument, according to the Bank's 1993–94 *World Debt Tables*, between 1980 and 1992 commercial banks reduced their proportional holdings of long-term third world debt from forty-three to twenty-six per cent of the total while the Bank's share of the total increased modestly, from seven to 11.6 per cent. Because the total debt of developing countries grew by two and a half times in twelve years – from 658 to 1,662 billion – all creditors held more debt in dollar terms in 1992 than they did in 1980. But during that twelve-year period the amount of commercial bank debt increased by only sixty-four per cent while the Bank's went up by 344 per cent.

The worst year for the commercial banks was 1987, when they held $435 billion worth of developing country debt. By 1992 they had reduced this amount by twenty per cent to $344 billion. The Bank's debt holdings had meanwhile risen from $122 billion in 1987 to $151 billion in 1992, an increase of 24 per cent.[10] Because money is fungible, structural adjustment loans from the Bank or the IDA free up funds for payments to commercial banks. In any event and for whatever reasons, debtors clearly now owe banks less and the Bank more and someone does seem to be bailing someone out.

Beyond its role in refinancing dubious commercial loans, some critics argue that the Bank was also one of the weapons used by the Reagan–Bush administrations to discipline the third world after a long series of humiliations for the US, including ignominious defeat in Vietnam, the Iranian hostage crisis and the successes of the OPEC cartel. The debt crisis offered an unexpected opportunity to apply the rollback policy, using SALs and SECALs to advance the US agenda. Walden Bello calls the practice 'blasting open' third world economies and cites a former US Deputy Treasury Secretary (Treasury is in charge of US policy in the Bank) on the case of the Philippines:

> We have not been particularly successful ourselves in winning policy reforms from the Philippines. Because it is something of a disinterested party, however, the World Bank has been enormously successful in negotiating important policy changes which we strongly support.[11]

Certainly the Americans can be heavy-handed when they want to – as in the Bank's 1987 Reorganization, demanded from Barber Conable by the Reagan administration in order to force through its worldwide free trade–privatization agenda. Can the Bank's board be expected to stand in the way of this or any such policy or to seek to lessen the influence wielded by the Bank's most powerful members? For several reasons this seems unlikely.

Governments of Part I countries on the whole share the US ethos, particularly its view of structural adjustment. Executive directors from Part II borrowing countries would hardly oppose SALs and SECALs, even at the risk of having their own economies 'blasted open', since acceptance of these loans, as well as the conditions that go with them, is a prior requirement for obtaining other credits elsewhere. If this means they must swallow the pill of the US or G-7 agenda, they will take a deep breath and swallow it. The very poorest countries get no IBRD money at all but depend entirely on the IDA. The IDA, in turn, depends on its donors: unlike the IBRD it cannot raise money on capital markets. Africa – but also India, China, Bangladesh and Pakistan – would be crazy to offend the G-7 and thus jeopardize a source of money on extremely favourable terms.

In addition to these pressures constantly at work on the Bank's borrowers, other serious constraints conspire to prevent the Bank's board from behaving like an independent body prepared to seize the policy initiative and grasp the political nettle. One is the 'I'll scratch your back if you'll scratch mine' syndrome which is the golden rule implicit among borrowing country EDs.

One ED confides, 'This board is never going to vote against a single loan' for the simple reason that if a loan ever had to go back to the drawing board, it might never find its way back to the board. Loans are already painfully slow in clearing all the procedural hurdles and borrowers despair of ever receiving one with less than a year and a half lead time. Executive directors are understandably interested in obtaining loans for their protégés without agonizing delays and thus will always lend a hand, and a vote, to their fellow-sufferers.

Perhaps the greatest obstacle of all to board independence and increased power is the sheer bureaucratic guile of the Bank's top layers of management prepared to do battle against *anybody* who might try to manage the Bank in their stead. Borrowers cannot afford to offend them and even Part I country directors may turn out to be 'no match for a usually brilliant group of professionals with decades of experience at the Bank'.[12]

One student of the Bank thinks the board's independence and power would be strengthened if executive directors were named for an irrevocable period of perhaps four years. He says the EDs should not be, as now, high-ranking bureaucrats but 'individuals with high visibility and prestige' at home.[13]

Such a measure would not help to heal an insidious and growing North–South split, although it might make the board's actions more newsworthy and thus attract more public attention and debate. The drawback is that people with high visibility and prestige usually want to remain visible and prestigious and might not, upon occasion, be above grandstanding to make their points.

Whoever is on the board, the sheer volume of the material the EDs are expected to handle means that no matter how smart they are individually, how rational their division of labour, or how streamlined their procedures (which are in fact said to be quite cumbersome), they can't possibly assess properly upwards of 220 new projects a year *and* keep an eye on projects under implementation *and* deal with ongoing and longer-term policy matters.

The directors necessarily rely on the Bank's professional staff and the information they obtain will be as good as the staff wants it to be. Since the board does not participate in the hiring (much less the firing) of the Bank's senior people, the latter are in no way dependent on its goodwill for their careers. The board may theoretically provide guidance but also receives it and must take what it gets. Secrecy has been, to date, one of the wily management's most effective weapons.

Even if by some fluke the EDs did attempt to challenge top Bank management and redirect the Bank's focus away from structural adjustment, they would be handicapped. Both on the board and in the Bank at large there exists an excessively narrow 'skills mix', as the Bank likes to call the variety of training and professional capacities in-house. Why should this highly trained, élite group of mostly male macroeconomists on the board put the environment, poverty or sustainable development at the top of their lists? Why should a senior management with largely the same credentials want them to?

As if these impediments did not suffice, the EDs' personal career constraints would make the cup overflow. The *Economist* gets it right when it explains that:

Rich country directors, mostly upper-middle ranking civil servants, know they have little to gain from confronting a Bank president who can get through on the telephone to their bosses, the finance ministers, at any time of the day or night. And poor-country directors hesitate to confront top management if they think it might jeopardize capital flows to their countries or compromise their comfortable compatriots inside the Bank.[14]

What if some strong directors decided to push Preston's poverty-alleviation agenda (he might then ring their finance ministers to praise them)? What is the real power of the *ex officio* chairman of this board, the President of the Bank?

Several Presidents have spent most of their first terms trying to figure out what was going on and then didn't get a second term to exploit their knowledge. It is no criticism of Preston to point out that he had zero prior experience of complex issues like the environment, development or poverty – his entire career until age sixty-five was spent as a top investment banker. In his pre-Bank existence he ran not a bureaucracy but a business and he was not obliged to deal with politics.

Still, Preston has a lot going for him. He is the ultimate East Coast WASP, born in 1926 when old money and *noblesse oblige* meant something in the United States. He went to St Paul's, an isolated Episcopal school in New Hampshire, an American version of Eton or Harrow, whose job was and is to train the aristocratic Christian gentlemen who, when not sailing or attending charity balls, would run America. Still only seventeen, Preston enlisted in the Marines in 1943 and served until the end of the Second World War in Okinawa. Afterwards, he went to Harvard and thence to J.P. Morgan – the ultimate WASP bank – where he remained until named President of the World Bank.[15]

The class into which Lewis Preston was born is dying if not dead. Part of its tradition was to run roughshod, when necessary, over its self-proclaimed social inferiors, a category encompassing most Americans and all foreigners except the British aristocracy. Another part of that tradition revolved, however, around loyalty to the nation's founding principles, service to the community and Doing the Right Thing in one's private and professional life.

Now these traditions are in the hands of a dwindling number of old – and increasingly older – boys and girls whose upbringing inculcated them with patrician ideals. Preston, having announced that 'sustainable poverty reduction is the benchmark by which the Bank's performance as a development institution will be measured', might have the right combination of compassion and indifference to the opinion of others to bring it off. If he decides to manage more than the financial side of the Bank, which he could probably do in his sleep, he might shake it up enough to surprise everyone, including the people who appointed him.

Preston underwent major surgery in 1993, leading to a some-what reduced schedule and to the odd vulture hovering over his chair. His term lasts until September 1996 when he will be seventy. Although not impossible, it is unlikely that at that age he would be reappointed. Here, then, is a man who has nothing to lose and whose institution, because of its fiftieth birthday, will be in the spotlight until the end of his reign.

Enough speculation. The bottom line is that the board can't really run the Bank and as of this writing the present President hasn't started to run it either. Before casting stones either at the EDs or at the President for not fulfilling their rightful destinies, let us take a closer look at a final set of constraints under which they labour. These arise from the hybrid nature of the Bank itself. The institution the President and the board are charged with guiding is neither fish nor fowl, nor any other recognizable Order.

It functions as a bank but does not take its chances in the market-place. Its portfolio is 'safe as houses', even if it makes one terrible loan after another, because its borrowers pay back, or else. Its board cannot act like the board of a private corporation where its job would be to keep the company on course – the Bank cannot, materially speaking, go *off* course, whatever the verdict of the market or the fate of the local people may be.

Under the guise of economics, the Bank is making more and more overtly political decisions which affect the lives of millions. Overstepping its initial mission, it is defining and imposing its own policies and weakening the state in its client countries. But it isn't like a government either because it is subject to no corpus of law, no political constitution (aside from its Articles) which, like a constitutional court, its board might be charged with honouring and protecting from abuse.

From whatever angle we examine the question, we are left with one of the world's most powerful entities in the control of a handful of career technocrats. Strictly speaking, the Bank is hegemonic; culturally speaking, it has a near-monopoly over development discourse, theory and practice and successfully propagates an increasingly fundamentalist ideology. There are people at the Bank who feel responsible literally for entire continents or sizeable chunks of them, theirs to 'save' or to 'lose' – in any case to shape to their own and their employer's design. Compared to some of them, Alexander the Great was a man of small ambitions.

There is a sense, however, that the Bank has taken over the world's development agenda by default, mostly because of other people's laziness or ineptitude. According to this argument, the Bank hasn't asked for leadership but has had, so to speak, leadership thrust upon it. This was particularly true in the 1980s when other donors got in the habit of linking their loans and lending conditions to those of the Bank, then slid down the slippery slope, following its lead on many other matters.

The Bank gradually took over the functions of the UN specialized agencies as well because the latter couldn't get the job – whatever the job might have been – done. According to this version, the Bank is hegemonic not because it wants such responsibilities but because nobody is challenging it.

This 'nature and the Bank abhor a vacuum' theory tells us exactly what is so scary about the Bank. The North has no policy worth mentioning, the relationship of one-sixth of humanity with the other five-sixths has fallen through the cracks, and ideological, 'empire vs. barbarian' fantasies are beginning to replace strategic thought.

In this empty space, devoid of leadership and ideas, whatever the Bank wants to do, it can do. By default, *structural adjustment plus Bank projects are Northern policy with regard to the poorer countries, the only policy on offer*. The Bank is a super-State Department or Foreign Office coupled with a powerful economic machine that can force dozens of countries to comply with its directives.

As for its projects, the Bank now says it intends to put implementation, as opposed to conception and design, at the top of its list and to make the country focus even stronger. Projects will be subordinated to the policy aims. The Bank's country point-man or woman will arguably be a more powerful, though more shadowy, figure than the country's nominal ruler. If the projects are harmful to people and to nature, the situation could become even worse than the one engendered by the 'push the money out the door' culture.

For the present, the only tenuous link to a structure of political control remains the executive directors (or, in a different register, the withholding by national legislatures of funds for the IDA and for general capital increases). At present, parliamentarians are not asking questions about the instructions their Bank EDs receive from their governments. Most NGOs are not lobbying to make sure that EDs responsive to poverty and environmental concerns are named to the board, or even to make sure that their votes are a matter of public record. With few exceptions, NGOs haven't a clue as to who their representative on the board is anyway, nor any idea of what s/he does all day.

Even if the board were strengthened there are no guarantees that democratic control could be exerted over the Bank, especially by people in the South on the receiving end of its projects. Insofar as the Bank is – as we have been arguing – like the Church, this is a misplaced hope. The Pope and the College of Cardinals are not the representatives of the faithful and they do not supply them with any justifications for their actions. During the Vatican Council in the early 1960s, many people harboured the illusion that base communities and liberation theologians could push their views upwards through the Church and change it: they have since been disabused.

In terms of decision-making power, there are no links at all between the faithful and the hierarchy. The upper reaches of the bureaucracy – whether of the Church or the Bank – are not there to serve the faithful or the poor but to make political decisions according to strategic and institutional objectives.

The Bank is not an international institution which represents its member countries and thus owes those countries and by extension their people some kind of accounting. Its senior people (managing directors or vice presidents) are like the Cardinals. When management jokes about the Mushroom Principle – feed everyone else shit and keep them in the dark – they are talking about their own power to do exactly that.

Like the Church, the Bank says in sum, 'I am what I am, you know what my doctrine is and you have given it your tacit consent.' If the tenets of the religion are accepted, there is no need to supply particulars. Who runs the Bank? Not the executive directors, not (yet) the current President and certainly not the civil societies of member countries, but top career managers who know that the Bank is not a public service organization but an enterprise for restructuring the world economy, indeed the world.

Chapter XI

The Bank Perceived:
Images and Self-Images

Like any modern corporation, the Bank is concerned about its image; unlike any modern corporation, it has no marketing problems. The Bank gets its product – loans and credits – out the door at the rate of two and a half million dollars an hour and its borrowing country clients don't much care how the Bank is perceived so long as the money keeps flowing. Whatever the appearances, these developing countries are not the Bank's real clients: the target audience it must favourably impress is in the rich North. Here are the governments that supply the capital for general capital increases for the IBRD and the Replenishments for the IDA; here, too, the widows, orphans and pension-fund managers who buy its bonds. If the Bank's image deteriorates too sharply in the rich countries, it will sooner or later feel the pain in its purse and its power will consequently be diminished.

One of the greatest threats of the 1990s to the Bank's image came from an unlikely quarter: the Bank. The Wapenhans Report, whose formal title is 'Effective Implementation: Key to Development Impact', was an in-house assessment of the Bank's entire loan portfolio. The gist of the Wapenhans Report is that a large and increasing number of Bank projects are failing, even when assessed only on narrow economic criteria. How did such a damning document come to be written?

When Lewis Preston became President of the Bank in late 1991, he wanted to make sure the institution's loans were actually delivering the benefits to borrowers that his staff claimed for them. He called on Willi Wapenhans, a Bank VP on the point of retirement and a veteran operations man, to lead a task force whose job was to survey the overall – as opposed to individual – performance of Bank loans. It was the first time in nearly fifty years anyone had entertained such an eccentric idea.

The task force judged the loans entirely on their own terms, with the sacrosanct rate of return as the yardstick. In other words the social or environmental impact of a dam or a road was not taken into account insofar as the dam produced the requisite kilowatts of electricity or the road carried the anticipated traffic. If the dam displaced several thousand people or the road led directly to forest destruction, these costs were not weighed as part of the Wapenhans mandate unless such considerations had been written into the terms of the loan agreement at the outset.

Even on this restrictive basis, the team discovered that the Bank's portfolio was in sad shape, its quality in marked decline. Overall, twenty per cent of the 1,800-odd projects in 113 countries contained in the Bank's $140 billion loan portfolio presented major problems. Worse still, the proportion of troubled projects was steadily increasing, from eleven per cent in the early 1980s to an alarming 37.5 per cent for projects completed in 1991. In the task force's judgement, 'The portfolio's deterioration has been steady and pervasive and is apparent in an increasing number of sectors' (water and sanitation and agriculture were the worst, with failure rates above forty per cent).

Other bad tidings from Wapenhans concerned the relationship between staff time and loan quality: the inquiry discovered that the longer it took Bank staff to prepare projects, the less successful they tended to be.[1]

This particular finding also reflected a lack of borrowers' commitment to projects, mostly dreamed up by Bank staff with little input from the countries concerned. Indeed, the team found that governments were routinely flouting their agreements with the Bank. Wapenhans leaves little to the imagination, noting that 'compliance' is 'startlingly low' or 'the evidence of gross non-compliance is overwhelming'. Borrowers respected their agreements in only twenty-two per cent of the loans examined. Furthermore, they ignored them with impunity, since non-compliance with contracts carried no discernible sanctions. As a result, 'the high incidence of non-compliance undermines the Bank's credibility'.

Lewis Preston deserves credit for ensuring publication of the

Wapenhans Report in late 1992, warts and all. True, by then everyone and his aunt had already had access to a leaked copy of the 'confidential discussion draft' and from the moment this draft began to circulate, the report sent tremors through the institution. It also forced the executive directors to take their policy-making function more seriously. The challenge to the board was to make sure that senior management did not, so to speak, simply shove Mr Wapenhans into a drawer. The directors did rise to this occasion, formally asking management what it intended to do about the Bank's sagging portfolio.

Management responded with a plan so patently inadequate that the board sent it back. The putative author of these halting 'Next Steps', as the plan was called, was a meek and mild Indian close to retirement; the real power behind it was said to be the ubiquitous Ernest Stern, the most powerful of Preston's three senior managing directors, the man the *Economist* calls the 'de facto head' of the Bank. As the *Economist* reported,

> the opacity and lack of conviction of this paper has so disappointed directors that no vote will now take place. The document, said one director, had 'Ernie's fingerprints all over it'.[2]*

The next 'Next Steps' was an improvement. It provided a more credible action plan which the board approved in July 1993. Announcing the plan to the press in his capacity as Acting President (Preston was in hospital), Ernest Stern demonstrated with consummate skill his ability to join the critics when clearly outnumbered:

> Central to the plan is the commitment to make the management of projects under implementation as important as making new loans. Only sound, on-the-ground results − the development impact of

---

* The covering letter by President Preston to 'Next Steps' had more substance than the document itself. He praised the Bank (actually it was his own idea) for undertaking a 'public self-examination', stating that the Bank should be a 'risk-taking institution'. 'As this ['Next Steps'] program is put in place, *we expect a change in institutional behavior and attitudes* over time which will reflect the crucial importance of managing the implementation of our operations well and of judging our effectiveness in terms of development impact' (emphasis added).

projects – are true measures of the Bank's contribution to sustainable development.[3]

The process initiated by Wapenhans comes down to an attempt to launch wholesale cultural change, to wrest the Bank from its entrenched 'approval culture' (Wapenhans's own term) and create one inspired by the desire to see projects actually work. This wrenching shift will have to be accomplished in the teeth of senior management which has always preferred, as Wapenhans reminds his readers, 'to focus on lending targets rather than results on the ground'.[4]

If the culture can indeed be wrenched, emphasis will shift from the money-out-the-door approach to implementation and the policy environment, a euphemism for making governments behave themselves and stop ignoring their obligations as defined in loan agreements. This orientation will also reinforce the Bank's preoccupation with adjustment and governance. Wrenching will be made easier if the proposed new guidelines on staff incentives and individual promotions are actually followed by encrusted senior people. The real test of a cultural revolution will be staff getting more points for following through on existing projects than for designing new ones.

Despite bombshells like the Wapenhans Report, the Bank's legitimacy has rarely been questioned and those who have questioned it have tended to lack legitimacy themselves. The odd academic or angry NGO is no match for such an institution. Furthermore, some extremely powerful interests have joined forces to add their own prestige, in a structured and orchestrated way, to an ongoing affirmation of the Bank's legitimacy.

The major advocacy group for the Bank is called the Bretton Woods Committee, with its headquarters in Washington not far from the Bank. The Committee comprises a select company of about 400 top US establishment figures, both Republicans and Democrats, occupying 'leadership positions in business, government, national associations and education'.

The members' list of this group reads like a Who's Who of American movers, shakers and policy makers: former presidents, vice-presidents and cabinet members, with emphasis on secretaries of treasury, state and defense; chairmen and governors of the

Federal Reserve; senators, congressmen and state governors; chief executive officers of dozens of major transnational corporations and of the top investment and commercial banking houses; senior partners of the country's most prestigious law or accountancy firms; with an assortment of university presidents, professors and a smattering of trade union leaders, NGO, think-tank or foundation officials.

In 1989 the Bretton Woods Committee sponsored a major conference on third world debt. The then Treasury Secretary Nicholas Brady chose this platform to launch the Brady Plan, the standard debt reduction framework used ever since. At this conference, Brady lauded the Bretton Woods Institutions as promoters of 'sound policies' (i.e. adjustment) and entrusted them with a major role as debt managers. This is an indication of the Committee's clout which it also uses for such tasks as lining up a 'network of businesses [which] is becoming an important force to build US support for the development banks'. American companies receive more Bank procurement contracts than those of any other nation.

Moreover, 'As a world leader, the United States ought to play a leadership role in these institutions'. To that end, the Bretton Woods Committee was set up to lobby the US Congress and other targets on behalf of the Bank and the IMF, because these institutions 'directly assist many countries key to America's strategic and national security interests', including 'several strategically key countries, such as Mexico and Brazil, that get little or no direct US economic assistance'.[5]

Capital has indeed flowed abundantly to such countries: in 1993, Mexico became the Bank's top all-time borrower when it received the largest environment loan ever granted – $3 billion to clean up the border zone between Mexico and the US.*

The Bank's role in promoting privatization across the planet is

---

* Somehow this loan seems not unrelated to the Clinton administration's frantic efforts in the autumn of 1993 to force through the North American Free Trade Agreement (NAFTA), roundly opposed by environmentalists. The cleanup loan was first announced not by the Bank but by US Trade Representative Mickey Kantor and is to be managed by the 'US–Mexican cooperation commission created within the framework of side agreements to NAFTA', according to Kantor. See Agence France Presse dispatch of 24 September 1993.

also of major interest to the members of the Bretton Woods Committee. In 1992 and 1993, ongoing privatization in Eastern Europe and the former Soviet Union was discussed and encouraged at a series of meetings and conferences. The Committee was also actively preparing for the Bank's fiftieth birthday in 1994, planning a major conference to be held – where else? – in Bretton Woods. Paul Volcker, former Chairman of the US Federal Reserve, is in charge of the Committee's contribution to these celebrations and – according to Washington gossip – positioning himself to become the next President of the Bank. The Committee's public stance is that 'US interests can be advanced by US participation in the international financial institutions'.

Despite the competence of the Bank's own External Affairs Department and major outside lobbying efforts exemplified by the Bretton Woods Committee, more and more people now question the Bank's world-view and no longer wholly accept its self-proclaimed legitimacy. Increasingly, they are even *serious* people, like legislators and newspaper editors, not merely dissident academics, eco- or human rights activists. The latter are also much better organized than they once were and can no longer be easily dismissed. The Bank is becoming visibly worried that rhetoric and the usual information channels will not do the image-burnishing job alone; it is poised to go out into the world and recruit more, new and different supporters.

An internal memo from President Preston's office to the Bank's executive committee summarizing 'Highlights from the President's February 22 (1993) Meeting with Vice-Presidents' notes that

> Mr Preston reported on his recent visit to Scandinavia, Switzerland and Italy. He said that *he was concerned by the limited understanding of the Bank's development work in much of the donor community and by the Bank's increasingly negative external image.* He stressed that the Bank needs to adopt a pro-active approach to external communications, rather than trying to defend itself *ex post* against criticism from well organized environmental and human rights groups (emphasis added).[6]

One of the three managing directors thereupon suggested that the Bank take advantage of all its fiftieth birthday events, as well as upcoming UN conferences on major development issues (Cairo 1994 on population; Copenhagen 1995 on social development): 'The Bank should become more active in shaping and using such events'.

The Financial Policy and Risk Management Vice-President observed that considering the 'difficult negotiations for the Tenth Replenishment of IDA' the Bank ought to convey

> a better understanding and a more positive image of its activities to key audiences in donor countries [and] develop country-specific strategies for managing relations with major donors.

Among 'key audiences', this gentleman doubtless had in mind the United States Congress. Three months after he spoke at this meeting with President Preston, the Tenth Replenishment of the International Development Association (the Bank's soft loan window) barely squeaked through.*

All the VPs at the meeting with Preston agreed that the Bank needed to 'counteract the negative image generated by NGOs and other critics'. They decided the Bank should look into such strategies as:

> reaching out to under-exploited constituencies in developed countries, such as private sector industrialists or major academic centers; taking a more pro-active role in defining the agenda for debate with Bank critics and using modern communications techniques such as mass media advertising.[7]

The Bank has also retained a corporate strategy and image consulting firm which in 1993 conducted in-depth interviews of dozens of representative people in several countries concerning their perceptions of the Bank.[8]

The Bank also has more subtle ways of building and promoting

---

* Despite US recalcitrance, the Bank obtained pledges of approximately $18 billion from 34 donors to fund the IDA from July 1993 through June 1996. Adding insult to injury, however, US legislators also approved by a hair's breadth $56 million in fresh capital for the Bank (IBRD), 20 per cent less than it wanted: the vote was 216 to 210 in favour but four of the 'yeas' came from delegates of US territories whose votes don't count.

its image. A close reading of its own documents with this institutional goal in mind can be an extremely instructive experience. We are, for example, semiologically speaking, entranced by the 1992 *World Development Report* and ask the reader to bear with us for a moment of critical content-analysis. The report begins with these stirring words:

> The achievement of sustained and equitable development remains the greatest challenge facing the human race.

Would anyone dare to argue with such a sentence? It has that unmistakable ring of truth, at once a sobering statement and a call to arms, all in fifteen words. Here indeed is the Voice of Authority and we would be both foolish and stubborn not to believe it.

But does this fine rhetoric perhaps conceal more than it reveals? We think it does, but let's begin by giving the Bank's rhetorician the benefit of the doubt. We'll grant that 'development' has a content and a meaning upon which all reasonable people (in the present case, the entire human race) can agree. This, by the way, is a huge concession. Dozens if not hundreds of definitions of development have been offered over the years to the point that many people (including us) now find the word meaningless if not suspect.

We'll gloss over this point and we'll accept the admonition as well – that achieving this universally agreed development, whatever it is, is the main thing all of us ought to be doing, right now, dropping everything else on our agendas, because it is the 'greatest challenge' facing us and we know this is true because the Bank says so.

So we must accept this challenge, no doubt about that. It's the only way to be responsible members of the human race, to do our duty, to go to bed with a clear conscience. The Bank has persuaded us. But how, then, as morally convinced people are we to go about meeting the challenge? Usually, a challenge is addressed to someone a bit more specific than the human race; one team challenges another for the cup, one swordsman another to a duel; you need an adversary or at least a partner. In the Bank's statement, however, as members of the human race, we're all in this thing together, so presumably if we accept the challenge, as we are now determined to do, the adversary we have to take on is whoever or whatever is preventing the achievement of development.

Maybe it's the transnational corporations or the CIA; the local landowners or the dumb natives; Oxfam field-workers or perhaps even the Bank itself. Here the rhetorician leaves us high and dry; he doesn't give us a clue who or what to target in order to take up this greatest challenge. We're out there in the field without a map or a strategy, looking for an adversary who has neither a face nor a name. True, the next sentence identifies 'acute poverty' and 'grossly inadequate access to the resources' which could give 'more than one billion people a chance for a better life', but this doesn't get us much further.

Thus we begin to wonder if deep-down the Bank really wants us – whatever the moral concern which its rhetoric has awakened in our breasts – to take up this 'greatest challenge'. Perhaps it just wants to go on doing so itself, on our behalf, representing the human race according to its own lights with the rest of us applauding from the sidelines? Certainly if we were to deal with this greatest challenge adequately, we would at least have to devote enough critical thought to the matter to figure out who or what is preventing those billion people from having access to resources; to discover what or who has condemned them to 'acute poverty'. Otherwise we cannot possibly take up the challenge with any hope of success. On closer examination, coming from the Bank, a statement like:

> The achievement of sustained and equitable development remains the greatest challenge facing the human race

may not be a call to arms at all – no telling where that might lead – but rather a call for conversion and an invitation to adhere to the Bank's own version of cause and effect; of events and ethics. Our moral consciousness is being awakened not so that we will go out and identify precise targets with a view to taking specific action against them; we are not even being asked to contribute to Oxfam. We are, rather, being encouraged to hold fast to certain truths as they may be defined by the Bank. From time to time, as in this example, the basic truth may be rejuvenated. Mere development will no longer do. It must also be sustained and equitable, adjectives – also undefined, but at this point who cares – which allow the Bank to cast its net wider, towards environmental and social justice constituencies.

Why should fifteen words deserve several paragraphs? Because they mean something different from what they pretend to say; because they are a reassertion of the Bank's right to define development and to trace the path that will eventually lead the human race there; because they serve as a kind of verbal recruitment poster like the famous 'Uncle Sam Wants YOU'. The Bank wants us to sign up and line up behind it.

The Bank is notifying us that: 1) it knows, and has known all along, what development is (including the sustained and/or equitable varieties); 2) it is self-authorized to remind us and other members of the human race of our moral obligations; and 3) among these is our obligation uncritically to let the Bank get on with doing whatever it considers necessary to achieve sustained and equitable development. The first sentence of the *World Development Report* is reaffirming the Bank's legitimacy and wants us to reaffirm it too.[9]

In the world of NGOs, however, positions are hardening and some have had enough of an institution which continues (as attested in the executive committee memo cited above) to treat substantive criticism as an 'image problem' to be countered with 'mass media advertising' or tried-and-true promotional techniques rather than as an incentive to change.

Some North American organizations most critical of the Bank have established frequent and reliable contact with counterpart NGOs in the South often representing communities on the receiving end of Bank projects. The best known example of their cooperation, though far from the only one, is the effort to stop the Sardar Sarovar dam in India. For many of these campaigners, the Bank's attitude in this case plumbed the depths of cynicism and it pushed them over the edge.

By 1993 some of these organizations were thinking the unthinkable and saying the unsayable: *Shut it down.* Actually, those three little words should be both thinkable and sayable: the Bank's own Articles of Agreement make ample provisions for its liquidation.

Lord Keynes even said rather wistfully of his Bretton Woods lawyers, 'I wish that they had not covered so large a part of our birth certificate with such very detailed provisions for our burial service, hymns, and lessons, and all'.[10]

In the United States, Friends of the Earth, among others, thinks efforts to reform the Bank are vain. Its spokesman testified to the Senate committee which oversees Bank funding:

> For ten years [working with citizens' groups from around the world] we have been accumulating more and more evidence of environments destroyed and economies undermined by World Bank loans . . . Now, on reviewing the past decade, and especially in light of the extraordinary events surrounding the Sardar Sarovar dam project in India, we regretfully conclude that these global efforts have failed . . . the World Bank is not reformable.[11]

Their strategy is to hit the Bank in the wallet; they urged the US Congress not to fund the IDA. In Canada, PROBE International takes much the same line. Already in September 1991 PROBE had written to the Canadian governor of the Bank that 'democratization of the World Bank [is] impossible'; it 'is neither reformable nor worth reforming'.

In addition to the familiar environmental and human rights arguments, PROBE added that the Bank's loans (like other foreign loans) have relieved third world governments from establishing legitimate tax régimes in their own countries and that the Bank itself is 'not a sound financial institution' because its AAA credit rating is not based on AAA-quality investments in its client countries but rather on government guarantees from the developed world.[12]

Foes like FoE and PROBE are among the irreconcilable radicals but not all NGOs have given up on the Bank. Some simply find the 'Shut it down' slogan politically unrealistic, given a Bank that has yet again outgrown its real estate and is moving into another costly ($100 million over the initial $186 million estimate) custom-built office complex. The G-7, and especially the United States, who control the money, show few signs of wanting to evict this tenant and so long as they want him to stay, he can. Those NGOs that take the Bank's continued existence for granted prefer to push for internal change whereas 'close it down' NGOs tend to cut themselves off from any further influence on those in a position to change Bank policy.

Reformist NGOs can sum up their goal in a word: democracy. Democratization of the Bank could, they believe, contribute to the defence of human rights (especially those of indigenous peoples), poverty alleviation and environmental protection. Many NGOs, particularly in the South, are against cutting off funds to the IDA since it provides one of the rare windows for soft loans, especially to Africa. The refusal of some of the radicals to accept this point has not always been conducive to good relations between Northern and Southern NGOs, a disagreement the Bank's own strategists have understandably sought to exploit.*

The Rainforest Action Network sums up the standard reformist NGO demands under the following headings: end the secrecy; ensure accountability; give the affected people a voice in their future; provide clear statements of the Bank's objectives for all loans; institute sound and rigorous economic analysis of projects; provide complete environmental assessment prior to making decisions on loans; encourage sustainable development rather than short-term, 'pay-off' economics; provide for independent auditing of the World Bank's operations; provide for independent technical reviews.[13]

'Vast programme!' as General de Gaulle is said to have remarked on hearing an aide cry, 'Death to imbeciles!' But still, perhaps, a feasible one, because the reformist ranks are swelling and there is movement within the Bank as well, to which we shall turn in a moment.

In the early 1980s critiques of the Bank tended to centre on the environmental devastation its projects caused but the environmentalists were pretty much alone. Now others have joined the chorus because of the Bank's concentration on structural adjustment which critics see creating widespread human damage. They resent the Bank's claim to be a 'purely economic institution' when its impact

---

* We hear (although we cannot prove) that the Bank encouraged African ambassadors in Washington to lobby the Black Caucus in the US Congress to support the IDA.

is so clearly social and political as well. And they believe it has failed in all three areas – social, political *and* economic, while simultaneously gaining greater and greater control over world affairs.[14]

Approaches to reform differ according to each organization's political analysis. The Bank can be 'reached' in basically four ways: 1) influence the votes of executive directors (many of whom, it is true, represent governments unresponsive to their own citizens) to cause them to reject policies or refuse projects; 2) mount international campaigns against specific projects; 3) create an 'image problem' for the Bank on a broader basis (e.g. poverty, the environment, human rights) which might make it change its behaviour; 4) hold a dialogue with the institution in good faith, putting one's grievances on the table.

All these approaches have met with some limited success but apparent victories may also be fragile so long as no legally binding mechanisms guarantee continued enforcement. Furthermore, historically speaking, every time the Bank has been effectively criticized, it has responded by expanding.

The Bank's previous disregard for women, or poverty alleviation or the environment have all led to the creation of new departments or units, increased staffing and programme levels; governance seems slated to play this expansionary role in the later 1990s. One cynical friend inside says that 'creating a unit' means putting all those with a professional interest in the issue in one place so that they can be more easily sidelined. NGO activists do not always seem entirely clear on their goals: do they want the Bank to reform itself by doing less, or more?

Here, briefly sketched, are examples of the approaches used by activists:

1. The US environmental movement has shown that the votes of executive directors can be legally mandated. This movement has pushed legislation through Congress obliging the US ED of each multilateral development bank to vote no or to abstain under certain conditions (usually documented environmental abuse, threat of future abuse or gross violations of human rights). From 1992 through mid-1993, these American MDB executive directors

actually did vote no or abstain on more than 170 occasions. This is no mean achievement, given that the United States controls 17.5 per cent of the vote at the Bank.[15]*

2. The best example of successful opposition to a specific loan has been described in Chapter VIII. Besides Sardar Sarovar, Northern and Southern NGOs are attempting to slow or halt other Bank dam/water management projects in Indonesia (Kedung Ombo), Thailand (Pak Mun), Argentina (Yacyreta), Chile (Bio-Bio River) and others. This approach can turn a momentary spotlight on some of the Bank's worst features; the disadvantages are its obviously Sisyphean nature and the risk that even if the Bank drops out, the host government will go ahead with the project anyway.

3. At the 'general issue' level, organizations like Greenpeace, the Environmental Defense Fund and Friends of the Earth wage ongoing guerrilla warfare against the Bank's frequent environmental lapses and overall policy, while the US-based Development Group for Alternative Policies has taken the lead in bringing together NGOs worldwide to campaign against structural adjustment. The Development-GAP is also actively celebrating, if that's the word, the Bank's Big Birthday, under the slogan '50 Years Is Enough!', rounding up a coalition of the 'usual suspects' – church-affiliated organizations, human rights activists, indigenous peoples' solidarity groups and ecologists.[16]

4. As for sitting down at the same table, twenty-five NGOs from North and South have formed an invitation-only coalition to carry on what they call a 'critical dialogue' with the Bank on subjects of mutual concern, particularly popular participation in development projects and the impact of structural adjustment. This NGO Work-

---

* Whether NGOs in other countries might be ready to attempt such a strategy is another question. Susan George has sometimes asked the generally well-informed audiences to which she speaks from time to time if anyone in the audience knows the name of the World Bank executive director for that country. As of November 1993, utter silence had been encountered in England, Germany, Belgium and Italy ... Swiss NGOs, however, have pursued this line since Switzerland joined the Bank in 1992. The other vital task is to target the people who tell the ED how to vote.

ing Group on the World Bank, whose secretariat is housed at the International Council of Voluntary Agencies in Geneva, has held several meetings with high-level Bank people to try to inject some NGO thinking into the Bank's analyses, since their common goal is to alleviate poverty. The results are patchy so far but both sides are said to be displaying goodwill and a capacity to listen.[17]

Organizations or individuals practising any of these strategies can draw on the resources of the Bank Information Center in Washington, an invaluable source for updates on Bank projects, environmental assessments and the like. The lively and irreverent quarterly publication *BankCheck* provides hard news and the occasional bit of gossip for a mailing list of about 2,000 and goes into high editorial gear when the Bank and the Fund hold their annual meetings in the autumn.[18]

The Bank is most vulnerable to criticism of its lack of internal democracy, because it does not practise what it preaches to client countries under the doctrine of governance. The fiction that the Bank is a purely economic institution is no longer tenable – and even if it were, the economy has such a huge impact on both people and nature that checks and balances would be considered normal and necessary in a national context with regard to an institution of comparable power. Making the democratic arguments stick at the international level is the challenge, particularly since no political machinery for doing so yet exists. The two big words for advocates of democracy are accountability and transparency.

In an attempt to make the Bank accountable to some external body, a proposal to create an Independent Appeals Commission was issued in September 1993 by two US and two Swiss NGOs. Drawing on the experience of the Morse independent review of Sardar Sarovar, they define some 'minimum characteristics' for such a commission: it should be permanent and independent from Bank management and board; it should receive and investigate public complaints 'regarding violations of World Bank policies, loans and credit agreements and violations of international human rights law in World Bank-funded projects'; it should have access to all relevant Bank documents and staff; its findings and recommendations should be binding unless reversed by two-thirds of the executive directors; it should be transparent, making its findings, recommendations and supporting documents simultaneously available to the EDs, the Bank's management, the complainant and the public.[19]

The organizations proposing an Independent Appeals Commission say its main function would be to help the Bank follow its own rules. This proposal is not especially revolutionary: it is well within the Board's power to create such a commission which would be comparable to similar bodies attached to national agencies (including the US State Department and the Peace Corps) whose role is to make sure that agency staff and operations conform to predetermined policies. The Swiss government immediately came out in favour of such a commission, albeit one with slightly reduced powers, which should, according to the government spokesperson, 'increase the World Bank's transparency and credibility'.[20]

At this writing, the only improvement in the accountability department occurred in September 1993 when the board decided to create a much more toothless affair than the one activists want. Even so, according to an internal European Commission memo, it 'has given rise to heated debates' among the executive directors. The European observer writes that:

> [U]nder pressure from US green lobby groups – known for their radicalism – and with the support of influential US Congressmen, the US proposed an independent inspection panel that could investigate complaints by groups which believe that they have been adversely affected by Bank projects ... There was opposition from some European EDs on the ground that the panel looked like an independent tribunal, but in the end the proposal was approved, albeit with some reduction of its independent character: the panel can review complaints only if it receives the green light from the Executive Directors.[21]

The green light may or may not be flashed.

Transparency is a problem for everyone. The Bank's line was always that it can't (won't) make most documents public in order to protect the confidentiality of its relationships with clients, which the clients demand – and which outsiders see as precisely the problem. In July 1989 the Bank completed a policy document on the disclosure of information. In his Foreword, Barber Conable says it tries to strike 'a careful balance' between the need for confidentiality and the fact that 'we [the Bank] want to share the wealth of available data with concerned parties and the general public'. The disclosure document leads off with:

> It is the Bank's policy to be open about its activities and to welcome, and to seek out, opportunities to explain its work to the widest audience possible . . . It follows that there is a presumption in favor of disclosure outside and within the Bank in the absence of a compelling reason not to disclose.[22]

So far so good. Unfortunately, the following forty paragraphs and sub-paragraphs contain so many restrictions as to render these fine principles virtually meaningless. Many of the restrictions are specific – for example, disclosure of the Bank's commodity price or financial forecasts is forbidden. (This may be a wise precaution because the Bank is so often wrong: see Chapter IV.)

One proviso, however, covers anything which could conceivably irk a borrower government just in case the specific restrictions missed it:

> [I]nformation should not be disclosed outside the Bank if, because of content, wording or timing, disclosure would be detrimental to the interests of the Bank, a member country or Bank staff, e.g. would adversely affect the Bank/country relationship because of the frankness of the views expressed.[23]

The Bank specifically refuses, for example, to disclose detailed information concerning the foreign debt of its borrowing countries, or the amount of debt held by creditor country A on debtor country B, or indeed anything else smacking of useful, disaggregated data.[24] In a rare blast, the *Financial Times* also let fly at the Bank's

> relationships with some of its African clients [which] are profoundly unhealthy: protective, secretive or defensive, sometimes all three . . . all too often, information that should be in the public domain remains secret. When information about grave mismanagement is withheld, confidentiality overlaps with complicity.[25]

By 1992 the debate on transparency had become noisy enough

to reach the cloistered offices of the executive directors, who split over the issue to tell or not to tell. A working group to review the information disclosure policy was named. It delivered its not very startling report in March 1993, including, however, an annexe by dissident group members advocating total transparency on some matters, in keeping with the 'intense and legitimate expectation of the interested public for information on environmental and social impacts of proposed loans'.[26]

In April 1993, twelve board members wrote to Managing Director Ernest Stern, 'strongly opposing open access to what they considered confidential documents' (in this case the National Environment Action Plans required by the Bank of its borrowers).[27] Even so, in August, the board came out in favour of expanded access to information partly on grounds that: 'The Bank strongly supports accountability and transparency in its borrower countries and, therefore, recognizes the importance of the Bank itself being – and being perceived as – an open institution'.[28]*

In January 1994 the Bank was expected to open a Public Information Center in Washington servicing its Paris, London, Tokyo offices and other field offices. A broader range of documents will be available in hard copy or on Internet. Projects under preparation are supposed to be much more fully described at the outset with descriptions periodically updated.

Although both *BankCheck* and the Bank Information Center remain dubious ('little new material will be accessible that NGOs can't already get') there does seem to be a will at work inside the Bank to open up, however cautiously. US legislators delaying renewed IDA funding have made it clear they want less secrecy in exchange for US taxpayers' dollars. As a spokesperson for the Bank told *BankCheck*, 'it's no coincidence that this [new policy on information disclosure] is coming at the time of the IDA replenishment'.[29]

* The Bank really should change its standard 'For Official Use Only' document distribution cover sheets. The title page of 'Expanding Access to Bank Information' has the usual box at the bottom stating: 'This document has a restricted distribution and may be used by recipients only in the performance of their official duties. Its contents may not otherwise be disclosed without World Bank authorization'. Perhaps the Bank just has a nice sense of irony.

Whether pushed by NGOs or by internal winds of change, whether willingly or under pressure, in 1992 and 1993 the Bank positively teemed with new initiatives. Never had poverty, the environment, hunger, NGOs, democracy – or the Bank's own performance – received such attention, or generated so many press releases. As so often happens with the Bank, the rhetoric/reality problem is here acute. Optimists outside and inside believe genuine change is under way – the Bank's head of operations policy calls it 'historic' – whereas sceptics remain sceptical. We reserve judgement, considering the wisest course is to trust the Bank one day at a time.

Habitual critics, too, are willing to keep an open mind. In its June 1993 newsletter, the Bank Information Center asks,

> Could NGOs have misjudged Lewis Preston? As strange as it seems, consider what the World Bank President told his senior management at a March 26 retreat. According to an internal Bank memo, Preston 'criticized the Bank for being elitist, resistant to change, reluctant to listen to criticism and reluctant to acknowledge its mistakes' and 'called for a corporate culture where change was welcomed'.

It was Preston who in 1992 made the pledge – which no one obliged him to make – that the Bank would and should be judged on sustainable poverty reduction. The 1992 operational directive to staff on poverty reduction affirms that the 1990s will be different from the 1980s when 'policy-based adjustment lending overshadowed the Bank's poverty reduction objectives, but eventually enabled the Bank to address more effectively the relationship between poverty and the policy environment'.[30]

Most NGOs would say that adjustment lending worsened and deepened poverty, but at least the Bank is turning over a new rhetorical leaf and has plans 'by the end of fiscal 1995' to have completed 'eighty-eight poverty assessments in eighty countries'.[31] It would be churlish to ask why this has taken nearly fifty years.

In late November 1993 the Bank hosted a monster Conference on Overcoming Global Hunger, with some thousand people in attendance. Preston opened it with the news that 'the more widespread and deep-rooted form of hunger is caused by people having neither the capacity to produce food nor the income to buy it. Fundamentally, hunger is caused by poverty.'*

On this occasion, the Bank also announced a $2 million grant to the Grameen Trust, an offshoot of the Grameen Bank in Bangladesh. Literally 'People's Bank', Grameen now services several hundred thousand village borrowers, mostly women, with loans averaging $75. The Bank grant will provide seed-money for replicating in other countries the remarkable success of Grameen in fostering 'micro-enterprise' among extremely poor borrowers.

We wish, however, to point out that it is precisely to this *individual* approach that the Bank now clings. Having spent the 1980s in a single-minded effort to reduce or annihilate the capacity of the state to improve anyone's life, it now wants people like Muhammed Yunus, founder and head of Grameen, and brilliant concepts like his bank to take up the slack. This helps to perpetuate the belief that development is somehow apolitical and government irrelevant.

The Bank doesn't need a positive image in order to sell anything but paradoxically it is more dependent on outside perceptions than a commercial company – for example, in the long run, the Bank may suffer more for Sardar Sarovar than Union Carbide did for Bhopal. The basic image problem of the International Bank for Reconstruction and Development is that reconstruction was taken over almost instantly, historically speaking, by the Marshall Plan and now the entire notion of development is running out of steam.

In less than fifty years, development has developed – from a kind of intellectual primeval soup into a fully-blown field and discipline – one from which the present authors, for example, have hitherto derived a major portion of their livelihoods. We are in the presence of a genuine industry which has spawned, by the hundreds, consulting companies, academic departments and university institutes;

---

* In her 1976 book, *How the Other Half Dies*, Susan George wrote: 'To state matters simple-mindedly, if you want to eat, you must be able either to grow your food, or to buy it, or a combination of both . . . Only the poor – wherever they may live – go hungry . . . deeply rooted patterns of injustice and exploitation, homegrown or imported, literally prevent them from feeding themselves'. Since the Bank has now officially recognized the first point, there is hope that it may also one day recognize the second.

think-tanks, government cooperation agencies and ministries; books, magazines and publishing houses; NGOs, UN specialized agencies and, not least, the smaller development banks and the Bank itself.

In pursuit of development, forests are felled to provide the paper for countless reports, millions of air miles are logged, lucrative procurement contracts are signed; thousands of jobs and billions of dollars are on the line – yet the whole business may be based on a myth. Once upon a time, alchemy and geocentric astronomy were also legitimate fields and disciplines.

The Bank pays the price for being the world's premier institution in this field. It is the cornerstone of the house of development. If people believe the house is solid, then it is. If they don't, those apparently firm foundations of 1818 H Street hold up nothing more substantial than a house of cards and of air. The Bank doesn't need to be understood but believed in, for what is perceived is.

Dr Gott's Formula

Or, a succinct guide for those who want to keep the Bank open for ever, for those who want to close it down right now and for those who aren't sure

Doug, John and Juliette were having a drink on the terrace at the Rondo on Q Street, off Dupont Circle. They had just come out of another meeting of the '50 Years Is Enough' campaign which had not ended in total harmony. The non-governmental organizations present hadn't sorted out what they wanted from the Bank and consequently the demands they had formulated were not likely to cause too many sleepless nights among the denizens of 1818 H Street.*

John left their table for a moment to go next door to Kramer Books and came back with a copy of the *Washingtonian* magazine. Leafing through it as the others desultorily sipped their drinks, he said 'Wow, would you get a load of this house for sale in Chevy Chase. Hey, let's buy it – listen to this – it's got "walls of glass, soaring ceilings and enormous room sizes". Maybe we can move the headquarters of "50 Years" there.

'These owners are really baring their souls. They're selling be-

---

*This conversation took place in mid-1993. A year later, the '50 Years is Enough' campaign had drawn up a detailed five-point platform, signed by over fifty US organizations, stressing openness, accountability, debt reduction, an end to environmentally destructive lending and to structural adjustment as now practised. Specific demands arising from this platform include the separation of the IDA from the IBRD, mandatory citizen input before any new loans are contracted, use of Bank–Fund reserves to write off debt and a moratorium on large dams. Copies are available from Development-GAP, 927 Fifteenth Street NW, 4th floor, Washington, DC 20005, fax (202) 898 1612.

cause they're having another house built. You guys won't believe this: "She will miss their long private drive, the bright and open floor plan and the wonderful decks overlooking the majestic trees. He'll remember the luxurious master suite complete with Jacuzzi, skylight, separate shower and circular windows, the grand first-floor library with fireplace and the impressive entry foyer. They'll both miss the dumb waiter which carries groceries direct into the kitchen." No, come on, this is too good to be true. Do you know whose house it is? None other than Armeane Choksi's – you know, he's the Bank's Vice-President of Human Resources Development and Operations Policy and he's put his title in the ad. Is his position at the Bank supposed to increase the value of his real estate or what?'

Juliette chimed in, 'Choksi is in charge of the Bank's anti-poverty programme. Choksi, have you no shame?'

Weary laughter greeted her remark. Doug said, 'That's just the point. These guys can get away with anything. We're never going to get rid of them. I'm doing the campaign but I don't expect to see any results in my own lifetime. It doesn't matter what the people want – we saw that with NAFTA. But what else is there to do?'

John said Doug was too pessimistic. It might take time, but in the end it's the people who make history. The people would eventually do away with the Bank, or change it so much as to make it unrecognizable.

Robert was walking by the café, saw the group and joined them. 'What were you talking about when I so rudely interrupted?'

'Basically about how long the World Bank is going to be around,' Juliette told him. 'Doug thinks it's going to last more or less for ever, John says we can close it if we try hard enough and I'm not sure. I just keep on pushing and I try not to worry too much about the outcome.'

Robert, the only scientist in the group, had a copy of *Nature* with him. 'I may have your answer,' he said. 'There's a piece in here by this Princeton astrophysicist who says he has a sure-fire formula for calculating how long things are going to last, whether they're species or systems or, I suppose, institutions. He applies what he calls the "Copernican Principle" which says there's nothing special about most objects – the species or the system or whatever. Like

Copernicus was the first to grasp that there's nothing special about the earth, that it's not the centre of the solar system, much less the universe.'

'Well, let's try it on the Bank,' said Doug. 'It can't be any worse than consulting the I Ching.' Robert wrote out the formula for them on a napkin. He explained that according to Professor Gott, statistical longevity-range calculations are based on the present age of the object, because the longer something has been around, the longer it is likely to survive. You don't have to know anything about how or why the phenomenon might end; you just have to be willing to accept that precious few, if any, phenomena are special. On this basis, Gott gives *Homo sapiens* a minimum future of 5,128 years and a maximum of 7.8 million. He says his formula squares remarkably well with actually observed lifespans of many species.

So Doug, John and Juliette decided they would each apply Gott's formula – which fortunately called only for simple arithmetic – to the institution of their choice. John chose the Catholic Church. 'Unless the Church is special,' he announced to the others, 'as of 1993, it has a minimum life expectancy of fifty-one years; a maximum of 77, 272.'

Doug naturally chose the Bank. 'This doesn't help a whole hell of a lot,' he told his friends. 'If the Bank is nothing special either, its life span will be somewhere between 1.25 and 1,911 years.'

Juliette said, 'Have I got news for you. You may both be right about the Bank. I didn't take 1993 as my baseline, but 1987. And I chose to apply the Copernican Principle to the Soviet Union. In 1987, if Dr Gott knows what he's talking about, we could have expected the Soviet Union to last from 1.8 to 2,730 years.'

J. Richard Gott III, 'Implications of the Copernican Principle for Our Future Prospects', *Nature*, vol 363 (27 May 1993), pp. 315–19. The *Financial Times* of 20 October 1993, p. 13, recounted Mr Choksi's full-page house advertisement under the title, 'Down and Out in DC'.

'The Thing'

In the late 1980s the Italian Communist Party was undergoing a full-blown identity crisis. Italian Communists had no idea what to call whatever future Party might emerge from the ruins of the post-Gorbachev world. In all the documents, in all the discussions of the time, this as-yet undefined Party was referred to as *la Cosa* – the Thing – an institution in search of a new personality. Since *The Godfather*, *Cosa Nostra* – Our Thing – has entered all our vocabularies, whatever our language. Calling the Mafia *Cosa Nostra* is one way of not having to say what it really is.

At Bretton Woods, the founding fathers didn't know what to call the Bank either – it got its name more or less by default and 'Bank' it has remained. Throughout these pages we have tried to determine what the Bank is and at the end of the enterprise we, too, are tempted to call it the Thing because, although we think we have made progress, to some degree it remains fascinating and mysterious. One of the chief attributes of power is not having to say what it is, not having to reveal its true identity, not having to give up its secrets to even the most diligent search.

Thus the question 'Why is the Thing so powerful?' is crucial. One thing about the Thing is certain: it is not powerful because it is a bank; that is, in ordinary language, a purely economic entity. Nor is it powerful because it has some of the characteristics one would expect of an international public service organization. It is a political and cultural enterprise, even a modern version of what the pioneer sociologist Marcel Mauss called the 'total social phenomenon' (*le fait social total*). The obvious, financial and economic side of the Bank is only the tip of the proverbial iceberg. The multiple roles it plays and the many functions of power it assumes, like the difficulty of defining it, make the Bank a total social phenomenon, a Thing.

This is why throughout the book we have spoken of beliefs, faith, doctrine, prophecy, and fundamentalism; of ancestors, initiation, *esprit de corps*, intellectual leadership and rule. This is also why, in addition to the facts and the documentary evidence, to the economic and political analysis we have tried to provide, we have made a few unorthodox sorties we called 'Interludes' into the world of the imagination. If the Bank were just a bank we would have had no reason to call on fiction.

We hope the reader will have found in each chapter and interlude partial answers to the question 'Why is the Thing so powerful?' This is the thread we have tried to follow, the one that should bind the book together.

Borrowing from French sociologist Pierre Bourdieu, we can say that the Bank is powerful because of its capacity constantly to exchange economic capital for symbolic capital and vice versa. Its economic activities generate money – well over a billion dollars a year in profits – but also immense prestige. Its prestige in turn generates more financial and economic power. The Bank has dug passageways and built bridges that allow it continually to shuttle between material and non-material wealth, to transform one kind of capital investment into another and to reap all the rewards of both.

The Bank is thus in a position to assume functions which are at once economic and symbolic: integration, guidance and, most important, maintenance of a programme of truth. The Bank is the visible hand of the programme of unrestrained, free market capitalism.

The Bank's first function is to be an instrument of integration through the market. This market is (or should be) co-extensive with the world; like that of the Church, its vocation is universal. All nations and all people must become ever more tightly bound to it. In this setting, the doctrine of export-orientation finds its natural home. All countries must trade as much as they can and rely for their subsistence first on the world market, last on their own resources.

Until quite recently, even in wealthy countries, communities provided for most of their wants from their domestic, local economies. What they could not find close at hand, they sought at the regional or national level. Only rarely, usually for luxury items, would they have recourse to the world market. This historical pattern has been turned on its head: we are now exhorted to satisfy our needs first from the international, global market, then the national or regional one and so on, down the ladder to the domestic economy, lowliest of all.

The Bank's second function is to act as a guide. Those who believe that its own doctrine is that of *laisser-faire* are mistaken. The Bank is, in fact, far more interventionist than the interventionist governments whose policies it seeks to transform. If the Bank were to leave people and societies alone, anything could happen – they might operate not on the basis of the marketplace but on principles of reciprocity, redistribution or solidarity. In modern societies, the state has attempted, with greater or lesser success, to organize redistribution and solidarity. Thus the state, like the traditional society based on reciprocity, is under threat from the Bank.

Here we face a contradiction. The marketplace cannot be the natural habitat of humankind. If it were, the Bank's interventions would be unnecessary. Everywhere the market would *already* be the sole guiding principle of society and, if it were, in the Bank's own view, there would be no underdevelopment, no South, no need for modernization or for structural adjustment – and no need for the Bank.

Why do we think we need the Bank? For the same reasons we think we need the Church. Frail, imperfect humanity needs constraints, guardrails, continual instruction in, and interpretation of, the doctrine. Those who have not yet reached the full expression of market capitalism and consequent development, those who fall by the wayside, must be goaded along the path to salvation.

To change society one must also change individual men and women. Man must be ontologically reconstructed and redeemed as *homo economicus*. What is redemption if not the passage from one state to another, from darkness to light? The virtues of the New Economic Man, whose dwelling place is the market, are the will and the capacity to accumulate, to follow self-interest and to maximize profit in all things. His wants are unlimited; to satisfy them, he must learn to struggle against his fellows. Scarcity is a fact of life. There is not enough to satisfy the unlimited desires of all nor to provide a place in the sun for everyone. If unemployment in their country is twenty per cent or more, the New Men and Women *will* pit themselves against each other to find work at any price, at all costs.

The Bank's third function is to be the standard-bearer of a programme of truth. If the world market is the Bank's fundamental organizing principle, price is its instrument. One of the Bank's major articles of faith is 'getting the prices right', which it translates in French as *la vérité des prix*, the truth of prices. A price has a metaphysical quality because it is supposed to be the invisible point at the intersection between hundreds, thousands, millions of individual transactions. Price, if governments do not meddle by providing subsidies and otherwise distort the natural balance of things, will regulate human activity and necessarily bring order out of apparent chaos.

Those who deny a programme of truth defy the law, in the case of the Bank the laws of economics, structural adjustment and the market. With the International Monetary Fund, the Bank is the keeper of laws which, like the Ten Commandments, are immutable. Once revealed, they must be followed. Defiant countries that refuse them outright are blacklisted, literally excommunicated from the international community. Governments which receive the law half-heartedly must be exhorted to better performance. The Bank will reward or punish them by the granting or withholding of loans and credits. Thus it helps return them to the straight and narrow path or, in its own words, puts them back on-track.

If the New Man finds his life in the market, what of his death? All great truths must in one way or another speak of last things; the Bank's is no exception. The Bank's nominal mission is to promote development. Development in its biological sense means an organism's attainment of its inherent potential, inexorably followed by decay and death. In the Bank's vocabulary, however, this biological meaning is replaced by a concept of never-ending growth. The Bank's priesthood specifically denies limits to growth and promises an ersatz eternity in the here-and-now.

If such endless growth is supposed to lead to an American or European middle-class standard of living for over five billion people today and who knows how many tomorrow, we already know this to be an ecological and biospheric impossibility, even assuming tremendous and rapid changes in technology. The Bank refuses to confront this last of all last things – not merely individual or societal death but the possibility of species extinction, including that of the human species. Incantations like 'sustainable development' stave off the moment when the finite must at last be faced.

The Church's traditional imagery of heaven and of hell is graphic and explicit. Although it cannot prove that anyone has ever gone there, it still issues the visas to the promised land. The Bank paints no pictures with saints, angels and demons but it does put up signposts pointing towards paradise, exhorting the faithful to imitate the blessed – the now-developed rich market-economy countries or at least those who are well on their way, like the Asian tigers.

The very vagueness of the concept of development and the great number of candidates who hope to attain it legitimize the Bank's functions, justify its existence and explain its power. As long as the fragile planet's heavenward journey lasts, as long as the poor are with us, as long as salvation is sought where it cannot be found, the World Bank will find for itself a role and a mission.

Thanks

Faith and Credit is part of the ongoing critical work on development undertaken by Fellows and associates of the Transnational Institute (TNI) in Amsterdam, with which Susan George has been affiliated in one capacity or another since it was founded in 1973. This book could not have been written without a budget, to which the Foundation for Deep Ecology of San Francisco generously contributed. Special thanks to Jerry Mander and to Doug Tompkins for their immediate understanding of this project and for the Foundation's utter absence of bureaucratic, time-wasting procedures. In the framework of its contributions to TNI's work on development, the Finnish Development Cooperation agency FINNIDA also provided part of the necessary funds. Neither donor exercised, or even thought of asking for, oversight of the manuscript.

Exchanges with several TNI colleagues were helpful and stimulating, particularly with Mariano Aguirre, Marcos Arruda, John Cavanagh, Jochen Hippler, Dan Smith, Basker Vashee and Howard Wachtel. Thanks to Laurian Zwart for managing our money and to Wim van der Schot for organizing meetings.

'It is Bank policy to be open and helpful to the news media' says a Bank in-house manual and we can attest that in our case the policy was not only strictly adhered to but exceeded: the Bank's attitude to our enterprise was beyond praise considering that it couldn't have expected the outcome to be all sweetness and light. Timothy Cullen, Division Chief of Information and Public Affairs, was absent when we were doing research in Washington but had clearly sent word round that we should be given appointments and we were. Special thanks also to John Clark and to John Mitchell and to archivist Charles Zeigler. How researchers obtain their documents is their own business, but we want to make clear that no one in the Bank gave us materials they weren't authorized to share with outsiders nor acted in any other way unprofessionally. We are grateful to the many people in the Bank who gave us their time and attention, helping both with 'deep background' and with specific queries.

Several colleagues and friends provided documents, comments and contacts. We're especially grateful to Robin Broad and (again) John Cavanagh, Juliette Majot who edits the lively *BankCheck*, Chad Dobson of the Bank Information Center, Doug Hellinger of the Development-GAP, Colin Stoneman and David Woodward. David Batker of Greenpeace's Multilateral Development Bank unit shared his knowledge of the Bank's environmental record; Bruce Rich generously gave us the manuscript of his book about the Bank, *Mortgaging the Earth*, and John Mihevc, whose perception of the Bank–religion tie parallels our own, let us have his thesis. Kirsten Garrett sent tapes of her Australian National Radio broadcasts and Pieter Smit collected several hundred pounds, it sometimes seemed, of documents by and about the Bank. Professor Nicholas Stern kindly sent a pre-publication copy of his chapter for the official Bank history. Thanks to Bob Lyons and the Greenpeace 'Greenbase' we had daily worldwide electronic press coverage of the Bank and all its works. The help of our informant in the European Community, a certain T.O. Moss, was invaluable. The same goes for two former Bank employees who do not wish to be named but whose patience and frankness are greatly appreciated.

For their help and encouragement, we would also like to thank in no particular order except alphabetical, Brent Blackwelder, Tony Bogues, Tony Bond, Peter Bosshard, Nicholas Claxton, Christian Coméliau, Kira Dale, Herman Daly, Cam Duncan, Jean-François Garnier, Doug Henwood, Stuart Holland, Marie-Dominique Perrot, Riccardo Petrella, Gilbert Rist, Jai Sen, Paul Sweeney, Jan-Joost Teunissen, Kay Treakle, Lori Udall, Frank Vogl, Joe Wampler, Sarah Williams, Matti Wuori.

Stefan McGrath at Penguin and François Gèze at La Découverte have made publishing in our common working languages a pleasure. Finally, there's nothing quite so awful for a personal *entourage* as putting up with someone who is living for long periods in a text. The people in our private lives are uncommonly nice and pretended not to notice that much of the time we weren't really there.

Notes

Introduction

1. Moises Naim, 'The World Bank: Its Role, Governance and Organizational Culture', 20 September 1993, a paper prepared for the Committee on the Future of the Bretton Woods Institutions, p. 5.

2. Susan George, *A Fate Worse than Debt* (New York, Grove Weidenfeld, 1987), pp. 258–9.

Chapter I: In the Beginning

1. On the ancestors of modern societies and institutions, see Fabrizio Sabelli, 'Les Ancêtres Sont Parmi Nous' in the volume of the same title, eds. J. Hainard, R. Kaehr and F. Sabelli (Neuchâtel, Musée d'Ethnographie, 1988).

2. Our account of this conference and the quoted material are drawn, unless otherwise noted, from US Department of State, *Proceedings and Documents of the United Nations Monetary and Financial Conference*, Bretton Woods, New Hampshire, 1–22 July 1944, USGPO 1948, two volumes, (publication 2866, International Organization and Conference series I, 3), hereafter *Proceedings*. All our references come from volume I which is over 1,100 pages long. It seemed fastidious and not especially useful to include a page reference for every quote and we have done so only occasionally.

3. Cited in Georges Valance, *Les Maîtres du Monde: Allemagne, États-unis, Japon* (Paris, Flammarion, 1992), pp. 24–6; Valance is himself quoting Elliott Roosevelt in *Mon Père m'a dit* [My Father Told Me], (Paris, Flammarion, 1947). We do not have Roosevelt's original text and have translated the cited French translation back into English.

4. Hearings of the House Special Committee on Postwar Policy and Planning, 78th Congress, 2nd session, 1944, pp. 1082–3, cited by Bruce Nissen, 'Building the World Bank' in *The Trojan Horse*, Steve Weissman (ed.), (San Francisco, Ramparts Press, 1974), p. 38.

5. Charles P. Taft, cited by Bruce Nissen, 'Building the World Bank', in Weissman, p. 39.

6. Keynes's address to the House of Lords, 23 May 1944.

7. World Bank in-house magazine *Banknotes*, July 1956, quoting an early 1942 typescript of White's kept at Princeton and also citing a biography of H.D. White by David Rees, Coward McCann and Geoghagen, 1973.

8. *Banknotes*, July 1956.

9. *Proceedings*, p. v.

10. Shirley Boskey, 'Bretton Woods Recalled', in the 10th anniversary issue of *Banknotes*, June 1956.

11. *Proceedings*, p. 71.

12. *Proceedings*, p. 1103.

13. Robin Broad, *Unequal Alliance: The World Bank, the International Monetary Fund and the Philippines* (Berkeley, University of California Press, 1988), p. 22 and notes concerning Keynes's diaries.

14. George Theunis, Reporting Delegate of Commission II to the Executive Plenary Session of the Conference, *Proceedings*, p. 1101.

Chapter II: The Other Ancestor

1. This period is exhaustively treated in Edward S. Mason and Robert E. Asher, *The World Bank since Bretton Woods* (Washington, DC, The Brookings Institution, 1973). See especially Chapters 3 and 4. The presidential terms and amounts loaned each year: Tables B–1 and B–2, pp. 798 and 799.

2. See Fred Pearce, *The Dammed* (London, Bodley Head, 1992), for accounts of several dams and water management projects financed by the Bank, in particular the Volta River project (Ghana) and its leonine arrangements with Kaiser Aluminum (pp. 123ff.).

3. Robert S. McNamara, *Address to the Board of Governors*, Nairobi, Kenya, 24 September 1973. IBRD pamphlet series, pp. 6–7.

4. William Clark, 'Robert McNamara at the World Bank', *Foreign Affairs*, Fall 1981, p. 168.

5. Deborah Shapley, *Promise and Power: the Life and Times of Robert McNamara* (Boston, Little, Brown & Co., 1993), p. 18. 'The Helper of the Largest Number' is the title of Shapley's first chapter.

6. Shapley, *Promise and Power*, pp. 478 and 567–8.

7. Shapley, *Promise and Power*, p. 48.

8. Shapley, *Promise and Power*, p. 435.

9. Clark, 'Robert McNamara at the World Bank', p. 168.

10. McNamara, Nairobi *Address*, 1973, p. 2.

11. OECD, *Financing and External Debt of Developing Countries, 1986 Survey* and *1992 Survey*, Paris, 1987 and 1993, Table V.1.

12. Susan George, *How the Other Half Dies* (Harmondsworth, Penguin, 1976 and subsequent editions), Chapter 10, p. 257.

13. Robert S. McNamara, *Address to the Board of Governors*, Manila, Philippines, 4 October 1976, pp. 18–20, plus the whole section on 'Resource Constraints' and the need to increase the Bank's capital and replenish the IDA, pp. 28–39.

14. McNamara, Nairobi *Address*, 1973, p. 8.

15. Robert S. McNamara, 'On Gaps and Bridges' in *The Essence of Security: Reflections in Office* (London, Hodder and Stoughton, 1968), pp. 107–21 *passim*: the chapter is based on addresses at two US colleges in 1966 and 1967.

16. Shapley, *Promise and Power*, p. 515.

17. Robert S. McNamara, 'On Gaps and Bridges' in *The Essence of Security*, pp. 110 and 115.

18. McNamara, 'On Gaps and Bridges' in *The Essence of Security*, p. 109.

19. Robert S. McNamara, 'Where Interests Collide' in *The Essence of Security*, pp. 29–30. (Although the sources in the Appendix to this book are not very clear, it appears that this chapter was initially testimony to Congress on the 1969–73 Defense Program and the 1969 Defense Budget supplied by Secretary of Defense McNamara in January 1968.)

20. Robert S. McNamara, 'Where We Stand' in *The Essence of Security*, p. 7.

21. Robert S. McNamara, 'The Essence of Security' in *The Essence of Security*, p. 146.

22. McNamara, 'The Essence of Security' in *The Essence of Security*, p. 149.

23. McNamara, 'The Essence of Security' in *The Essence of Security*, p. 148.

24. Interview with Frank Vogl, one of Clausen's closest aides, Washington, DC, 30 March 1993.

25. McNamara, Manila *Address*, 1976, p. 13.

26. Structural adjustment was mentioned in McNamara's *Address to the United Nations Conference on Trade and Development* (UNCTAD), Manila, 10 May 1979, p. 29, and elaborated on a few months later in his *Address to the Board of Governors*, Belgrade, 2 October 1979, pp. 38–43.

27. Willi Wapenhans (former Bank Vice-President, since 1993 a private

consultant), 'The Political Economy of Structural Adjustment: an External Perspective', paper presented at the International Seminar *Structural Adjustment and Beyond*, organized by the Directorate General for International Cooperation (DGIS), Dutch Ministry of Foreign Affairs, The Hague, 1–3 June 1993.

28. Robin Broad, *Unequal Alliance: The World Bank, the International Monetary Fund and the Philippines* (Berkeley, University of California Press, 1988), p. 79, citing World Bank, *Report and Recommendations* (by McNamara), 21 August 1980; see also Chapter 5, 'Adjustment in Action'.

Chapter III: Structural Salvation

1. *Adjustment and Poverty in Africa*, presented by the United States Agency for International Development to the Donors' Meeting, Special Programme for Assistance to Africa, Brussels, 21 October 1992, Conclusions, pp. 35–7.

2. François Bourguignon and Christian Morrisson, *Adjustment and Equity in Developing Countries: A New Approach* (Paris, OECD, 1992).

3. A concentrated expression of the NGO position is *The Other Side of the Story: The Real Impact of World Bank and IMF Structural Adjustment Programmes*, the product of a 1992 forum of highly representative development and environment NGOs, available from the Development-GAP, 927 Fifteenth Street NW, Washington, DC 20005, fax (202) 898–1612. See also the Oxfam Report, *Africa: Make or Break* (Oxford, Oxfam, 1993). Susan George has also written extensively on the social and environmental impact of structural adjustment in *A Fate Worse than Debt* (Harmondsworth, Penguin, 1988) and *The Debt Boomerang* (London, Pluto Press, 1992).

4. A detailed and subtle rendering of this dialectics will be found in Paul Mosley, Jane Harrigan and John Toye, *Aid and Power: The World Bank and Policy-Based Lending* (2 vols., London, Routledge, 1991).

5. The document from the Japanese Overseas Economic Cooperation Fund (OECF) was issued in Japan in October 1991 and published in English as 'Implications of the World Bank's Focus on Structural Adjustment', *Third World Economics*, 16–31 March 1993 (Third World Network, 87 Cantonment Road, 10250 Penang, Malaysia).

6. See Mosley, Harrigan and Toye, *Aid and Power*, especially volume two, containing nine case studies.

7. Colin Stoneman, 'The World Bank, income distribution and employment: some lessons for South Africa', proceedings of a conference at the University

of East Anglia, 25 March 1993; see also his 'Policy reform or industrialisation? The choice in Zimbabwe' in R. Adhikari, C. Kirkpatrick and J. Weiss (eds.), *Industrial and Trade Policy Reform in Developing Countries* (Manchester, Manchester University Press, 1992).

8. Colin Stoneman, 'The World Bank and the IMF in Zimbabwe' in Bonnie K. Campbell and John Loxley (eds.), *Structural Adjustment in Africa* (New York, Saint Martin's Press, 1989), pp. 37–66; the quote is from p. 44.

9. Stoneman, 'The World Bank' in Campbell and Loxley, *Structural Adjustment in Africa*, p. 46.

10. The Bank almost invariably judges that a country's currency is overvalued because its standard package includes devaluation so as to bring local prices more into line with international ones. Colin Stoneman explains how, in doing so, it lowers DRCs, for if the currency unit was worth, say, US$0.25 before devaluation, domestic costs will have been divided by 4 so as to get their US$ equivalent, giving, say, a value of 2.5 for a particular industry. This would mean that it is a very inefficient industry, as 10 units or US$2.5 are used in creating only US$1 in value. After devaluation reduces the currency unit to, say, US$0.20, 10 units are now only US$2, so the DRC for the industry in question improves from 2.5 to 2. The trouble for the Bank when it investigated the competitiveness of industry in Zimbabwe in 1982 was that it 'knew' that industry was uncompetitive because it was protected and the Bank intended to use this 'fact' to recommend removal of protection. But unfortunately, it found the average industrial DRC to be the lowest yet in Africa at 1.27, i.e. at the current exchange rate, US$1.27 were being used to produce goods valued internationally at US$1. But if the currency was overvalued by 20 per cent, devaluation by this amount would reduce the average DRC almost to unity, signifying efficiency – an impossibility in a protected economy. Therefore, in this case, the currency could not be overvalued and the report duly claimed this!

11. Stoneman, 'The World Bank' in Campbell and Loxley, *Structural Adjustment in Africa*, p. 55.

12. Colin Stoneman, 'Zimbabwe Opens up to the Market', *Africa Recovery*, October–December 1990, p. 3.

13. OECD, *Financing and External Debt of Developing Countries, 1992 Survey* (Paris, OECD, 1993), table on Zimbabwe, p. 212.

14. Personal communication to Susan George from CamFed's Ann Cotton, 31 October 1993. Anyone wishing to aid the Womankind Zimbabwe Project which is helping girls to stay in school without resorting to such

extremities may send contributions to CamFed, 25 Wordsworth Grove, Newnham, Cambridge, CB3 9HH.

15. Colin Stoneman, 'The World Bank demands its pound of Zimbabwe's flesh', *Review of African Political Economy*, March 1992.

16. Internal memorandum to the Director General of Directorate V for Employment, Industrial Relations and Social Affairs from (Mr —, Unit V/B/1), 'ILO Policy Seminar on Employment and Training Dimensions of Adjustments in Central and Eastern Europe (Turin), 30 March – 2 April 1992', Brussels, 6 April 1992.

17. The World Bank, *Current Questions and Answers*, Information and Public Affairs Division, External Affairs Department, Washington, DC, World Bank, April 1993) response to question 'What is adjustment lending?', p. 10.

18. Paul Mosley, Jane Harrigan, John Toye, *Aid and Power*, vol. I, p. 11.

19. This is the premise of Walden Bello (with Shea Cunningham and Bill Rau) in *Dark Victory: The US, Structural Adjustment and Global Poverty* (London, Pluto Press and the Transnational Institute, 1993).

20. See, among the 'formalists' who hold that every individual, in all societies, is in fact a profit-maximizing, self-interested capitalist (or at the very least proto-capitalist), Robbins Burling, 'Maximization Theory and the Study of Economic Anthropology', *The American Anthropologist*, 64 (1964), pp. 168–87, and Melville J. Herskovits, *Economic Anthropology* (New York, Knopf, 1952).

Chapter IV: False Prophecies

1. Percy S. Mistry, 'African Debt: Options for the Future', a background paper for UNICEF (distributed by the Netherlands Forum on Debt and Development – FONDAD), February 1993.

2. For a description of the Mexican debt crisis, see Susan George, *A Fate Worse than Debt* (Harmondsworth, Penguin, 1988), Chapter 2.

3. World Bank, *World Development Report 1981*, pp. 60 and 61.

4. World Bank, *World Development Report 1982*, p. 34, plus Table 4.3, 'Net financing flows, all developing countries 1970–1990'.

5. OECD, *Financing and External Debt of Developing Countries 1991 Survey* (Paris, OECD, 1992), Table III.1 'Total net resource flows to developing countries'.

6. World Bank, *World Development Report 1983*, pp. 21–3.

7. Masood Ahmed and Lawrence Summers (at the time of writing, the Bank's chief economist), 'A Tenth Anniversary Report on the Debt Crisis', *Finance and Development* (the World Bank/IMF magazine), September 1992, p. 2.

8. Ahmed and Summers, 'Tenth Anniversary Report', p. 4.

9. Ahmed and Summers, 'Tenth Anniversary Report', p. 4.

10. World Bank, *World Development Report 1986*, p. 56, Table 3.4, 'Current account balance and its financing in developing countries, 1985 and 1995'; actual debt figures from OECD, *Financing and External Debt of Developing Countries, 1992 Survey* (Paris, OECD, 1993). Table v.1, which places total developing country debt, including short term, at \$1.534 billion in 1992.

11. *World Development Report 1991*, p. 12, p. 27 and Box 1.4, pp. 28–9.

12. Primary commodities as a percentage of total exports in GATT, *International Trade 89–90*, vol. I, Appendix Table 4, 'Product composition of merchandise trade by region, 1980 and 1988'.

13. Sources: Projections: World Bank, 'Accelerated Development in Sub-Saharan Africa', 1981, Table 3.6, 'Projected Price and Volume of World Trade in Selected Commodities'. Actual: World Bank, 'Revision of Primary Commodity Price Forecasts and Quarterly Review of Commodity Markets – September 1991', 7 November 1991, Table 3, 'Weighted Index of Commodity Prices'. Although this is not specified, we assume the 1981 Bank document ('Accelerated Development') used constant dollars for its 1990 index projections. We therefore used the constant dollar index in the Bank's 1991 commodity document. But even if one were to refer to this document's table for current dollar price indexes (which naturally register 10 years of inflation since 1980) the Bank's 1981 predictions for 1990 were still way off: minerals and metals by 112.7 per cent; petroleum 76.6; fats and oils 67.9; beverages 60.6; timber 121.7; agricultural non-food 85; total food and beverage 77.3.

14. World Bank, 'Revision of Primary Commodity Price Forecasts', Table 2, 'Commodity Prices and Price Projections in Current Dollars'; column of projections for 1993 plus relevant *International Herald Tribune* and *Financial Times* indexes in late August 1993.

15. World Bank, *Report of the Joint Audit Committee*, 14 November 1989, paragraph 94.

16. Telephone conversation with an official in this division, September 1993.

17. John Cavanagh and Robin Broad, 'Flawed World Bank Report Could

Cause Wrong Policies for Third World', in *Third World Network Features*, September 1987. In the same piece, economists Cavanagh and Broad demolish the methodology which the Bank uses (in the 1987 *World Development Report*) when it attempts to prove that the most 'strongly outward oriented' economies are doing better than more inwardly oriented ones. See also the estimate of the 1982 *WDR* which forecasts export growth 1980–90 at 3.5 per cent (low case) to 6.8 per cent (high case), Table 4.1, p. 33.

18. These figures are (we suppose) unpublished and are found in one of the documents supplied by the Bank to the participants in the Special Programme of Assistance to Africa donors' meeting of 19–22 October 1992 in Brussels. The figures for 1993 are thus the Bank's projections and consist of unweighted averages. The weighted averages for the 26 countries are: exports up by 3.7 per cent; consumption down by 0.1 per cent per year for 1991–3.

19. Hans W. Singer, 'Alternative Approaches to Adjustment and Stabilisation' (adapted from a series of lectures organized by the Food and Agriculture Organization – FAO); reproduced in *Third World Economics*, 72 (1–15 September 1993).

20. The closest approximations to a comprehensive study we have been able to obtain, having queried a member of the Bank's policy research staff, International Trade (International Economics Department), are commodity-specific rather than general and concern only Africa: *How policy changes affected cocoa sectors in Sub-Saharan African Countries* and *Should Sub-Saharan Africa expand cotton exports?* (Working Paper Series, Nos. 1129 and 1139). See footnote to p. 86 for the Transnational Institute examination of African commodity prospects, including the views of commodity traders. The latter are not optimistic: South Asia is gaining market share at Africa's expense, African suppliers are often seen as unreliable and their products may no longer be adapted to evolving consumer tastes.

21. Stuart Holland, 'Towards a New Bretton Woods: Alternatives for the Global Economy', A Report for the Forecasting and Assessment in Science and Technology (FAST) Programme of the Directorate General Science, Research and Development, Commission of the European Communities, May 1993, pp. 13ff.

22. Drawn directly or calculated from *World Investment Report*, 'Foreign direct investment inward flows by region and country, 1980–1990', (New York, UN Center on Transnational Corporations, 1992).

23. Holland, 'Towards a New Bretton Woods', footnote p. 13.

24. Susan George, *A Fate Worse than Debt*, 2nd edn (Harmondsworth, Penguin, 1989), pp. 269–70.

25. Percy Mistry, 'African Debt'.

26. World Bank *Annual Report* 1992, Statement of Income, and Statement of Changes in Retained Earnings, p. 200; and World Bank, *Annual Report*, 1993, p. 192.

27. As in Ahmed and Summers's *Finance and Development* article cited above, although it skirts around the issue of the Bank's own responsibilities in the debt crisis and its treatment.

Chapter V: The Fundamentalist Freedom Fighter

1. John Mihevc, 'The Changing Debate on Structural Adjustment Policies in Sub-Saharan Africa: Churches, Social Movements and the World Bank', dissertation for Ph.D. in theology, University of St Michael's College, Toronto, Canada, 1992.

2. Mihevc, 'The Changing Debate', pp. 4 and 12.

3. Franz Hinkelammert, cited in Mihevc, 'The Changing Debate', p. 11.

4. Julio de Santa Ana, 'Sacralization and Sacrifice in Human Practice', in World Council of Churches' Commission on the Churches' Participation in Development, *Sacrifice and Humane Economic Life* (Geneva, WCC, 1992), p. 20; in Mihevc, 'The Changing Debate', p. 17.

5. Lawrence Summers, internal Bank memo, 12 December 1991, commenting on the 1992 edition of the Bank's *Global Economic Perspectives*.

6. 'The In-Your-Face Economist at the World Bank', *Business Week*, 11 May 1992.

7. Michael Weisskopf, 'World Bank Official's Irony Backfires', *Washington Post*, 10 February 1992.

8. Summers's speech was recorded at the October 1991 Bank–IMF annual general meeting in Bangkok by Kirsten Garrett of the Australian National Radio: 'Background Briefing', Australian Broadcasting Company, National Radio, broadcast on 3 and 10 November 1991 and transcribed here from the tape.

9. Celestine Bohlen, 'Social Fabric Frays as Russian Society Remakes Itself', *The New York Times* (also in the *International Herald Tribune*), 31 August 1992.

10. Bohlen, 'Social Fabric'.

11. Summers, broadcast by Kirsten Garrett, 'Background Briefing'.

12. Summers is speaking to Oswald Johnston, 'World Bank Economist Takes a Different Tack', *Los Angeles Times*, Business Section, 7 May 1991.

13. A seminar conducted at the École des Hautes Études en Sciences Sociales in Paris by Christian Coméliau, of the Geneva University Institute of Development Studies, in the spring of 1992 was particularly helpful in making explicit the (usually) unstated assumptions of the market; some of his observations are freely adapted here.

14. Larry Summers, recorded at the 1991 Bangkok meeting in an interview with Kirsten Garrett, 'Background Briefing' on the ABC, 10 November 1991.

15. Michael Prowse, 'Save Planet Earth from Economists', *Financial Times*, 10 February 1992.

16. Lawrence Summers, 'Summers on Sustainable Growth', a page-long letter to the *Economist*, 30 May 1992.

17. Summers, 'Summers on Sustainable Growth'.

18. Donella H. Meadows, Dennis L. Meadows, Jorgen Randers, *Beyond the Limits* (Chelsea Green Publishing Company, PO Box 130, Post Mills, Vermont 05058, USA, 1992), and Lawrence H. Summers, 'Is the World Beyond Its Limits?', undated (first half of 1992) and, to our knowledge, unpublished.

19. Summers, 'Is the World Beyond Its Limits?', conclusion of unpublished review.

20. Summers, 'Summers on Sustainable Growth'.

Chapter VI: L'Esprit de Corps

We are grateful to David Batker who, having seen the Bank from inside as an intern, now studies it from outside as part of the Greenpeace Multilateral Development Bank unit and who gave us much useful information. Other informants, presently or previously employed by the Bank, cannot be named for obvious reasons but we thank them for their help, insights and candour which have greatly contributed to this chapter.

1. Aart van de Laar, *The World Bank and the Poor* (The Hague, Martinus Nijhoff Publishing, 1980), Chapter 4, 'Bank Staff'.

2. Atsuko Horiguchi, pictured and quoted in the *Young Professionals Program*, 'Working for Global Development', n.d. The previous citations concerning requirements for the YP programme also come from this brochure.

3. Edward S. Mason and Robert T. Asher, *The World Bank Since Bretton Woods* (Washington, DC, The Brookings Institution, 1974), p. 71.

4. Amon J. Nsekela, 'The World Bank and the New International Economic Order', *Development Dialogue*, Dag Hammarskjöld Foundation, 1 (1977), p. 76.

5. Van de Laar, *The World Bank and the Poor*, p. 102.

6. The World Bank Group Staff Association, *A Sense of Common Purpose: The Staff Association at 20*, August 1991, p. 1.

7. Staff Association, *A Sense of Common Purpose*, p. 1.

8. Draft Report of the Subcommittee, 13 June 1978, office memorandum to: Task Force on the Reorganization of the Staff Association; from: Subcommittee on Fostering Participation in the Bank.

9. Karen S. Thomas, 'Communication and Decision-Making in International Organizations: A Cross-Cultural Perspective on Organizational Behavior in the World Bank', Ph.D. dissertation, University of California, Berkeley, Political Science Department. The quotes are all derived from Thomas's 'Executive summary', dated 4 November 1980.

10. Thomas, 'Communication and Decision-Making'.

11. Shapley, *Promise and Power*, pp. 532–3.

12. The name of this official, whom insiders will recognize, is of no importance; his trajectory is. See also Bruce Rich, *Mortgaging the Earth* (Boston, Beacon Press, 1994), pp. 307ff.

13. For the following account of the 1987 Reorganization, unless otherwise noted, we draw on the staff association's account in *A Sense of Common Purpose*, and especially on the Bank's own official, though unpublished account, 'Reorganizing the Bank: an Opportunity for Renewal: Report to the President from the Steering Committee on Reorganization of the World Bank, April 1987'. Many interviewees spoke spontaneously or at our request about this event; the press also paid it a good deal of attention at the time.

14. 'Conable's Year of Living Dangerously at the World Bank', *Business Week*, 20 July 1987.

15. Anatole Kaletsky, 'When a Shake-out Fails to Shape Up', *Financial Times*, 4 August 1987.

16. 'Reorganizing the Bank: An Opportunity for Renewal, Report to the President from the Steering Committee on Reorganization of the World Bank, April 1987', paragraphs 2.05 and 2.06.

17. 'Reorganizing the Bank', paragraph 2.07.

18. G.-A. Cornia, Richard Jolly, Frances Stewart (eds.), *Adjustment with a Human Face* (Oxford, UNICEF and Oxford University Press, 1987).

19. 'Reorganizing the Bank', paragraph 3.34.

20. 'Reorganizing the Bank', paragraph 4.05.

21. Staff Association, *A Sense of Common Purpose*, p. 31.

22. Dr Ned Rosen, 'Staff Survey Report', submitted to the World Bank/IFC Staff Association, 18 July 1988.

23. Rosen, 'Report'.

24. Rosen, 'Report'.

25. Rosen, 'Report'.

26. The World Bank Group, 'Attitude Survey '93, Institutional Summary Report' (QUESTAR Organizational Consulting and Research, 1993).

27. Naim, 'The World Bank: Its Role'.

Chapter VII: Governance: The Last Refuge?

1. Jean-Christophe Rufin, *L'Empire et les Nouveaux Barbares*, (Paris, Editions J.-C. Lattès, 1991), p. 132, our translation.

2. Samuel P. Huntington (Director of the Olin Institute for Strategic Studies at Harvard), 'The Clash of Civilizations?', *Foreign Affairs* (Summer 1993), pp. 22 and 29, and his interview in *New Perspectives Quarterly*, 10:3 (Summer 1993).

3. For a sampling of the Bank's literature on poverty, see *World Development Report 1990*, of which poverty is the central theme; Operational Directive 4.15 on Poverty Reduction, 1992 (accompanied by the *Poverty Reduction Handbook* and available from the External Affairs Department in five languages); *Implementing the World Bank's Strategy to Reduce Poverty*, April 1993. We return to this theme in Chapter IX.

4. World Bank Press Summary, 'Preston says poverty reduction is benchmark for performance as new directive to staff is published'. This document is not dated but comparison with other sources shows it must be 10 or 11 May 1992.

5. See Ibrahim F.I. Shihata, 'The World Bank and "Governance" Issues in its Borrowing Members', in Ibrahim F.I. Shihata, *The World Bank in a Changing World* (The Hague, Martinus Nijhoff, 1991).

6. World Bank, *Governance and Development* (Washington, DC, World Bank, 1992), p. 1.

7. Pierre Landell-Mills and Ismail Serageldin, 'Governance and the External

Factor', paper for the World Bank's Annual Conference on Development Economics, Washington, DC, 25–6 April 1991. The paper does 'not necessarily represent the views of the World Bank, its Executive Directors or the countries they represent'.

8. *Sub-Saharan Africa: From Crisis to Sustainable Growth* ('A Long-Term Perspective Study') (Washington, DC, World Bank, November 1989), principal authors Pierre Landell-Mills, Ramgopal Agarwala, Stanley Please.

9. *Sub-Saharan Africa*, p. 5.

10. Shihata, 'The World Bank and "Governance"', p. 54.

11. Shihata, 'The World Bank and "Governance"', p. 79.

12. The quotes from the British are, in order: letter from the Permanent Representative, United Kingdom Delegation to the OECD to the General Secretary of the OECD, 1 July 1991; letter from Douglas Hurd to Jacques Delors, President of the EC Commission, 10 June 1991; speech by Lynda Chalker to the Overseas Development Institute, 25 June 1991.

13. Conable is cited in Carol Lancaster, 'Governance and development: The Views from Washington', *IDS Bulletin*, 24:1 (1993), p. 10.

14. Shihata, 'The World Bank and "Governance"', pp. 82–3, emphasis added.

15. World Bank, *Governance and Development*, pp. 6 and 10; also pp. 53 and 55.

16. Cf. Lancaster, 'Governance and Development', p. 11.

17. Hans W. Singer, 'The Bretton Woods System: Historical Perspectives', a paper presented at the North–South Roundtable meeting in New York in 1993 and reprinted in *Third World Economics*, Third World Network, 71 (16–31 August 1993).

18. Quoted in the *IMF Survey*, 14 December 1992.

Chapter VIII: The Environmental Battlefield

1. Richard Webb is also a former governor of the Central Bank of Peru. This quote is from 'The World Bank: Mission Uncertain', a case study prepared for the Harvard Business School by Professor George C. Lodge (Case N9–792–100), 1992.

2. Webb, 'The World Bank: Mission Uncertain'.

3. Vice-President of External Relations José Botafogo G. is quoted in Marjorie Messiter, 'In the Eye of the Environment Storm', *The Bank's World* (the Bank's in-house magazine) (November 1986).

4. World Bank, *Annual Report 1993*, Table 5–4, p. 100. The exact figure, rounded, is $1.377 billion: it includes the categories of staff costs ($876 million); consultants ($112); contractual services/representation ($45); travel ($132); overheads ($212).

5. Internal note to the Acting Director General of the Commission of the European Communities Directorate General for Development, 28 May 1993, plus covering letter. We wish to stress that we did not obtain this document either from the person who carried out the mission or from his superior who wrote the covering letter, neither of whom we have ever met.

6. World Bank, *Current Questions and Answers*, Information and Public Affairs Division, April 1993, p. 51.

7. World Bank, *Annual Report on the Environment, FY 1993*, and organizational charts.

8. World Bank, Staff Appraisal Report, India National Thermal Power Corporation Power Generation Project, 4 June 1993, cited in Peter Bosshard, 'Energy from Dante's Inferno', a memorandum of the Berne Declaration and Greenpeace Switzerland, Zurich, 16 November 1993.

9. World Bank, Operations Evaluation Department, Performance Audit Report, India (concerning four thermal power projects), 3 February 1993, Report no. 10854, cited in Bosshard, as above.

10. World Bank, 'India: Sustainable Development in the Singrauli Region, Towards an Action Plan', May 1992, cited in Bosshard as above.

11. David Batker, in attachments to 'General Comments on the World Bank Environmental Assessments' conveyed on behalf of Greenpeace USA to the Office of Multilateral Development Banks, United States Treasury Department, 27 September 1991 (the project in Java is the Suralaya Thermal Power Project).

12. Those interested in the Bank's official environmental assessments may call upon the Bank Information Center, 2025 I Street NW, Suite 522, Washington, DC 20006, fax (202) 466–8189. The BIC regularly publishes lists of upcoming loans most likely to have a detrimental impact on the environment. For a small fee it can supply copies, particularly to NGOs in the borrowing countries concerned.

13. This line of argument is to be found throughout the Bank's 1992 *World Development Report*. Summers was responsible for this report and is cited in the UPI dispatch of 18 May 1992 covering its release which we quote here.

14. World Bank, *Current Questions and Answers*, p. 51.

15. See also the aftermath of the Wapenhans Report described in Chapter

x, echoed here by el-Ashry. He is cited by the (US) Bureau of National Affairs (BNA) news dispatch, 'New annual review of World Bank projects said to include environmental matters', Washington, DC, 26 July 1993.

16. World Bank, *Annual Energy Sector Review FY 1991*, 1991. Since the Bank uses the terms 'energy conservation' and 'energy efficiency' interchangeably (cf. World Bank, *Energy Efficiency and Conservation in the Developing World*, 18 March 1992), we assume that the 1% includes 'efficiency' loans as well.

17. David Hopper, 'The World Bank's Challenge: Balancing Economic Need with Environmental Protection', the World Wildlife Fund, United Kingdom, World Conservation Lecture, delivered in London, 3 March 1988.

18. See House of Commons, Canada: 'International Financial Institutions', Nineteenth Report of the Standing Committee on Finance, First Report of the Sub-Committee on International Financial Institutions, June 1993; paragraphs 210–13 concern David Hopper's testimony and involvement with the Bank's Sardar Sarovar project.

19. Press release of the Independent Review, 'Massive Dam Project in India Criticized for Environmental and Human Rights Violations', released 18 June 1992.

20. *Narmada Bachao Andolan* (Save Narmada Movement), *Towards Sustainable and Just Development, The People's Struggle in the Narmada Valley*, 1991–92 (NBA, 58 Gandhi Marg, Badwani, Madhya Pradesh 451551, and C17/A Munirka, New Delhi 110067, India).

21. *Sardar Sarovar: Report of the Independent Review*, published by Resource Futures International, Ottawa, 1992. Sardar Sarovar is the name of one of the huge centre-piece Narmada dams; this is why people refer interchangeably to the project as Narmada or Sardar Sarovar. The quoted material is from the 'Letter to the President' accompanying the review, addressed by Chairman Morse and Deputy Chairman Berger to Lewis T. Preston, President of the World Bank, 18 June 1992, pp. xi–xxv of this volume.

22. *Sardar Sarovar*, pp. xxiii and xxiv.

23. Cited in 'Statement of Friends of the Earth before the Senate Appropriations Subcommittee on Foreign Operations Concerning Foreign Aid Appropriations for the World Bank [and other agencies]', 15 June 1993, p. 14; also at the time of the vote in Jim Lobe, Inter-Press Service dispatch of 23 October 1992. Lobe reports also on the Bank's 11 September 'confidential memo to its Executive Directors' urging that the Narmada project go forward and attempting to push it through on 1 October,

a date the board delayed until 15 October, without, however, mustering the necessary votes to defeat the project.

24. Bradford Morse, Chairman, and Thomas Berger, Deputy Chairman of the Independent Review, *Letter* dated 13 October 1992 to World Bank President Lewis T. Preston with copies to the executive directors of the Bank. Morse and Berger state at the end of their letter: 'Our Review no longer has any formal existence. All of us have returned to our private lives. We make this suggestion [to meet with Preston and the EDs to discuss the matters raised], however, because we wish to preserve the integrity of the Independent Review's findings'. To our knowledge, no such meeting ever took place.

25. Press Trust of India news agency is quoted in an AP dispatch from New Delhi, 30 March 1993.

26. AP–Dow Jones dispatch from New Delhi, quoting the *Asian Wall Street Journal*, 28 June 1993.

27. *The Price of Progress* was broadcast on Central Television in June 1987. The following quotes are from the soundtrack, transcribed by the authors from the cassette which Nicholas Claxton kindly made available.

28. Carter Brandon and Ramesh Ramankutty, 'Towards an Environmental Strategy for Asia', World Bank, December 1993. Our quotes are from the Bank's News Release (no. 94/S31 EAP) concerning the paper, which appeared too late for us to include an analysis in this book.

Chapter IX: Intellectual Leadership and the H Street Heretics

1. 'Reorganizing the Bank', especially paragraphs 2.11 and 3.04.

2. European Community office in Washington, DC, note to the Director General of DG VIII (Development Directorate) from Andreas van Agt, 'World Bank Research: an Overview', 20 February 1992.

3. van Agt, 'World Bank Research'.

4. Joel Samoff, 'The Intellectual–Financial Complex of Foreign Aid', *Review of African Political Economy*, 53, March 1992, pp. 60–75.

5. Samoff, 'The Intellectual–Financial Complex, p. 73.

6. Nicholas Stern with Francisco Ferreira, 'The World Bank as "Intellectual Actor"', forthcoming in Volume II of the official history of the Bank, prepared at the Brookings Institution, Washington, DC, by Richard Webb and John Lewis, typescript dated 18 March 1993; page numbers refer to this draft.

7. Stern, 'The World Bank as "Intellectual Actor"', pp. 17, 24–5.

8. Stern, 'The World Bank as "Intellectual Actor"', p. 30.

9. Stern, 'The World Bank as "Intellectual Actor"', pp. 39–40.

10. Stern, 'The World Bank as "Intellectual Actor"', p. 60.

11. Stern, 'The World Bank as "Intellectual Actor"', pp. 74–5.

12. Stern, 'The World Bank as "Intellectual Actor"', p. 79.

13. Stern, 'The World Bank as "Intellectual Actor"', pp. 81–2. The passage is Stern's; the work cited is T.N. Srinivasan, 'Database for Development Analysis: an Overview', *Journal of Development Economics*, forthcoming.

14. Stern, 'The World Bank as "Intellectual Actor"', pp. 83–7.

15. David Woodward, *Debt, Adjustment and Poverty in Developing Countries* (2 vols., London, Pinter Publishers in association with Save the Children, 1992) and David Woodward, Anthony Costello, Fiona Watson, *Human Face or Human Façade? Adjustment and the Health of Mothers and Children* (London, Institute of Child Health, 1994).

16. World Bank, *World Development Report 1993: Investing in Health*, (Washington, DC, World Bank, July 1993).

17. The best known of UNICEF's publications in this area is also the earliest, Cornia, Jolly and Stewart's *Adjustment with a Human Face*. The series of 'Innocenti Papers' produced at UNICEF's research centre in Florence has continued the critique of the impact of adjustment on maternal–child welfare.

18. World Bank, *World Development Report 1993: Investing in Health*, p. 46.

19. David Woodward, personal communication to Susan George, 10 January 1994: the book he refers to in the Bank's bibliography is *Debt, Adjustment and Poverty in Developing Countries*. The Bank's bibliography for the short *WDR* section on adjustment impact is on p. 178 of the 1993 *WDR*, first column.

20. Stern, 'The World Bank as "Intellectual Actor"', 'Conclusions', p. 147.

21. Stern, 'The World Bank as "Intellectual Actor"', p. 117.

22. Stern, 'The World Bank as "Intellectual Actor"', p. 109.

23. World Bank, *Annual Report 1993*, p. 90.

24. This and other discrepancies in poverty measurement are brought out in Robert W. Kates and Viola Haarmann, 'Poor People and Threatened Environments: Global Overviews, Country Comparisons and Local Studies', a Research Report of the Alan Shawn Feinstein World Hunger Program at Brown University (Box 1831, Providence, Rhode Island 02912), 1991.

The two differing studies are the World Bank, 1990 *World Development Report* which estimated 630 million 'extremely poor' people and Alan Durning of the Worldwatch Institute who in 'Poverty and the Environment' *Worldwatch Paper*, 92 (1989) put the number of those 'living in absolute poverty' at 1,225 million.

25. Amartya Sen, *Poverty and Famines: An Essay on Entitlement and Deprivation*, (Oxford, Clarendon Press, 1981), and also his journal articles far too numerous to list.

26. This is certainly the case in the United States: see Kevin Phillips, *The Politics of Rich and Poor: Wealth and the American electorate in the Reagan aftermath* (New York, Random House, 1990). The anecdotal evidence for Latin America, Africa and the former Eastern bloc points in the same direction.

27. These concerns were addressed forthrightly by the Dutch World Bank Executive Director Evelien Herfkens in the discussion at the symposium sponsored by several Dutch NGOs at the Dutch Parliament on 12 March 1993, transcription kindly supplied by Pieter Smit who recorded and translated the participants' remarks.

28. See the letter and annexe from US NGOs to James Adams of the Bank concerning 'Next Steps' (follow-up to the Wapenhans Report, see Chapter XI), 21 May 1993, available through the NGO Working Group on the Bank, c/o ICVA, CP 216, 1211 Geneva 21.

29. Kates and Haarmann, 'Poor People'.

30. Quoted in Mark Tran, 'American Notebook: World Bank Must Act on Brave New Words to Help Poor', *Guardian* (London), 11 May 1992.

31. Max Planck, *Scientific Autobiography* (New York, 1949), pp. 33–4, cited in Thomas Kuhn, *The Structure of Scientific Revolutions*, 2nd edn (Chicago, University of Chicago Press, 1970), p. 151.

32. Frances Cairncross, *Costing the Earth* (Boston, Harvard Business School Press, 1992), deals with these issues. In Europe the work of the Dutch economist Roefie Heuting on full-cost accounting is also considered outstanding (though we confess to not having read him). Inside the Bank, Salah el-Serafy is the chief exponent of environmental accounting.

33. Lester Brown, Sandra Postel, Christopher Flavin, 'From Growth to Sustainable Development', in Robert Goodland, Herman Daly and Salah el-Serafy (eds.), *Population, Technology and Lifestyle: The Transition to Sustainability* (Washington, DC, UNESCO and the Island Press, 1992), p. 122.

34. Herman E. Daly, 'Farewell Lecture to the World Bank', 14 January 1994, in J. Cavanagh, D. Wysham, M. Arruda (eds.), *Beyond Bretton*

Woods: Alternatives to the Global Economic Order (London, Pluto Press, TNI and IPS, 1994). See also Daly's 'The Perils of Free Trade', *Scientific American* (November 1994), pp. 24–9.

35. This proposal has been worked out in detail in Ernst-Ulrich von Weizsacher, *Ecological Tax Reform* (London, Zed Books, 1992).

Chapter X: Ruling the Realm

1. Articles of Agreement, Article V, Section 4e.

2. Articles of Agreement, Article V, Section 2b, iii and vi: there are five other specific duties which the governors cannot delegate to the executive directors.

3. So as not to encumber the reader with needless detail, we use throughout the voting strength figures for the IBRD (hard loan) part of the Bank. Voting shares in the IDA, the more charitable wing of the Bank, are somewhat different, particularly in the case of Japan (6.74% of IBRD, 10.29% of IDA) which has been quietly building up its multilateral aid capacity during the 1990s.

4. Country groups and voting strength in World Bank *Annual Report 1993*, Appendix 2, p. 232.

5. Naim, 'The World Bank: Its Role'.

6. Cf. World Bank *Annual Report 1992*, section on the executive directors, pp. 25 and 62–3.

7. Walden Bello, 'The Role of the World Bank in US Foreign Policy', *Covert Action*, 39 (Winter 1991–2).

8. Cited in Paul Sweeney, 'Who's in Charge at the World Bank', *Global Finance*, (September 1993).

9. Interview with Patrick Coady, Washington, DC, 29 March 1993.

10. Calculated from World Bank, *World Debt Tables 1993–94*, Summary Table 5, p. 171.

11. Bello, 'The Role of the World Bank'. The quote initially appeared in a volume published by the Bretton Woods Committee, *The World Bank, the US and the Developing World* (Washington, DC, 1988). Bello, with Shea Cunningham and Bill Rau, elaborates on the Reagan–Bush administrations' use of the Bank in *Dark Victory: the US, Structural Adjustment and Global Poverty* (London, Pluto Press, 1994).

12. Naim, 'The World Bank: Its Role', p. 25.

13. Naim, 'The World Bank: Its Role', p. 33.

14. 'Not There Yet', *Economist*, 16 May 1992, p. 112.

15. A portrait of Preston and an informative account of his career at Morgan will be found in Robert Teitelman, 'The Man behind the Morgan Mask', *Institutional Investor*, October 1991.

Chapter XI: The Bank Perceived: Images and Self-Images

1. Portfolio Management Task Force, 'Effective Implementation: Key to Development Impact', Confidential Discussion Draft, 24 July 1992, *passim*.

2. World Bank, 'Portfolio Management: Next Steps', R93–62, prepared for the executive directors' meeting of 4 May 1993; 5 April 1993. 'H-Street Blues', *Economist*, 1 May 1993, p. 91.

3. Stern is quoted in George Graham, 'Action Plan for World Bank', *Financial Times*, 13 July 1993.

4. Task Force, 'Effective Implementation', paragraph 57, but see also the preceding pages on 'Quality of Portfolio Performance Management' from paragraph 37.

5. From the Bretton Woods Committee information brochure, pp. 3 and 8. Literature from the BWC, 2029 K Street NW, Suite 300, Washington, DC 20006, USA (202) 331–1616; also its separate report on the conference on Third World Debt: A New Look, held on 10 March 1989.

6. World Bank Office Memorandum, 23 February 1993, from Jane Armitage, EXC (Executive Committee) 'Subject: EXCMEMO "Highlights from the President's February 22 (1993) Meeting with Vice-Presidents"'.

7. 'Effective Implementation', note 1.

8. Seigel and Gale; a letter from a senior consultant in its London office thanking Mr X for participating in this process, 30 July 1993.

9. For more on the latent content of institutional clichés about development, see Marie-Dominique Perrot in Gilbert Rist and Fabrizio Sabelli (eds), *Il Etait une Fois le Développement* (Lausanne, Editions d'En Bas, 1986).

10. *Proceedings*, p. 1110.

11. 'Statement of Friends of the Earth before the Senate Appropriations Subcommittee on Foreign Operations Concerning Foreign Aid Appropriations for the World Bank [and other agencies]', 15 June 1993, pp. 13–14.

12. Letter to the Hon. Donald Mazankowski, MP, Minister of Finance and Canadian Governor to the World Bank, from Walter Pitman, Chairman of PROBE International, 23 September 1991. These same positions were forcefully argued in Patricia Adams (Executive Director of PROBE), *Odious*

Debts (London and Toronto, Earthscan, 1991). The argument about the Bank's financial solidity seems weak to us: surely guarantees from the rich countries do just what Keynes intended them to do – underpin the Bank's financial credibility in capital markets.

13. Rainforest Action Network, *Action Alert* 80 (January 1993).

14. See Lisa Jordan and Peter van Tuijl, 'Democratizing Global Power Relations: Steps towards a political foundation for a global NGO campaign to reshape the Bretton Woods Institutions' (July 1993), (unpublished, for copies contact the authors at INGI, PO Box 11609, 2502 AP, The Hague, Netherlands). This paper provides an excellent summary of the various NGO *problématiques* with regard to the Bank, stressing the concerns shared by environmental, human rights and poverty-alleviation NGOs.

15. Bruce Rich, in *Mortgaging the Earth* (Boston, Beacon Press, 1994), explains how this legislation was achieved. We are grateful to Lori Udall, then of the Environmental Defense Fund, for supplying us with the complete list of the US executive director's negative votes and abstentions from 1992 through mid-1993. This list from the US Treasury ('International Financial Institutions' Quarterly Transactions') concerns US votes at all the regional multilateral development banks as well as the IFC, the private enterprise lending wing of the World Bank Group. The Bank – IBRD and IDA – accounts for over fifty per cent of these 'nays' and abstentions, usually, but not always on environmental grounds.

16. Development-GAP can be contacted at 927 15th Street NW, 4th Floor, Washington, DC 20005, fax (202) 898–1612.

17. Information available from NGO Working Group on the World Bank, c/o ICVA, 13, rue Gautier, 1201 Geneva, Switzerland, fax (41–22)738 9904.

18. Addresses as of mid-1994: Bank Information Center, 2025 I Street NW, Suite 522, Washington, DC 20006, fax (202) 466–8189; *BankCheck*, c/o International Rivers Network, 1847 Berkeley Way, Berkeley, California 94703, fax (510) 848–1008.

19. An initial 'Draft Provisions for an Independent Appeals Commission to Oversee the World Bank' – effectively statutes – was circulated by the Environmental Defense Fund and the Center for International Environmental Law, 6 April 1993. An 'International NGO Policy Paper', 'Creating an Independent Appeals Commission at the World Bank', arguing the case for an IAC, was issued by these same two organizations, plus the Berne Declaration and Greenpeace Switzerland in September 1993.

20. *Neue Zuercher Zeitung*, 7 September 1993, p. 20.

21. From a confidential report on the Development Committee Meeting from the European Commission Washington delegation, 28 September 1993, p. 3.

22. World Bank, 'Directive on Disclosure of Information', July 1989, paragraphs 2 and 3 under 'Policy'.

23. World Bank, 'Directive on Disclosure', paragraph 4.

24. World Bank, 'Directive on Disclosure', paragraphs 26, 28 and 29.

25. Michael Holman, 'World Bank's Worst-Kept Secrets', *Financial Times*, 2 March 1993.

26. World Bank, 'Report of the Working Group on the Review of the Directive on Disclosure of Information', 29 March 1993, with annexe, 'Access to Information: an Alternative View', p. 3.

27. According to a European Community *Note* for the attention of the Acting Director of DG VIII (the Development Directorate), 28 May 1993, the letter to Stern was shown by Bank personnel to an EC man on mission to the Bank.

28. World Bank, 'Expanding Access to Bank Information', approved by the executive directors on 26 August 1993, SecM93–927, 31 August 1993, p. 3.

29. Bank Information Center, 'New World Bank Policies Set on Information and Appeals', *Early Warning* (September 1993), and Juliette Majot, 'Unclear on Disclosure', *BankCheck* (September 1993).

30. World Bank, Press Summary, 'Preston says poverty reduction is benchmark for performance as new directive to staff is published', n.d. but most likely 11 May 1992.

31. World Bank, 'Implementing the World Bank's Strategy to Reduce Poverty: Progress and Challenges', April 1993, p. xiii.

Index